JOHN POLLARD SEDDON

Portrait of John Pollard Seddon from *The Building News* 17 January 1890

Catalogues of Architectural Drawings in the Victoria and Albert Museum

John Pollard SEDDON

by Michael Darby

Victoria and Albert Museum

Front wrapper
Design by J. P. Seddon for part of Victoria Terrace,
Aberystwyth, Dyfed. c.1868 (D.1389–1896)

Back wrapper
Design by J. P. Seddon for the Dunraven Arms Hotel, 1852
(D.873–1896), later called the Southerndown Hotel and now
the Welsh Sunshine Home for Blind Babies, Glamorganshire.

Published in 1983
by the Victoria and Albert Museum
London sw7 2rl

ISBN 0 905209 41 9

Designed by Graham Johnson

Printed by Lund Humphries

Contents

Acknowledgements 8

Foreword 9

Introduction 11

Abbreviations 15

Chronology 17

CATALOGUE
Topographical Drawings 27

Architectural Designs 29

Unidentified Designs 31
For specific clients 100
Cottages, stables, a toll house, etc 102
Ecclesiastical including monuments 103
Houses and villas 105
Public buildings 107
Roofs 107
Schools 107
Miscellaneous 107

Designs for Applied Arts 108
Ceramics 108
Furniture 108
Metalwork 114
Stained glass 115
Textiles 116
Tiles 116

Index 119

In Memoriam
Ann Lorenz Van Zanten

Acknowledgements

My greatest debt of gratitude is to Seddon's surviving relatives Colonel R. N. Seddon, the Misses Alison and Margaret Birch and their brother John who have not only provided me with hospitality and useful advice, but who have also been extremely generous in allowing me to borrow material in their possession.

Peter Howell generously permitted me to use the card index of Welsh buildings he compiled while writing with Elizabeth Beazley their pioneering Companion Guides to North and South Wales. Joanna Heseltine and Margaret Richardson of the Royal Institute of British Architects Library (Drawings Collection) kindly allowed me to use the manuscript of their catalogue which included Seddon and Christopher Pickford sent me details of the holdings of Seddon material in the Hereford Record Office. My colleagues in the museum have, as always, been full of encouragement and good advice and I would particularly like to thank John Physick, Michael Kauffmann, Michael Snodin, Clive Wainwright, Garth Hall and Nicky Bird.

I must also thank Keith Kissack for going through the drawings in Monmouth Museum with me and for providing useful information about Seddon's work in Gwent and Herefordshire, and my wife whose work on 19th century sculpture has constantly turned up new Seddon references for me. Lastly I would like to express a special debt of gratitude to the late Lyn Allen who read the manuscript and made several useful additions and corrections, and to Graham Johnson for designing this catalogue and seeing it through the press.

Foreword

The Museum began to collect architectural drawings on a large scale as long ago as 1863 when over 2,500 designs were bought from C J Richardson, Sir John Soane's assistant. The collection grew rapidly thanks to generous gifts and bequests during the latter part of the last century and now consists of over 35,000 architects' drawings. Indeed, it constitutes the most important collection in London after the R.I.B.A. and the Soane Museum and we have felt for some time that it deserves to be more widely known.

Accordingly, we planned to produce detailed catalogues of the holdings, calling upon specialists both within the Museum and outside. We have benefited from the ready co-operation of some of the leading scholars in the field, and, under the general editorship of Michael Snodin, a programme of catalogues was set in train.

The present volume is the first fruit of this programme and I should like to welcome it most warmly both as a major contribution to 19th century architectural studies and as the foundation stone of an extensive series of such catalogues. Indeed, it was Michael Darby who drew up the initial plans and it is fitting that his contribution should be the first to appear in print.

Other catalogues now in the press are by Alistair Rowan on Adam, Pierre de la Ruffinière du Prey on Soane and Alexandra Wedgwood on Pugin. For each volume a complete set of microfiche illustrations will be available separately from Ormonde Publishing at 76 Clancarty Road, London sw6 3AA.

Grateful acknowledgement must be made for much help received from John Physick, the Museum's senior architectural scholar, and Nicky Bird, the Publications Officer, without whose enthusiastic support this series would never have materialised.

C. M. Kauffmann

Keeper of Prints & Drawings and Paintings

Design submitted by Prichard and Seddon in the competition for the War and Foreign Offices, Whitehall, London in 1857, which won fourth prize. Plate from the *Illustrated London News*. 12 Sept 1857. p.276.

Photograph of Seddon's model submitted in competition for the Law Courts, 1867, and now destroyed.
Photograph courtesy of the Royal Institute of British Architects: Drawings Collection.

Introduction

There is no comprehensive study of John Pollard Seddon. Although architectural historians are aware of the reputation which he enjoyed amongst his contemporaries and stress the importance of his publications for the study of the Gothic revival, general accounts of nineteenth century architecture and design have so far devoted comparatively little space to him. The fullest records of his life and work remain the obituaries which appeared in the *Builder* and the Royal Institute of British Architects' *Journal* in 1906 (1).

Perhaps one of the main reasons for Seddon's anonymity has been the absence of a corpus of work which could be positively attributed to him. The designs he submitted unsuccessfully in competition for the Government Offices (with John Prichard) in 1856-57 and for the Law Courts in 1867, and the University College of Wales at Aberystwyth from 1864, are well known, but his name has until recently been linked with few other projects and buildings. This catalogue of nearly two thousand drawings depicting numerous different works, the majority of which were presented to the Museum in 1896 by Seddon's daughter Margaret Birch, help to restore the balance. The list of drawings is supplemented by a chronology incorporating a considerable amount of material relating to other works by Seddon, and it is hoped that together they will provide a basis for a much fuller study in the future. In the meantime it is, perhaps, pertinent to record some of the more interesting facets of his life and career here.

John Pollard Seddon was born on 19th September 1827 at London House, Aldersgate where his father Thomas Seddon had a large furniture manufactory. The business had been founded in the mid 18th century by George Seddon, John Pollard's great, great grandfather, and had flourished to such an extent that by the end of the century it was one of the largest in the country. In the early 19th century, after the upholsterer Nicholas Morel had been taken into partnership, the firm was commissioned to carry out work at both Buckingham Palace and Windsor Castle.

Although John Pollard designed furniture for the firm and many drawings survive in the Museum's collection, this interest appears to have evolved as a result of his architectural work. He records in a memoir of his brother Thomas, the minor Pre-Raphaelite painter, that Thomas certainly designed furniture for his father before travelling to the East where he died, and it was, perhaps, to his younger son rather than to John Pollard that Thomas senior looked for the continuance of the business. Although there are several published accounts of the firm these all suggest that it ceased trading in the early 19th century. Their authors were apparently unaware of the drawings in the Museum, so that very little is known of its history in the 1850s and 60s. (2)

After receiving his education at Bedford Grammar School, Seddon became a pupil of the architect T. L. Donaldson in 1847, and remained with him until 1851 when he went on a tour of the Continent and returned to set up in practice in London. It was at about this time that he was appointed architect of a hotel at Southerndown on the south coast of Glamorganshire during the building of which he met John Prichard, his future partner. Seddon later recorded their meeting: 'while so engaged [on the Southerndown hotel] I made enquiries as to what objects of architectural interest there might be in the neighbourhood, and being told of the Cathedral at Llandaff, the restoration of which had been commenced, and was then in progress, and furnished with an introduction to Mr John Prichard, the son of the Vicar of the Cathedral and resident architect in charge of the work, I accordingly visited him there, and was most graciously received, and shewn all there was to be seen by him. Immediately afterwards on my return to London, I was surprised, and I may say gratified, to receive an offer of partnership from

---

[1] *Builder*, 10 February 1906, p. 150. Royal Institute of British Architects *Journal*, 1905-06, p. 221.

[2] The main sources for the history of the firm are:— Ambrose Heal, 'The Firm of Seddon', Country Life, 20 January 1934, pp. 72–73; G. B. Hughes, 'George Seddon of London House', *Apollo*, May 1957, pp. 177–181; R. Edwardes, 'A Great Georgian Cabinet Maker—New Light on the Firm of Seddon', *Country Life*, 21 October 1933, pp. 415–18; notes in the Department of Furniture and Woodwork. A portrait of George Seddon was presented to the Department of Prints and Drawings by Miss A. Birch in 1927 (p. 21–1927).

him which I accepted [and] I went down there at once, and took up my residence in Llandaff with him'. (3)

Prichard's upbringing in the confines of the cathedral ensured that he was acquainted not just with ecclesiology but also with Gothic architecture at an early age. It was hardly surprising, therefore, that having chosen architecture as a career he should have articled himself firstly to Augustus Pugin and later to Thomas Walker, both confirmed Gothicists. Prichard was apparently very fond of drawing and in both offices he worked on the plates for Pugin's *Examples of Gothic Architecture*. Seddon's education by comparison, in the office of the classicist Donaldson, does not appear to have equipped him with any great knowledge of Gothic, and since it was as an advocate of this style that he was later to become famous, the influence of Prichard on his work was considerable.

If one compares Seddon's designs for John Hales's houses at Tulse Hill, which are rather bland Italianate villas with Romanesque and minimal Gothic detailing of 1851, with the very competent and skilfully handled gothic design which he and Prichard submitted only four years later for the Government offices, the degree of this influence is clear. Even in the different designs for the Southerndown hotel Prichard's influence is evident. Seddon's first drawings, prepared before he met Prichard, are for a simple building in the tradition of Hales's villas, but after their meeting he soon altered them to include many elements—local materials and detailing of windows, porch and doors, for example—which are reminiscent of some of Prichard's earlier designs, and were to become standard in Seddon's later gothic work.

It would seem that Seddon looked upon Prichard as his next master. He was certainly prepared to do menial tasks in order to work with him for it has been said that Seddon undertook the role of 'housekeeper' and that in the early days at least he called himself Prichard's 'oldest pupil' (4). Unfortunately, very few details have come to light about the practical working of the partnership. It has been suggested that the two architects worked independently, Seddon mainly confining himself to church restoration in Monmouthshire. As Diocesan Architects, however, the partners were called upon to build schools, parsonages and other buildings as well as churches, and as the collection of drawings in the Museum makes clear, Seddon designed many of these buildings himself.

It is not clear why the partnership ended so suddenly in 1863. Seddon's statement that 'the financial rewards were insufficient for two people' appears over-simplified. Prichard had always preferred drawing to keeping accounts, and his involvement with the design of a mansion in Jerez de la Frontera for the sherry magnate Señor Gonzalez meant that he was out of the country for some time in the early 1860s. Consequently, Seddon was left to settle Prichard's Eatington Hall contract, which coupled with his need to keep the business going, must have imposed a considerable strain on him. The partners had opened an office at 6, Whitehall in London of which Seddon had assumed control, so that the travelling must have been arduous too. Furthermore, Seddon had married in 1862 and bought a house at 12 Park Street, Westminster.

While both architects remained on friendly terms after the partnership ended and seem to have worked in harmony on new buildings, this should not be allowed to obscure the fact that they held radically different views on the subject of restoration. Prichard declined to restore work which he did not consider authentic, and to judge by his design for the southern tower of Llandaff Cathedral and his virtual rebuilding of St. Cathwg's Church at Pentyrch in the Decorated style, for example, he was prepared to invent new designs when no precedent existed. Seddon, on the other hand, attempted to 'replace matters nearly as he found them', and became well known for the 'loving care in which he preserved the ancient details, and for his skill in designing such furnishings as font covers, pulpits and stained glass'. (5) He was also famous for the expertise he brought to bear in solving complex structural problems, the shoring of the tower of the church of St. Nicholas at Grosmont being a notable example.

[3] *Public Library Journal*. Quarterly Magazine of the Cardiff and Penarth Free Public Libraries, and the Welsh Museum, VI, March 1903, p. 29.

[4] L. Allen, 'Some Notes on the Architectural Work of John Prichard and John Pollard Seddon', prepared for the Victorian Society's Aberystwyth weekend, 1976, p. 4.

[5] ibid., pp. 5 and 10.

Although he resided in London from the early 1860s Seddon's ties with Wales were not entirely severed. In the Spring of 1864 he became involved with Thomas Savin over the building works at Towyn and Borth which led to the commission to design the Castle Hotel, now the University College of Wales, at Aberystwyth, his best known work. The full story of the College is told in the catalogue, how Savin's plans changed daily, and how Seddon was obliged to keep five hundred men in work by making drawings in the evening for building the next day. Although a major fire and later alterations some of which were carried out by Seddon himself, now make assessment of his original work difficult, it must be admitted, nevertheless, that the college bears clear indications of its rather random and hurried development. If Seddon had had more time to work on his plans he would have perhaps produced a more cohesive and integrated design.

Abermad, the house which Seddon built a few miles outside Aberystwyth for Lewis Pugh Pugh provides a clearer indication of Seddon's independent abilities than the University College of Wales. The design is certainly more unified but it is at the same time structurally and aesthetically far less satisfactory than Prichard's Eatington Park a house of similar scale. Seddon shows greater concern for the individual details than the overall design; the porch, for example, appears to have been added to the front facade rather than being conceived as an integral part of it. In several of Seddon's large houses such as the Chigwell Row parsonage, the articulation of the wall surfaces and arrangement of the plan conveys a 'boxy' quality which is lacking in the smaller buildings he designed during the partnership, and contrasts with the rhythmic play of solid and void, and form the pattern which so distinguish Prichard's designs. Indeed, Seddon himself seems to have sensed a certain deficiency in his abilities as an architect for after leaving Prichard he increasingly concerned himself with restoration, and the design of furniture, metalwork, tiles and stained glass, while leaving more and more of the architectural work to a succession of partners and collaborators including J. Murray, E. W. Godwin, R. Phené Spiers, J. Coates Carter, W. H. C. Fisher, H. Roumieu Gough, H. Crisp, E. Beckitt Lamb, and L. Harvey. One should not underestimate Seddon's architectural ability however. In his treatment of Gothic detail, decorative and structural, he was both original and successful. The use of columnar forms like those on the Aberystwyth College and Abermad porch, which owe something to Venetian precedents, are very striking. Indeed, J. Coates Carter, at one time his partner, believed that 'he was, in fact, far the most original of the Gothic revivalists; for though among the strongest in his love for and belief in the revival, he was always a modern rather than a mediaevalist, even though he himself might not altogether have been willing to admit it; and in his work almost alone among the early revivalists was it impossible to trace the origin of the detail to any particular mediaeval style or building'. (6)

One of the most interesting facets of Seddon's career, and one which deserves further research, concerns his involvement with the Pre-Raphaelites. Towards the end of his life Seddon recalled how his brother had set up a drawing school in Camden Town 'to provide for his artist friends amongst whom were all the Pre-Raphaelites, facilities for studying the figure from life; and the occasion of their meetings for that purpose were usually prolonged as social gatherings, wherein much animated discussion took place upon artistic subjects, and I of course felt it a great pleasure and privilege to be allowed though quite their junior, to form one of the party' (7). After leaving London direct contact with these artists ceased, but Seddon took with him fond memories of the meetings, and when Prichard provided him with the opportunity to commission works for Llandaff Cathedral, he wasted no time in getting in touch with them again. Thomas Woolner was asked to provide models for the pulpit, and Rossetti designed the reredos. Seddon recalled that 'I had . . . formed a very high opinion of D. G. Rossetti's early imaginative and religious paintings, and particularly of his 'Girlhood of the Virgin Mary', 'The Annunciation', etc., and became enamoured of his bold and rich colouring. Indeed I looked upon him as the most promising of the fraternity to develop a high class

6 Royal Institute of British Architects *Journal*, 13, 1905-06, p. 221.

7 *Public Library Journal*. Quarterly Magazine of the Cardiff and Penarth Free Public Libraries, and the Welsh Museum, VI, March 1903, p. 29.

of Ecclesiastical decorative art' (8). This admiration had earlier led Seddon to commission from Rossetti *Giotto painting the portrait of Dante*, which hung with Ford Madox Brown's *King Lear* and *View of Hampstead* which he had purchased at auction, on the walls of the house in which he and Prichard lived at Llandaff.

After Seddon's return to London he took up again with the Pre-Raphaelites, particularly with Ford Madox Brown. William Michael Rossetti in his *Some Reminiscences* recalled that 'the ladies of the Seddon family were at all times on the most cordial terms with those of the Madox Brown household' (9), and after Dante Gabriel Rossetti's death—in a bungalow which Seddon had provided for him at Birchington-on-Sea— he and Madox Brown designed together the monument to Rossetti on the Embankment at Chelsea. Another, earlier example of their collaboration, which also involved other members of the Brotherhood, is King René's Honeymoon Cabinet in the Museum's Victorian Primary Gallery. This large oak cabinet which Seddon designed as a desk and receptacle for his drawings in 1861, includes painted panels contributed by the Pre-Raphaelites, and is an important early example of the mid Victorian taste for 'mediaeval' furniture. The panels depict imaginary, often amusing incidents during the honeymoon of King René of Anjou (1409–1480) of whom Sir Walter Scott wrote 'a prince of very moderate parts, endowed with a love of the fine arts, which he carried to extremity, and a degree of good humour which never permitted him to repine at fortune'. The top is inscribed with the punning motto 'Non sono sed dono', and the sides inlaid with scenes showing Seddon as a lobster settling disputes with a client and builder depicted as snakes. Such jocular scenes may have been the responsibility of Seddon's pupil William Burges who is known to have worked on the cabinet.

King René's Honeymoon Cabinet illustrates Seddon's passionate belief in the unity of the arts, a topic which formed the subject of several of his lectures and articles. Throughout his working life Seddon was a prolific writer. From January 1849 when a lecture entitled 'On Monumental Architecture' was published in the *Builder*, a constant stream of books and articles flowed from his pen. Most were concerned with aspects of the Gothic revival but their scope ranged over other topics too—Memoirs of his grandfather and brother; published lectures on painting, sculpture, restoration, polychromy, ornament, competitions and photography; books on his travels, and architectural progress; and pamphlets on furniture, church fittings and Kent cottages. His abilities as a writer and critic led to his appointment as Editor of the *Building World* in 1887. Seddon was also a good committee man and was at different times Vice-President, member of Council and Honorary Secretary (with C. Forster Haywood) of the Royal Institute of British Architects; Secretary and Vice President of the Architectural Museum; Vice President of the Westminster School of Art; and either a committee member or consultant to many organisations including the Church Crafts League, The Architectural Photographic Society, the Architectural Association and the Incorporated Society for Promoting the Enlargement, Building and Reparation of Churches and Chapels. His connection with the Architectural Museum lasted for more than twenty five years. After negotiating the transfer of the Museum's collections to the Architectural Association in 1902, and publishing a catalogue entitled *A Casket of Jewels* in the same year, he was presented with a silver bowl by the Committee.

In April 1904 at the age of seventy six Seddon finally retired from his appointment as Surveyor for the Archdeaconry of Monmouth. Some small church works followed, but failing health soon overtook him and he died after an operation in St. Thomas's nursing home on February 1st 1906.

Whatever one may feel about Seddon's abilities as an architect *per se*, his decorative work, his belief in the unity of painting, sculpture and architecture, and the frankness and honesty with which he expounded the merits of the gothic style ensure his continuing interest. Few architects have explained so lucidly in print the motivations which lay behind their work. Seddon's many books and articles taken together with the Museum's large collection of drawings covering all aspects of his work constitute, therefore, an important source for the study of 19th century art and design.

8 ibid., p. 29.
9 W. M. Rossetti, *Some Reminiscences*, 1906, p. 144.

List of Abbreviations

A	*The Architect*
AA	The Architectural Association
AR	*The Architectural Review*
BA	*The British Architect*
Br	*The Builder*
BN	*The Building News*
CEAJ	*Civil Engineer and Architects Journal*
CB	*The Church Builder*
c.	Circa
d.	Dated
Eastlake	C. Eastlake, *A History of the Gothic Revival*, edition edited by J. Mordaunt Crook, 1970
Ecc	*The Ecclesiologist*
Exhib.	Exhibited
Haslam	R. Haslam, The Buildings of Wales: *Powys*, 1979
Howell and Beazley	Peter Howell and Elisabeth Beazley, *Companion Guide to South Wales*, 1977
Illus.	Illustrated
ILN	*Illustrated London News*
Insc.	Inscribed
'*Marble Halls*'	J. Physick and M. Darby, '*Marble Halls*', *Drawings and Models for Victorian Secular Buildings*. Catalogue of the V&A Exhibition, 1973
PH	Peter Howell's card index of Welsh buildings
Plans and Prospects	J. Hilling, *Plans and Prospects, Architecture in Wales 1780–1914*. Catalogue of the Welsh Arts Council Exhibition, 1975
RA	Royal Academy
RIBA	Royal Institute of British Architects
RIBA *Catalogue*	Catalogue of the Drawings Collection of the Royal Institute of British Architects. S. Edited by Margaret Richardson. 1976
s.	Signed
VCH	Victoria County History
Wm.	Watermark

Chronology

(Note. Buildings are listed at time of initiation rather than completion).

1827   Born 19 September at London House, Aldersgate

       Educated at Bedford Grammar School

1847   Becomes pupil of T. L. Donaldson

       Elected member of the AA

1849   Makes a journey to North Wales with his brother Thomas

       Lecture on 'Monumental Architecture' to the AA (Reprinted *Br*, 6 January 1849' pp.4, 5 and 13 Jan., pp.14–16)

1850   Made Honorary Secretary of the AA

1851   Completes apprenticeship to Donaldson

       Makes tour of the Continent

       London, Tulse Hill. Two house for John Hales (p.76)

1852   Becomes Associate of the RIBA

       Begins partnership with John Prichard

       Publishes *Progress in Art and Architecture*

       Exhibits at the Architectural Exhibition:
         Interior view and details of St. Marks, Venice (16)
         Doorway in the choir at Tour-en-Bessin, nr. Bayeux (19)
         Details of the Doges Palace (29)
         Finial, sacristy doorway, choir aisle, Evreux Cathedral, Normandy (34)
         View of the Doges Palace (42)
         Design submitted in competition for laying out the grounds belonging to the Governesses Institution in Kentish Town (79 and 178)
         Views of the central octagon, Coutances Cathedral, and the tower and spire of St. Pierre, Caen (141)
         View of the SW angle, St. Mark's Church, Venice (162)
         Design for entrance to a cathedral suggested by the Western portals of Bayeux (265)
         Design for two houses now in course of erection upon Lower Tulse Hill, Surrey faced with Suffolk bricks and stone dressings (284)
         Chapel, Cathedral of St. Lo, Brittany and sculpture S. Maclon, Rouen (310)
         A study (336)

       Southerndown, Glamorganshire. Dunraven Arms Hotel (pp.92, 93)

       Llandaff, Glamorganshire. Cathedral (p.69)

       Mottingham, Kent. Additions to house for H. Baines (p.80)

       Note: all buildings listed until 1862 are recorded as by Prichard and Seddon.

1853   Provides illustrations for J. E. Jackson, *History of the ruined Church of St. Mary Magdalene Doncaster*, 1853

       Cwmafan, Glamorganshire. All Saints church (p.54)

       Donnington Priory, Newbury, Berkshire. Cottage for John Hughes (p.56)

       Hentland, Herefordshire. St. Dubricius church restored (p.59)

       Orcop, Herefordshire. School (p.84)

       Pentyrch, Glamorganshire. St. Catwg's church restored (*Br*, 5 Dec. 1857, p.709)

1854   Gwerneshi, Gwent. St. Michael's church restored (PH)

       Llanfair Discoed, Gwent. St. Mary's church restored (PH)

       Llanfihangel Torymynydd, Gwent. Church restored (PH)

       Llanisien, Gwent. St. Denis's church restored (*Br*, 20 May 1854, p.269 and 3 June, p.294)

       Trellech, Gwent. Church (PH)

       Tynant, Glamorganshire. Church for Thomas Booker, not executed (p.96)

1855   Lecture 'The Fine Arts', at the Cardiff Exhibition (*Public Library Journal*, June, 1903, p.52, Cardiff, IV, pt.3)

Shows at the Architectural Exhibition:
W. elevation of church about to be erected by Thomas Booker MP at Tyn-y-nant in parish of Radyr, nr. Cardiff (includes list of materials) (309)
W. elevation of church now being erected at Canton, nr. Cardiff (includes list of materials (310)
Tynant church E. elevation (311)
Canton church E. elevation (312)
Tynant church S. elevation (313)
Canton church S. elevation (314)

Cardiff, Canton, Glamorganshire. St. John's church and school (p.49)

Llandysoe, Gwent. Parsonage (*Br*, 12 May 1855, p.224)

Pinner, Middlesex. Cottage for W. Barber (p.88)

1856   Shows a portfolio of drawings at the Architectural Exhibition

Eatington Park, Warwickshire. House for E. P. Shirley (p.56)

Keynsham, Somerset. House (c.1856) (p.66)

Llanfrechfa, Gwent. Parsonage (p.73)

London, Tulse Hill. Church submitted in competition (p.75)

Southerndown, Glamorganshire. Houses (pp.93, 94)

Turkey, Istanbul. Design in competition for the Crimea Memorial church (p.99)

1857   Takes charge of the Whitehall office

Shows at the Architectural Exhibition:
Design for a marine chateau at Kilpayson, nr. Milford Haven (98)
Designs for Crimea Memorial Church (227–230)

Aberavon, Glamorganshire. St. Mary's church (and school?) (*Ecc*, XVIII, 1857, p.258)

Cardiff, Glamorganshire. Post Office (*BN*, 9 & 16 October 1857, pp.1063, 1065, 1099)

Cymmer, Glamorganshire. Schools and master's house (*Ecc*, XVIII, 1857, p.395)

Llanddewi Fach, Gwent. St. David's church rebuilt (PH. Haslam, p.244. Latter gives date as 1860)

Llandeilo Gresynni, Gwent. Church restored (PH)

Llandysoe, Gwent. Design for restoration of church not carried out. (*Ecc*, XVIII, 1857, p.397)

London. Government Offices. Design submitted in competition (*ILN*, 12 September 1857, p.276)

Merthyr Dyfan. St. Dyfan's church restored. (*Br*, 10 Oct. 1857, p.583)

Peterston super Ely, Glamorganshire. Parsonage (p.87)

Pontnewydd, Gwent. Holy Trinity church (p.88)

1858   Lecture on 'Ancient and Modern Architectural Ornament contrasted' (*BN*, 29 January 1858, pp.109–112)

Beckford Hall, Beckford, Warwickshire. Alterations and additions for Hattil Foll (pp.35, 36)

Grosmont, Gwent. St. Nicholas's church restored (p.58)

Hentland, Herefordshire. Parsonage for Rev. Poole (pp.59, 60)

Kentchurch, Herefordshire. St. Mary's church rebuilt (p.65)

Llandeilo, Dyfed. Decoration for J. Charles Morris (p.71)

Llandeilo Bertholau, Gwent. Parsonage (p.71)

Llanelen, Gwent. School (c.1858) (pp.72, 73)

Llangwm Isaf, Gwent. St. John's church restored (p.74)

Llangwm Uchaf, Gwent. Church of SS Jeremy and John, re-arranged, nave rebuilt (p.74)

Llanharan. Church of SS Julius and Aaron. (D. J. Francis, *History of Glamorgan*, VII, 214)

Llanmartin, Gwent. St. Martin's church (p.74)

Mottingham, Kent. Villas for H. R. Baines (pp.80–82)

Templeton, Dyfed. St. John's church. Alterations (p.96)

Whitchurch, Herefordshire. Schools (p.99)

1859   Publishes *Memoirs and Letters of the late Thomas Seddon*

Exhibits at the RA:
   Christ's College, Brecon (1050)
   Eatington Park (1109)

Bridgend, Glamorganshire. School (p.42)

Cardiff, Glamorganshire. Church of Eglwys Dewi Sant (pp.47–49)

Cardiff, St. Fagans, Glamorganshire. Rectory (p.50)

Croydon, Surrey. Alterations and additions to Birdhurst for Mrs P. J. Fearon (pp.53, 54)

Cynwyl Gaio, Dyfed. Church restored. (p.54)

Dingestow Court, Dingestow, Gwent. Alterations and additions (p.55)

Hentland, Herefordshire. School (pp.60, 61)

Joldwynds, Holmbury St. Mary, Surrey. For Champion Wetton (pp.63, 64)

Llandenny, Gwent. St. John's church restored (p.71)

Llandogo, Gwent. St. Douchau's church. (Eastlake, appendix no. 197. *Ecc*, xx, 1859, p.71. *BA*, 17 July 1855, p.31)

Llandough, Glamorganshire. School (pp.71. 72)

Newport, Gwent. St. Woolos cathedral alterations and additions (p.83)

Newport, Maindee, Gwent. Church of St. John the Evangelist (p.83)

Norwood, Surrey. The Rylands, addition for C. F. Leaf (p.84)

Oxted, Surrey. East Hill House (p.85)

1860   Becomes Fellow of the RIBA

Exhibits at the RA:
   Llandaff (647)
   Church at Cardiff (664)

Caerleon, Gwent. Parsonage (p.46)

Gelligaer, Glamorganshire. Parsonage (p.57)

Kentchurch, Herefordshire. Parsonage (p.65)

Llampeter Velfrey, Dyfed. St. Peter's church (p.71)

Llanddewi Felfre, Dyfed. St. David's church (p.71)

Marshfield, Glamorganshire. School (p.79)

Mountain Ash, Glamorganshire. St. Margaret's church (pp.82, 83)

Newton. Church restored (PH)

Tintern, Gwent. St. Mary's church rebuilt (*Ecc*, xxi, 1860, p.49. Burnt down 1977)

Weston under Penyard, Herefordshire. School (pp.97, 98)

Whitsun, Glamorganshire. Church restored (*Ecc*, xxi, 1860, p.329)

Ystradowen, Glamorganshire. St. Owain's church (*Ecc*, xxi, 1860, p.324)

Designs for metalwork for Hart & Son (pp.114, 115)

Designs for furniture for Thomas Seddon (pp.108–113)

Design for a tomb (p.104)

Design for an ironwork screen (p.115)

1861   Article 'What is a Griffin?' (*Br*, 5 January 1861, p.15)

Article 'To "the Gargoyle of St. Mary Anne's"' (*Br*, 19 January 1861, p.45)

Lecture 'On the Grotesque in Art' (*BN*, 8 March 1861, pp.212–213)

Lecture 'The Dark Ages of Architecture' (*BN*, 14 and 21 June 1861, pp.507–509, 526. *Br*, 15 & 22 June 1861, pp.408 & 424. *CEAJ*, 1 September 1861, pp.259–264. RIBA *Papers*, 1860-2, pp.266–79)

Exhibits at the RA:

   Llandough Schools (683)
   Church of St. John the Evangelist at Newport, Mon. (704)

Berthwyd, Glamorganshire. St. Cynon's church (*CB*, 1862, pp.168-9)

Dixton, Gwent. Stained glass for church (pp.55, 56)

Droitwich, Worcestershire. St. Peter's parsonage, addition (p.56)

Little Dewchurch, Herefordshire. School (and parsonage?) (pp.66, 67)

Llanfabon, Glamorganshire. St. Cynon's church additions (*Br*, 27 July 1861, p.515)

Nash, Gwent. Church, chancel rebuilt (*Ecc*, XXII, 1861, p.206)

1862   Dissolves partnership with John Prichard

Marries

Becomes Hon. Sec. of the RIBA (until 1867)

Lecture 'Conventionalism in Ornament' (*CEAJ*, 1 August and 1 September 1862, pp.221–222, 275–276)

Lecture 'Sundry Notes upon some Miscellaneous Subjects'

Exhibits at the RA:
    Organ for 1862 Exhibition (910)
    Design for a stained glass window (914)

Exhibits at the Architectural Exhibition:
    Sketch of the Subject of the Crucifixion in the Easternmost window of the triforium of the apse to the chancel of St. Rhemi, Rheims (193)
    Sketches of color from the painted glass in the windows of the west front of Rheims Cathedral
    Design for a painted glass window (914)

Brecon, Powys. College (pp.40, 41)

Caerleon, Gwent. St. Cadoc's church (p.47)

Cork, Ireland. St. Finn Barr's cathedral. Design submitted in competition (pp.52, 53)

Great Yarmouth, Norfolk. St. Nicholas's church restored (p.58)

Holdgate, Shropshire. Parsonage (pp.62, 63)

Llandysoe, Gwent. Parsonage (p.72)

Llanfaches, Gwent. Church restored (PH)

Llanfair, Glamorganshire. St. Mary's church restored

St. Mary Church (village of), Glamorganshire. Church restored and enlarged (*CB*, 1864, p.38)

Design for an organ for Charles Meeking (p.101)

Design for a chandelier for W. Leaf (p.101)

1863   Moves to 12 Park Street, Westminster (later 1 Queen Anne's Gate)

Article 'Abbey Dore, Herefordshire' (*CEAJ*, 1 October 1863, p.283)

Article 'Some Practical Remarks upon Wall Masonry' (*CEAJ*, 1 March, 1 April, 1 May, 1 June, 1 July 1863,   pp.65–66, 92–93, 126–127, 156–157, 192–193)

Exhibits at the Architectural Exhibition:
    Competition designs for St. Finn Barr, Cork (1, 2, 3, 4, 5, 245)
    Elevation and plan of design submitted in competition for the Langham Hotel (110)
    Additions to Joldwynds, Surrey (252)
    Alterations to Birdhurst House, Croydon (253)
    Design for encaustic tile pavement for Holmer chancel, Nr. Hereford. Tiles by Godwin (379) (RIBA, *Catalogue*, p.35)

Llanddewi Rhydderch, Gwent. St. David's church restored (*CB*, 1863, p.184)

Designs for furniture for W.F.N. Moore (p.101)

Designs for furniture for R. L. Chance (p.100)

1864   Lecture 'On Architectural Competitions' at the RIBA, 15 February (*Ecc*, xxv, 1864, pp.110–111)

Lecture 'On St. Nicholas church, Great Yarmouth, Norfolk' read to the Cambridge Arch. Soc. (*Ecc*, xxv, 1864, pp.376–377)

Article 'Church of Notre Dame, Chalons-sur-Marne' (*CEAJ*, 1 February 1864, pp.38–39)

Article 'Grosmont Church' (*CEAJ*, 1 January 1864, p.7)

Aberystwyth, Dyfed. Castle House Hotel (p.31, 32)

Bonvelstone. Church rebuilt (*CB*, 1864, p.35)

Borth, Dyfed. Hotel completed (p.31)

Cardiff, Glamorganshire. St. Andrew's church (pp.47–49)

Charlton. Parsonage (p.50)

Chigwell Row, Essex. All Saints church and parsonage (pp.51, 52)

Guernsey (possibly). Studio for P. Naftel, alterations and additions (pp.58, 59)

Newchurch, Gwent. Church rebuilt (p.83)

Newport, Christchurch, Gwent. Church rebuilt (p.83)

Oldcastle, Gwent. St. John's church (p.84)

Design for tiles for Maw (p.116)

Design for screen for Allan Brock (p.100)

1865   Lecture 'On St. Nicholas church, Great Yarmouth' repeated (*Ecc*, xxvi, 1865, pp.124-5. RIBA *Papers*, 1864-5, pp.75-84)
Exhibits at the RA:
    St. Nicholas church, Great Yarmouth (788)
Exhibits at the Architectural Exhibition:
    Church of S.M. della Salute, Venice. Sunset (263)
    Central lantern of Coutances cathedral, early morning effect (268)
    Sketches of Dinan in Brittany, early morning effect (283)
    St. Nicholas church, Great Yarmouth (315–318)
    Sketches of Holdgate parsonage, Shropshire, recently built and School-Church about to be built at Glewstown in the parish of Goodrich, Herefordshire (319) (RIBA, *Catalogue*, p.35)
    Designs for encaustic tile arrangements for Maw (320, 324, 325)
    Sketches for fireproof warehouses (321)
    Sketch of church in mountain district (322)
    Designs for furniture for Messrs Seddon and Co (323)

Cholmodon. Church

London, Westminster. Christchurch (*CB*, 1865-66, p.40)

Penarth, Glamorganshire. Church, not carried out (p.86)

1866   Exhibits at the Architectural Exhibition:
    Design for Llandaff cathedral font (166)
    Design for a fountain proposed to be executed in Ransome's Patent Stone, for Australia (167) (p.104)

Bristol. Competition design for the Assize Courts (pp.42, 43)

1867   Lecture 'On the photographs taken for the Architectural Photographic Society in the year 1867' (RIBA *Papers*, 1867-8, pp.47–60)
Exhibits at the RA:
    Design for Law Courts, London (880)
    do. Central Hall (920),
Exhibits at the Architectural Association photographs of the Law Courts design as follows:
    Interior of the library (318)
    Perspective principal front (319)
    Four general views of the model (320)
    Interior view of central suitors hall (321)
    Two birds eye views of model (322)
Exhibits at the Paris Exhibition:
    A study for street architecture (group I, Class 4, no.39)

Caerleon, Gwent. St. Cadoc's church restoration (p.47)

Broadstairs, Kent. St. Peter's orphanage (p.44)

1868   Publishes *Rambles in the Rhine Provinces*

Visits Thornhill church (p.49)

Exhibits at the Architectural Exhibition:
    Views of selected competition design for church at Great Yarmouth (66, 216–219) (p.00)
    Design for Park Lodge, labourer's cottages, etc. at Dytchley, Oxon, for the Rt. Hon. Lord Dillon (68)
    Design for a block of model dwellings for the labouring class now being erected at Fulham for the Rt. Rev. the Lord Bishop of London (73)
    Design for proposed almshouses at Fulham (74)
    Design for altering an old house into school house and master's residence at Hoarwithy, Herefordshire (76)

Archway to the sacristy, Abbey of Romersdorf nr. Coblenz (113)
Plan of St. Mathias chapel, Cobern on the Moselle (114)
Fountain of the Abbey of Sayn nr. Coblenz (122)
Font of Limberg on the Lahn (123)
Font at Bingen on the Rhine (124)
Part of the Sexton's house at St. Florian's, Coblenz (125)
Broncroft Castle, Salop as proposed to be completed (163) (p.00)
Llanbadern church near Aberystwyth, about to be restored (164)
Competition design for St. Swithin's church, Lincoln (220–223)

Aberystwyth, Dyfed. Victoria Terrace (p.33, 34)

Monmouth, Gwent. Hospital enclosure (p.80)

1869   Lecture 'Some recently discovered examples of Ecclesiastical Decoration' (RIBA *Papers*, 1869–70, pp.207-8)

Exhibits at the RA:
University College, Aberystwyth (1003)

Exhibits at the Architectural Exhibition:
Powell's almshouse, Fulham as now in course of erection (23)
St. Nicholas church, Great Yarmouth (55, 56)
Competition designs for Slough church, with R. P. Spiers (99, 100)
Frame of sketches.
1. New hall, Nr. Halifax
2. Garden and entrance fronts
3. Old house at Boppard on the Rhine
4. Old house at Rhense on the Rhine (133)

Bradford. Design for Town Hall submitted in competition (*Br*, 30 October 1869, pp.858-9)

Grosmont, Gwent. St. Nicholas church, further restoration (p.58)

Design for eight cottages for S. C. Wilde (p.102)

1870   Exhibits at the RA:
Bradford Town Hall (778)
Exhibits at the Architectural Exhibition:
Sir A. Powell's almshouses Fulham (52)

Aberystwyth, Dyfed. Abermad house (p.30, 31)

London, Kentish Town. School (p.74)

Monmouth, Gwent. Schools (p.80)

Overmonnow, Gwent. School (p.80)

Ridgeway, Herne, Kent. Double cottage for G. Dering (p.61)

Kingston Hill, Kingston, Surrey. Parsonage (p.66)

Great Yarmouth. St. James's church (p.58)

Designs for cottages for T. H. Burroughs (p.100)

Design for lamp for Hart Son, Peard and Co. (p.114)

1871   Lecture 'On the University College of Wales and other Buildings at and near Aberystwith) (RIBA *Papers*, 1870-1, pp.148–55)

Lecture 'Principles of Chromatic Decoration' (RIBA conference)

Article 'Ancient Brick and Flint Cottages at Broadstairs in the Isle of Thanet' (*BN*, 3 March 1871, p.167)

Exhibits at the RA:
Victoria Terrace, Aberystwyth (880)
Design for the decorations of Christ's College chapel, Brecon (927–929)
Chancel, Grosmont church, Monmouthshire (964)

Bishopsbourne, Kent. Parsonage for Rev. C. W. Sandford (p.38)

Fishponds, nr. Bristol. Parsonage for Rev. A. B. Day (p.57)

Lacey Green, Buckinghamshire. St. John's church additions (p.66)

Designs for cottages for Mr Poole (p.101)

1872   Exhibits at the RA:
Windows for church at Fishponds near Bristol (1168)
University College, Aberystwyth (1205)

Wyesham, Gwent. St. James's church (p.99)

Design for a house for Rev'd Matthews (p.101)

1873   Lecture 'On the shoring of Grosmont Church Tower' (*BN*, 7 February 1873, pp.149–151. RIBA *Papers*, 1872-3, pp.101–10)

Exhibits at the RA:
St. James's church, Great Yarmouth (1123)
Stall work in St. Nicholas, Great Yarmouth (1140)
Staircase at University College, Aberystwyth (1205)

Kennardington. Vicarage for Rev. S. B. Lobb (p.65)

Redbrook, Gloucestershire. Church

Ullenhall, Warwickshire. Vicarage (pp.96, 97)

Design for an unidentified school (p.107)

1874   Exhibits at the RA:
St. Peter's orphanage, Isle of Thanet (1076)
Interior of a chapel (1106)

Adforton, Herefordshire. St. Andrew's church (*BN*, 2 October 1874, p.400, RIBA *Catalogue*, p.34)

Ayot St. Peter, Hertfordshire. St. Peter's church (p.35)

Broadstairs, Kent. St. Peter's church. Boundary walls, etc. (p.44)

Hoarwithy, Herefordshire. St. Catherine's church rebuilt (pp.61, 62)

Ingham, Norfolk. Holy Trinity church, additions (p.64)

London, St. Andrews church, Wells St. Designs for frontals (pp.74, 75)

Pinner, Middlesex. Barra Point (p.87)

Ware, Hertfordshire. Billiard room for Gwyn Jeffries (p.97)

1875   Kenmare, Co. Kerry. Rossdohan House (pp.90, 91)

Ullenhall, Warwickshire. St. Mary's church (p.97)

Upavon, Wiltshire. St. Mary's church. Nave restored (p.97)

Design for a house for H. J. Powys Keck (c.1875) (p.102)

Design for an Archbishop's throne (p.111)

1876   Addington, Surrey. School chapel (p.34)

Arminghall, Norfolk. St. Mary's church restored (p.35)

Cynwyl Gaio, Dyfed. Church. Further work (p.54)

Design for embroidery (p.116)

1877   Exhibits at the RA:
Chancel, Ullenhall church, Warwickshire (1148)
Screen, Ingham church, Norfolk (1156)
Restoration, Lambeth Palace Chapel (1166)

Arklow, Co. Wicklow. Town Hall

Rockfield, Gwent. Lychgate for St. Kenelm's church (p.90)

Sunningwell, Berkshire. St. Leonard's church restored (RIBA *Catalogue*, p.36)

Inscription on tomb for Sir Percy Burrell (p.100)

1878   Receives bronze medal at the Paris exhibition

Exhibits at the RA:
Queen's College, Oxford, etc. (1051) (RIBA, *Transactions* 1879–80, p.141)
Screen, Llangwm church, Monmouthshire (1061)
Queen's College, Oxford, window (1077)

Northampton. St. James's church, altar frontal (p.84)

1879   Great Kimble, Buckinghamshire. St. Nicholas's church, restoration (p.57)

Llanddewi Ysgyryd, Gwent. Church rebuilt (*BA*, 1879, p.239)

Designs for additions to cottage for Sir George Verdon (p.102)

1880   Lecture 'On the Polychromatic Decoration of Various Buildings' (RIBA *Transactions*, 1879-80, pp.129–148)

Birchington, Kent. Houses, hotels, bungalows, etc. (pp.36–39)

Birkenhead, Lancashire. North and South Wales Bank (*BN*, 17 June 1890, p.115)

London. Ecclesiastical Art Exhibition (*Br*, 21 August 1880, p.245)

Melbourne, Australia. Bank (p.99)

Truro, Cornwall. Church (p.96)

1881 Betchworth, Surrey. St. Michael's church (c.1881)

London, Aldersgate. St. Botolph's church. Font cover (*BA*, 13 May 1881, p.246)

1882 Lecture 'On Sundry Working Drawings' (*BA*, 8 December 1882, pp.584–586; 29 December 1882, pp.621–624)

Lecture at Architectural Association on St. Paul's Cathedral (?)

Henley in Arden, Warwickshire. Conservatory winter garden at Burrell's Park for H. G. Newton (*BA*, 8 December 1882)

Kilpeck, Herefordshire. Designs for porch for church (not executed) and parsonage (p.66)

London, Albert Embankment. Exterior decoration for Messrs Rust (*BA*, 16 June 1882, p.284)

London, Hammersmith. St. Paul's church (with H. Roumieu Gough) (*Br*, 2 December 1882, p.727)

1883 Camrose, Dyfed. Stained glass for church (p.47)

St. Arvan's, Gwent. Church restored (PH)

1884 Takes into partnership John Coates Carter

Burnley. Municipal buildings (*BA*, 31 October 1884)

Epsom, Surrey. Street designed for G. White (p.57)

Goodrich, Herefordshire. Church additions (*BA*, 3 July 1885, p.6)

Redruth, Cornwall. Church (p.90)

Swansea, Glamorganshire. Free Library, Art Gallery, and Science and Art Schools (*BA*, 21 November 1884, p.246)

1885 Chalfont, Buckinghamshire. Interior decoration for G. Robinson (p.50)

London. St. Paul's Cathedral. Scheme for painting dome (*Br*, 31 January 1885, p.164)

Paisley, Coats Memorial church (*Br*, 8 August 1885, p.186. *BA*, 31 July 1885. Water-colour interior belonging to Miss A. Birch)

Penarth, Glamorganshire. Conservative club (p.86)

Swindon, Gorse Hill, Wiltshire. St. Barnabas's Church (p.95)

1886 Appointed architect for the rebuilding of University College of Wales

Appointed Cathedral Architect, Llandaff after death of John Prichard

Exhibits at the RA:
  Memorial church, Paisley (1567)

Birmingham, Warwickshire. Competition design for Assize Courts (*Br*, 20 March 1886, p.438)

London, Chelsea. Rosetti Memorial fountain (*Br*, 17 April 1886, p.574)

Norwich. St. Peter Mancroft church, reredos

Design for a lodge for G. Robinson (p.102)

1887 Becomes Art Editor of *Building World* (*BN*, 17 January 1890, p.115)

Exhibits at the RA:
  University College Aberystwyth (1734)

Bath. St. Saviour's church, reredos

London. Design for a People's Palace (with E. W. Godwin) (*Br*, 12 February 1887, p.250)

1888 Moves to 23 Grosvenor Road, Westminster

Cardiff, Grangetown, Glamorganshire. St. Paul's Church (pp.49, 50)

London, Westminster. Christchurch vicarage (*Br*, 17 November 1888, p.360)

London, Westminster. Monumental Halls (pp.78, 79)

1890   Lecture 'On Church Fittings' (*Br*, 19 April 1890, p.285; RIBA *Transactions*, n.s. VI, 1890, pp.287–293)

Exhibits at the RA:
St. Catherine's church, Melincryddan (1919)

Article on church fittings

Briton Ferry, Glamorganshire. St. Mary's church rebuilt (p.44)

Chepstow, Gwent. St. Mary's church restored (pp.50, 51)

Chester, Cheshire. Designs for stained glass windows for church of St. Mary on the Hill (p.51)

Eythorne, Kent. Church restored (*BN*, 17 January 1890, p.115) (p.56)

Hereford. Proposals for west front of Cathedral (p.61)

Little Yeldham, Essex. Rectory (p.68)

Norwich, Norfolk. Pulpit and other work in Cathedral (*BN*, 17 January 1890, p.115. *Br*, 5 September 1891, p.193). At an earlier date Seddon had reported on west front

Penarth, Glamorganshire. All Saints church (p.86)

Stroud, Gloucestershire. School of Art with W. M. C. Fisher (pp.94, 95)

1891   Exhibits at the RA:
Welsh Church, Briton Ferry (1752)
Church of St. Mary, Chepstow (1764)

Cardiff, Glamorganshire. Warehouse in Frederick Street

Mexborough, Yorkshire. Church (p.79)

1892   Exhibits at the RA:
All Saints church Penarth, Glamorgan (1826)
Drawing of the Crucifixion of St. Remi, Rheims (1758)

Stutton, Suffolk. Rectory (p.95)

1893   Superintended execution of W. H. Smith Memorial Window, St. Margaret's church, Westminster

Superintended execution of Crucifixion window for Taormian Convent, Sicily for Sir Edward and Lady Hall

1894   Tredegar, Glamorganshire. St. Dingate's church (*Academy Architecture*, 1895, Supplement)

1898   Publishes *King Renés Honeymoon Cabinet*

1899   Southerndown, Glamorganshire. Additions to Marine Hotel

1900   Elected Vice President and Member of Council of the Architectural Museum (July)

1901   Re-elected to above

Elected Member of the Committee of the Church Crafts League (*Br*, 10 February 1906, p.150)

Elected to the Board of the Westminster School of Art

Llandaff Cathedral. Designs and presents two memorial windows to late Dean Williams and late Jonas Watson (*Br*, 10 February 1906, p.150)

1902   Receives silver bowl for services to the Architectural Museum and publishes *A Casket of Jewels* a descriptive work on the Museum

Cardiff, Adamstown, Glamorganshire. All Saints church (*Br*, 7 February 1903, p.146)

Blaina, Gwent. Mission room (*Br*, 10 February 1906, p.150)

Preston. St. Leonard's church restored

1903   Article 'The Works of the PRB in Llandaff Cathedral' (Cardiff Free Public Library and Museum *Journal*, IV, 1903-04)

Llandaff Cathedral. Organ screen (*Br*, 10 February 1906, p.150)

Rogiet, Gwent. Church restored

Walton-le-Dale, Lancashire. Church restored (Photo belonging to Miss A. Birch)

1904　Pamphlet with E. B. Lamb *Imperial Monumental Halls and Tower at Westminster*

Retires as Surveyor to the Archdeaconry of Monmouth

Dissolves partnership with Carter (April 12)

London, Paddington. St. David's Welsh church, gateway. Canon Edwards Memorial (*Br*, 29 October 1904, p.441 and 10 February 1906, p.150)

1905　Bristol. Christ church. Scheme for decorating one bay in the Renaissance manner with Mr Murray (*Br*, 10 February 1906, p.150)

Chalgrave. All Saints Church, restored (*Br*, 8 July 1905, p.34)

1906　Dies 1 February. Buried on 5 February at St. Mary le Park, London

Buildings, etc. of uncertain date

Aberdare, Glamorganshire. St. Fagan's church. (Correspondence and papers re. new church and parsonage. Plymouth Estate Archives)

Addington, Surrey. Cottages (p.34)

Barfrestone, Kent. St. Mary's church restored (*BN*, 17 January 1890, p.115; *Br*, 10 February 1906, p.150)

Brecon, Powys. Priory church, now the Cathedral (p.40)

Brookfield. National schools (p.46)

Dinas, Dyfed. Houses (after 1884) (*Br*, 10 February 1906, p.150)

Glewstone, Herefordshire. Altar. (RIBA *Catalogue*, p.35)

Holmer, Herefordshire. St. Bartholomew's church. Altar rails (RIBA *Catalogue*, p.35)

Hook, Surrey. St. Paul's church. Window and font. (RIBA *Catalogue*, p.35)

Llantrisant, Gwent. Church (p.74)

London, Kensington. 115–117 Lansdowne Villas, Brompton Road. Interior decoration (p.74)

London, Kentish Town. Middleton and Hungerford Roads. Houses (p.74)

London, Tulse Hill. Parsonage (p.76)

London, Westminster. St. Margaret's church porch and font (p.78)

Margate, Kent. Church. Seats (RIBA *Catalogue*, p.36)

Narbeth. The Grove (*BN*, 17 January 1890, p.115)

New Tredegar, Glamorganshire. Church (p.84)

Penge, Kent. Church (p.86)

Peterstone, Glamorganshire. Schools (p.87)

St. Lythans. Glamorganshire. Church restored (p.91)

Shotley Hall. Furniture (p.91)

Catalogue

Place (if place not known, name of client or subject of drawing. See index)

General note of aspect treatments (photographs, perspectives, plans, elevations, sections, and details). Number of sheets involved. Dates of drawings when known.

Inscriptions, signatures, etc. when they appear on more than one drawing in a series. Occasionally an individual inscription may be included when it relates directly to a preceding series. Dates and scales are not included here.

Techniques

Museum object numbers

Details of individual drawings including scales and dates (only mentioned when they appear on sheet), and any inscriptions not mentioned above. The drawing in this series are arranged in the aspect treatment order indicated above and in chronological order when possible.

Sizes of sheets in inches and centimeters (height before width).

Details of exhibitions, etc.

Literature

Note. In every case where 'etc.' appears after *Prichard and Seddon* it stands for the address *Llandaff and 6 Whitehall, London* or similar.

The volumes of drawings by John Pollard Seddon also include works by the following: H. H. Armstead; J. de Oates; R. W. Edis; H. Gaye; F. V. Hart; H. A. Kennedy; H. G. Murray; J. Prichard; G. B. Reynolds; E. R. Robson; J. T. Trench.

Travel sketch of the Church of St. Etienne at Caen D.1068–1907

Topographical Drawings

Sketches (277) of architecture and architectural details in England including buildings at Canterbury, Blythburgh, London (Westminster); Lichfield, Gloucester, Chester, Droitwich, St. Albans, Ely, Elland (Yorkshire W. Riding), Worstead (Norfolk) and Irstead (Norfolk); in Italy including Venice, Verona, Mons, Florence, and Milan; in Switzerland including Andermach and Lucerne; in Belgium including Louvain, Liege, Ostend, Ghent, Malines and Alost; in Holland including Maestricht; in Wales including Conway; in France including Rouen, Noyon, Bayeux, Beauvais, Caen and Dinan; and on the Rhine including Mannheim, Oberwesel, Mainz, Bacharach, Heilbron, Cologne, Coblenz, Freiburg, Aix la Chapelle, Oppenheim and Worms.
c.1849–1852.

Several are s. *John P. Seddon* or initialled *J.P.S.* Many of the Continental drawings are d. *June* or *July 1851* and one D.1146 of Malines is d. *2 July 1850*. D.1000 and D.1001 of Beauvais are insc. *from sketch by W. Burges.* D.905 of a cottage at Elland is insc. *reduce this so as to come within 2 cols of Building News;* and D.962 is insc. *P. Naftel Conway Castle* and d. *August 1849*.
Pencil, pen and ink, and water-colour. Some are on tracing paper. D.1920A, 1921A engraved.
D.1920, 1921, 1921A, 1923, 1935, 1936, 1941–1943—1896
D.894–899, 901–908, 910–1154, 1165–1172, 1175–1178—1907

D.914, 924, 927, 931, 933–935, 942–945—1907 and D.1943–1986, appeared as plates in J. P. Seddon, *Progress in Art and Architecture*, 1852.
D.1649–1896 depicts part of the interior of the drawing room at no. 8. Kensington Palace Gardens, London, a house designed and built by Owen Jones in 1843 for John Marriott Blashfield, a speculative developer.

Sketchbook including 83 leaves (some tipped in, some with engravings pasted on) of notes and sketches primarily of churches at Coblenz, Bendorf, Sayn, Romersdorf, Boppard, Andernach, Laach, Altenburg, Munster, Heimersheim, Swartz Rheindorf, Limburg, Arzheim, Louh, Alken, Bacharach and Cologne, made by Seddon during a tour on the continent. The sketches include plans, elevations and details, many inscribed with measurements. Some are reproduced in J. P. Seddon, *Rambles in the Rhine Provinces*, 1868. 1851. Several are s. *John P. Seddon* or initialled *J.P.S.*
Pencil, pen and ink, and water-colour. Some are on tracing paper.
$8 \times 6\frac{1}{2}$ (20.3 × 16.5) D.1190–1259—1896

LONG MELFORD, Suffolk. Church

Sketches of stained glass (3 sheets mounted on 1) Insc. *from Long Melford Ch. Suffolk*. Initialled *J.P.S.* d. *Feb. 61*.
Pencil and water-colour
$6\frac{5}{8} \times 10\frac{1}{4}$ (16.7 × 26.1) D.1712–1714—1896

THORNHILL, Church

Sketches (on 2 sheets) of stained glass. D.1716 d. *Sept. 68* and insc. *Thornhill Ch*. and D.1715 *Thornhill 68*
Pencil and water-colour
$6\frac{3}{4} \times 4\frac{3}{8}$ (17 × 11.2) D.1715, 1716—1896

It is not clear which Thornhill this is.

UNIDENTIFIED

Sketch of a spandrel panel depicting the Expulsion (?)
Pencil and pen and ink
$10\frac{1}{8} \times 8\frac{1}{8}$ (25.7 × 20.6) D.1921A—1896

Lithograph after a more finished version of the above.
s. with a monogram of the letters J.P.S.
$13\frac{3}{4} \times 8\frac{7}{8}$ (34.7 × 22.5) D.1921—1896

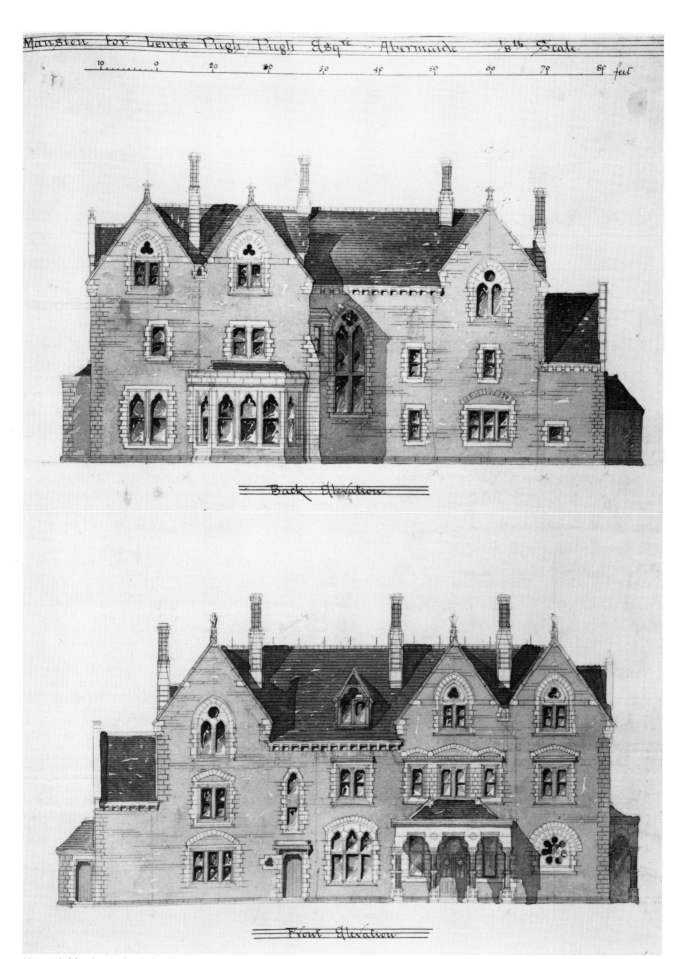

Back Elevation

Front Elevation

Abermad. Mansion for Lewis Pugh D.1397–1896

Architectural Designs

ABERMAD, Dyfed

Elevations, sections and details (on 14 sheets). 1870–1872
D.1304, 1397–1400, 1557, 1558 insc. *Mansion for Lewis Pugh Pugh Esq. Abermaide* or similar. D.1991 insc. *L. P. Pugh.* D.1399, 1400, 1557, 1558, 1991 s. or insc. *J.* or *John P. Seddon Archt.* D.1557, 1558 addressed *12, Park Street, Westminster.* D.1399, 1584, 1585, 1991 pencil. D.1400 pencil, and pen and ink. D.1304, 1397 pencil and water-colour. Rest pencil, pen and ink, and water-colour.
D.1304, 1397–1400, 1557–1559, 1582, 1584, 1585, 1601, 1620, 1991–1896

Garden elevation. Back elevation. Entrance elevation. Scale ⅛th
23¼ × 16¼ (59.2 × 41.4) D.1400–1896

Front elevation. Back elevation. Scale ⅛th and linear
20¾ × 14½ (52.6 × 36.7) D.1397–1896

End elevation. Elevation towards garden. Scale ⅛th and linear
20⅛ × 15 (51 × 38) D.1398–1896

Porch. Sketch plan, elevations, sections and details. Scale ½in
22½ × 29¼ (57 × 74.2) D.1304–1896

Design for entrance & porch. Plans, elevations, sections and details. Scale ½ inch and ¼ full size. d. *April 1870*
22 × 28¾ (55.8 × 73) D.1399–1896

Front door. Plan. Elevation. Section. Insc. with a note initialled *JPS. I think this would do for the 5ft doorway*
19 × 13¼ (48.2 × 33.6) D.1557–1896

Sketches of *Wrt iron hinges front entrance door.* Scale ½ *full size*
29½ × 20¼ (75 × 51.4) D.1991–1896

Plan, elevations and detail of *entrance doors to corridor.* Scale *1 inch.* Insc. *Door of teak*
20 × 13⅞ (50.8 × 35.2) D.1601–1896

Plan and elevation of front door. Insc. *A working drawing of this door & frame wanted (not doorway)* and initialled *J.P.S.*
15⅛ × 8 (38.4 × 20.3) D.1582–1896

Folding doors. Plan. Elevation. Section. Scale *inch*
19 × 13⅛ (48.2 × 33.2) D.1558–1896

Sketch plan, elevation, section and details of folding doors
13⅞ × 11¼ (35.3 × 28.5) D.1584–1896

Best internal doors. Plan, elevation, section and details. Scale *one inch*
18¾ × 12¾ (47.5 × 32.5) D.1559–1896

Plans, elevation, section and detail of doors
14 × 11¼ (35.6 × 28.6) D.1585–1896

Hall chimneypiece. Plan, elevations and details. Scale *Inch.* Alterations added in pencil
28½ × 21⅝ (72.2 × 55) D.1620–1896

Abermad is situated about four miles out of Aberystwyth on the road to Aberayon. Pugh Pugh employed his own workmen under the direction of David Williams for the construction, and spared little expense and trouble. A wide range of local materials were used, some of which, the stone for the impressive hall fireplace, for example, were very hard and difficult to carve. The walls are of dark purplish Schistose stone, the dressings of Doulting stone, columns of Shap granite and Bridgend green sandstone, the hall paved with Maw's tiles, and the garden steps of red conglomerate from Radyr, near Cardiff. One interesting feature is a stained glass window depicting Ruskin's Seven Lamps of Architecture for which a design is also preserved in the Seddon collection (catalogued under Hart, F. Vincent D.1173–1896).

Much of the internal woodwork was painted over earlier in this century but the present owner is now restoring this to its original state.

A, 12 Oct. 1872, p.203.
BA, 21 July 1882, p.342
Howell and Beazley, pp.65–66

ABERYSTWYTH, Dyfed
Castle House Hotel, later the University College of Wales

Detail of door. Plan, half elevations and section. Scale *inch.* (2 on 2 sheets D.1567 is a tracing of D.1566) Insc. *Castle House Aberystwith* and D.1567 *Billiard R. door detail* (the remainder is illegible) *P.P.E.*
D.1566 pen and ink and pencil. D.1567 pen and ink, and water-colour on tracing paper; torn.
D.1566 17¾ × 12⅜ (45 × 31.4) D.1567 13⅜ × 9½ (34 × 24.2)
D.1566, 1567–1896

Printed plans for the restoration of the College after the fire of 1885 appear on the back of several other drawings. These have not been catalogued because they are pasted directly to the pages of the volumes containing the collection, and can only be seen when the pages are held up to the light.

The story of the building of the Hotel and of its conversion, before completion, to the University College of Wales was told by Seddon in a lecture before the Royal Institute of British Architects entitled 'On the University College of Wales and Other Buildings at and near Aberystwyth'. How he was consulted by Thomas Savin, a railway entrepreneur, in the spring of 1864 about some proposed works at Towyn and the completion of an unfinished hotel at Borth, and how Savin then asked him to undertake the conversion into a hotel of Castle House, the mansion which Nash built for Sir Uvedale Price, and which Savin had just purchased. Seddon's work began with the design of a large public restaurant with a flat roof forming a promenade over-looking the sea. Everything was to be done very quickly. He prepared some sketches during the day, they were approved by Savin in the evening, and the foundations were laid out the next morning, while Seddon worked on more detailed drawings.

This method of working involving great speed and haphazard development set the pattern for the remainder of the building. Savin soon wanted a further storey to the restaurant to provide bedrooms, and in the Autumn he asked Seddon to design a much larger extension to the north with suites of rooms on the American model. These were followed by additions to Castle House itself, a ten storey tower, and the reconstruction of the sea wall, the last a huge task. Seddon was expected to keep five hundred men in work, and explained that he never was able to make any complete drawings. 'A rough wooden model was all I could prepare for general guidance, with the requisite working drawings for details as they were required'. As if these were not complications enough, the materials he specified could often not be obtained in time, and he would return to the site to find that building had already begun in others. His discovery that ordinary brickwork and cement rendering were being used on the south wing in place of what he had specified, for example, was what caused him to design the upper storey with timber framing, and incised and coloured cement panels.

In 1866 after Savin had spent some £80,000 he was declared bankrupt, and the building was purchased in an unfinished state by the Committee of the proposed University of Wales for the sum of £10,000. They were very slow in continuing the unfinished work, and much still remained to be done in September 1884 when a report was circulated that they intended to employ another architect. By June in the following year, however, after the *Builder* had supported Seddon's case, he was re-instated, and all seemed ready to proceed, when on 8 July a disastrous fire broke out in the chemistry laboratory completely gutting the north wing. The question of Seddon's employment then arose again. The Committee arranged for a competition for a new college on another site, but after premiums had been awarded and tenders received, Seddon submitted a long report showing how the buildings could be restored for under £18,000, several thousand pounds cheaper than the lowest quotation for a new building. At a meeting of the Committee on 29 July 1886 his report was accepted, and he and Carter were unanimously

The University College of Wales, Aberystwyth, as it appears today. Photograph courtesy of Richard Brinckley, University College of Wales.

chosen to undertake the work. A tender from S. Belham and Co. for £17,900 was accepted and work began almost immediately. By 28 April in the following year the *Builder* could report that the rebuilding was 'approaching completion'.

The College exterior remains substantially as completed by Seddon although his timber framing, and some later additions in the same style to the south wing, have been replaced with stone. Inside, the 'Quad' was formed by roofing in the main corridor in 1889-90, and in 1892 C. J. Ferguson designed the interior of the library. Ferguson was also the architect in 1894 of the present central block, replacing Castle House which had for some time been used as the Principal's residence. C. F. A. Voysey, Seddon's pupil, is reported to have designed the cement panels on the exterior of the south wing.

Few detailed drawings of the buildings survive because, of course, Savin did not give Seddon time to prepare them.

Br, 3 Sept. 1864, p.659; 27 Sept. 1884, p.850; 13 June 1885, p.825; 15 Aug. 1885, p.215; 7 Nov. 1885, p.634; 12 June 1886, p.847; 14 Aug. 1886, p.226; 26 Feb. 1887, p.335; 28 April 1888, p.229.
BN, 28 Dec. 1866, p.871; 14 April 1871, pp.278-9; 30 June 1871, pp.511, 515; 4 June 1886, p.930; 11 June 1886, p.968; 20 Aug. 1886, p.292; 22 Oct. 1886, p.627.
BA, 14 July 1882, p.331 etc. Eastlake, pp.47, 253, 360.
Catalogue of the University College of Wales Centenary Exhibition, 1972.
RIBA *Transactions*, 1870–71, pp.148–152
Howell and Beazley, pp.59–60

The University College of Wales, Aberystwyth.
Photograph taken during the original building works.
Photograph courtesy of the National Library of Wales.

The University College of Wales, Aberystwyth, after the fire of 1885.
Photograph courtesy of the National Library of Wales.

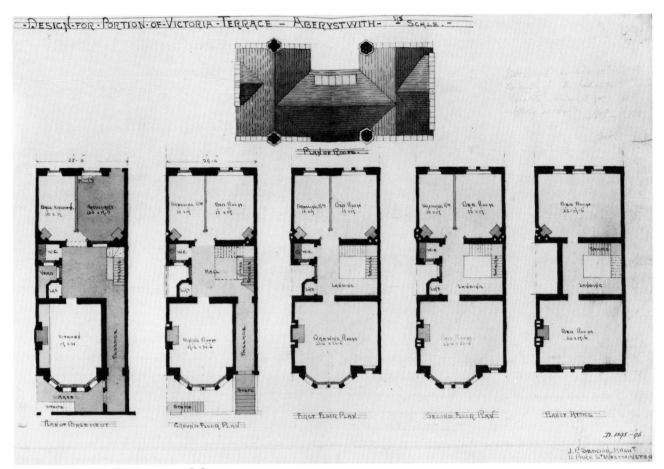

Aberystwyth. Victoria Terrace D.1395–1896

ABERYSTWYTH, Dyfed. Victoria Terrace

Plans, elevations, sections and details (on 9 sheets). Begun
1868.
D.1393, 1395, 1396, 1551 s. or insc. *J. P. Seddon* and D.1393,
1395, 1551 addressed *12 Park St. Westminster.* D.1389,
1391–1396 insc. with measurements.
D.1390–1394, 1396 pencil and water-colour. D.1395 pencil,
ink and water-colour. Rest pencil, pen and ink, and water-
colour.
D.1389–1396, 1551–1896

*Design for portion of Victoria Terrace Aberystwyth. Plan of basement.
Ground floor plan. First floor plan. Second floor plan. Plan of attics.
Plan of roofs.* Scale ⅛. Insc. with names of rooms and *Not
executed as being rather too costly for the particular locality—
arranged for letting in suites* initialled *J.P.S.*
15¾ × 22½ (40 × 57.2) D.1395–1896

Front elevation of a single house.
16¼ × 8¾ (41.2 × 22.1) D.1389–1896

Part elevation of a single house.
20 × 8½ (50.7 × 21.7) D.1390–1896

Plan, elevation and section of a curved window.
13⅝ × 13⅜ (34.6 × 34) D.1391–1896

Front elevation. Elevation of area wall. Single house.
32⅛ × 19⅛ (81.5 × 48.5) D.1392–1896

Part front elevation of a single house. d. *May 29th 18* (the rest
torn off)
22½ × 19¾ (57 × 50.3) D.1393–1896

Part front elevation of a single house.
22⅝ × 15 (57.4 × 38) D.1394–1896

End elevation. Scale ½ *inch*
39 × 22¼ (99 × 56.5) D.1396–1896

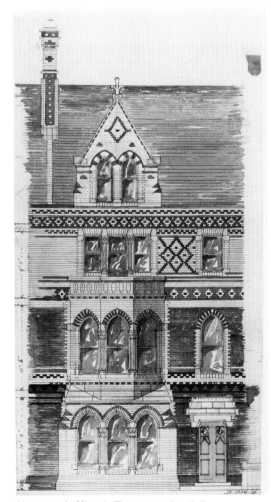

Aberystwyth. Victoria Terrace D.1389–1896

Victoria Terrace. Aberystwyth, as it appears today. Photograph courtesy of Richard Brinckley. University College of Wales.

Entrance door. Dining room and best door. Chamber floor door. Plans, elevations, sections and details. Scale *one inch.* d. *November 26th 1870.* Insc. *Mr Scott, Victoria Terrace, Aberystwyth.*
13⅛ × 19 (33.5 × 48.2) D.1551–1896

In 1865, in an article entitled 'Mr Seddon in Aberystwith', the *Building News* noted: 'Mr Seddon, not satisfied with the erection of a splendid hotel, appears ambitious to remodel Aberystwith. Seeing that that town is likely to become the favourite watering-place of Wales, he wishes to make it as attractive as the beautiful scenery which surrounds it. To accomplish this, Mr Seddon has called a meeting of the town authorities and submitted a comprehensive plan, involving considerable reconstructions and improvements. He suggests the erection of a new crescent of modern and noble houses, and another half crescent of villas. The residences are proposed to be of a superior character to attract permanent residents; also to erect a market-house, public slaughter houses, a laundry and bath-house, and additional church accommodation. He also proposed to apply to Parliament for an act for enlarged powers, not only to improve the town, in a general sense, by paving, better sewerage, additional light, and supply of water, but with compulsory powers to remove any obstruction to the beauty of the place. Another item in the plan was to rebuild the Belle Vue Hotel, so that it may vie with the other two hotels in course of erection. Mr Seddon proposes that much of this work should be done by a company, in whose name he apparently spoke. The town authorities listened to Mr Seddon with great satisfaction and unanimously resolved to give the proposed gigantic company their cordial co-operation'.

Nothing seems to have come of these grandiose proposals except the erection of Victoria Terrace, partly, no doubt, because of Savin's financial troubles with the Castle Hotel. The terrace, stretching northwards from Hayward and Davis's Queen's Hotel, was bounded by a quarry behind and by the recently completed esplanade in front. By June 1868 the *Building News* reported that the terrace 'consisting of twenty five houses' was 'about to be commenced'. It is not known when it was completed but work must have progressed fairly slowly because by March 1871, when the same periodical illustrated the corner house, only two others had been finished. These were built by Thomas Williams of Cardiff who was also the lessee, and estimated to cost £2,000 for the six storey corner block, and £1,600 for the five storey others.

Seddon explained in his lecture 'On the University College of Wales and other Buildings at and near Aberystwith' that he was commissioned by the Corporation to prepare the plans for the Terrace 'so that builders who may take leases might be compelled to conform to my designs'. He also explained that he had tried to meet 'the peculier requirements of a sea-side place, by making each floor contain a sitting room, bed and dressing rooms, and to be as complete in itself as possible. It is intended to diversify the houses, and to introduce among them several larger ones, with rooms on each side of the entrance'.

Perhaps the most striking aspect of Seddon's designs is their bright polychromy. The Queen's Hotel was built in the local purplish stone, a colour which was echoed again in the quarries defacing the green hills behind, while the remainder of the frontage of the town to the sea was occupied by 'a monotonous row of mediocre houses covered with drab-washed cement'. 'In consideration of these circumstances' explained Seddon, 'I chose a rich brick from the neighbourhood of Cardiff, as the material for the general groundwork. This is so used up to the underside of the topmost stories where I have changed it for a ground of buff brickwork, and I have relieved the former by the introduction of blue Staffordshire bricks, and the latter by carrying up some of the red into it. The columns forming the mullions of the windows are, like those of the college, of various delicately tinted sandstones; the capitals are all treated differently, with a small amount of carving. As Aberystwith faces Westward, the Parade is mostly in shade during the heat of the day but towards evening it catches the rays of the setting sun. I hope, therefore, that the effect of this terrace will be brilliant at a time of day when such can be tolerated'.

Victoria Terrace still survives although many details have been removed and a particularly unsympathetic window inserted at the Seabank Hotel.

BN, 24 November 1865, p.833; 17 March 1871, p.203 (illus) Howell and Beazley, p.60.

ADDINGTON, Surrey. Cottages

Plans, elevation, sections and details (on 4 sheets) including accommodation for a curate.
Insc. *Cottages at Addington, Surrey*
Pencil and water-colour. Inscriptions in ink
D.1459–1462–1896

Ground plan. First floor plan. Front elevation. Back elevation. End elevation. End elevation. Linear scale.
18¼ × 12¼ (46.3 × 31.1) D.1459–1896

Roof plan. Transverse section. Longitudinal section.
17⅞ × 12 (45.3 × 30.3) D.1460–1896

Plans, elevations and sections of window and door. Linear scale.
12¼ × 18 (31 × 45.9) D.1461–1896

Plans, elevations and sections of window and chimney. Linear scale.
18¾ × 12⅞ (47.7 × 32.7) D.1462–1896

School chapel

Addington School chapel. Part plan to be tiled. Scale ½ in. s. *J. P. Seddon.* Insc. with notes about the tiles to be used
Pencil and wash on tracing paper
9¼ × 13¼ (23.5 × 33.8)
D.2116–1896

Elevations (on 3 sheets) of ceiling, and north and east walls showing internal decorations. Scale ½ inch.
Insc. *Decorations* or *Proposed decorations chapel at Addington* or similar. s. *John P. Seddon* and d. *June 1876*
Pencil and water-colour
14¾ × 21¼ (37.5 × 54.6)
D.1689–1691–1896

ARMINGHALL, Norfolk. Church of St. Mary

Sections (2) of roof. Scale *1″*. 1876
Insc. *Arminghall Church.* D.1520 insc. in ink *I agree to this roof.*
Initialled *G.L.*(?) and d. *9.8.76.* D.1521 insc. with width of
span *16. 6″*
Pencil and water-colour. D.1520 on tracing paper
D.1520. $19\frac{1}{2} \times 25$ (49.5×63.2) D.1521. $18\frac{3}{8} \times 24\frac{5}{8}$ (46.7×62.5)
D.1520, 1521 1896

The Archaeological conference held in Yarmouth and Norwich
in 1879 visited the church when the *Building News* noted that it
had been 'completely restored by Mr J. P. Seddon—the floor,
seats, roof, plaster internal faces to walls, and fittings are new, the
only remains of the old structure worth notice being some good
poppy-heads which have been judiciously fixed on to the chancel
benches'.

There is a design for the seats in the RIBA, illus. in RIBA
Transactions N.S. VI, 1890, p.179.

N. Pevsner, *North-West and South Norfolk*, 1962, p.75
BN, 22 August 1879, p.233.
RIBA *Catalogue*, p.34

AYOT ST. PETER, Hertfordshire.
Church of St. Peter

Plans, elevations, sections and details (on 8 sheets) of roofs,
tower doorway, and entrance gateway. 1874-5.
D.1525, 1526, 1544-6, 1576 insc. *Ayot St Peter's Hertfordshire* or
similar. D.1526, 1545 insc. *John P. Seddon Architect.* D.1525,
1526, 1534, 1576 insc. with measurements, notes, etc.
D.1501, 1534, 1576 pencil. D.1544-6 pencil and water-colour.
Rest pencil, pen and ink, and water-colour.
D.1501, 1525, 1526, 1534, 1544-6, 1576–1896

Section of nave roof. Scale *1 inch*. Torn
$19\frac{3}{8} \times 28$ (49.2×78.1) D.1525–1896

Details of roofs. Nave roof. Chancel roof. Sections and details.
Scale $\frac{1}{2}″$ *to a foot.* d. *October 1874.*
Stamped *Incorporated Church Building Society. Plans approved* the
date *17 Nov. 1874* has been added in manuscript.
$23\frac{1}{2} \times 16\frac{1}{4}$ (59.7×41.2) D.1526–1896

Section of nave roof. Scale $\frac{1}{2}$ *inch*
$17 \times 14\frac{1}{2}$ (43×36.7) D.1534–1896

Section and part elevation of roof. Insc. *Dane Hill* (the next
word is illegible)
$13\frac{3}{8} \times 19\frac{1}{4}$ (33.9×48.9) D.1501–1896

Tower Doorway. Details. Scale $\frac{1}{2}$ *inch* and *full size*
$13\frac{1}{2} \times 14\frac{1}{4}$ (34.2×36) D.1544–1896

Pallisading. Plan. Elevation. Plan of top of pier. Elevation of pier &
section of wall. Scale *1″.* d. *March 75.*
$12\frac{1}{8} \times 17\frac{1}{2}$ (31×44.3) D.1545–1896

Details of Gate. Plans, elevations and details. Scale *details full*
size
28×18 (71.2×45.6) D.1546–1896

Elevations and details of gateway and pallisading. Scale $\frac{1}{2}$ *in*
$10\frac{3}{8} \times 12\frac{1}{2}$ (26.3×31.7) D.1576–1896

After the destruction of the old church at Ayot St. Peter by fire in
July 1874, Seddon won a competition for the design of a new
building which was dedicated on 26 October 1875. The *Building*
News noted that the new church was Early Decorated in style and
that the plan was without aisles: 'The chancel arch is the principal feature of the interior. The unusual stone facing is displaced
by pottery of the "Gris de Flandre" type, the design, which may
be termed an imitation of the thirteenth century, including birds
and flowers after life, unconventionally treated. The chancel is a
spacious one, and is of circular apsidal-ended form. The ceiling
is a simple curve, sky toned and otherwise partly, but richly,
decorated. The pavement is of Godwin's encaustic tiles . . . The
inner walls of the church are built entirely of bricks from the old
building, and are plastered. The external facing is of new red

brick in conjunction with Bath stone dressings. The roof is of
rather high pitch and is covered with local red tiles, with ridge of
terra-cotta . . . The total amount subscribed for the new building
was £2,800 besides gifts'.

Designs for the pulpit and seats are in the RIBA. A collection
of Seddon's letters relating to the rebuilding are temporarily
deposited in the Hertfordshire County Branch Library,
Campus West, Welwyn Garden City.

BN, 5 November 1875, p. 518
N. Pevsner, *Hertfordshire*, 1953, pp.46-7
RIBA *Catalogue*, p.34
Information from R. J. Busby, Reference Librarian, Welwyn

BECKFORD HALL, Beckford, Worcestershire

Plans, elevations, sections and details (on 12 sheets) for
alterations and additions for Hattil Foll. 1858.
D.855–865 insc. *Alterations to Beckford Hall, Gloucestershire for*
Hattil Foll Esq., or similar. D.856, 857 s. *Hattil Foll* and
J. Norman Brown. D.856-858, 860, 861, 863-865 insc. *Prichard*
& Seddon etc. D.866 lettered *J. R. Jobbins.*
D.866 engraving. D.865 pencil. D.860, 861, pencil and water-
colour. D.855 pen and ink. D.862-864 pen and ink, and water-
colour. Rest pencil, pen and ink, and water-colour. D.855, 861,
863 on tracing paper.
D.855–866–1896

Ground plan. Basement Plan. Scale $\frac{1}{8}$ *inch*
$16 \times 23\frac{1}{2}$ (40.8×59.5) D.857 × 1896

South elevation. Section. Scale $\frac{1}{8}$th. d. *1858*
$14\frac{1}{8} \times 19\frac{1}{4}$ (36×49) D.856–1896

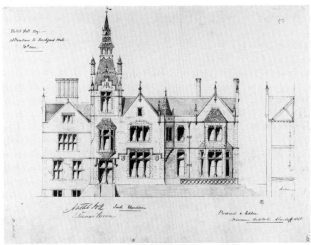

Beckford Hall D.856–1896

South elevation showing revised arrangement for terracing
Scale *3/16th*
$16\frac{5}{8} \times 22\frac{1}{8}$ (42.8×56.3) D.855–1896

End elevation. Transverse section on line AB. Scale $\frac{1}{8}$ *inch.*
Alterations indicated in pencil.
$12\frac{1}{2} \times 19$ (31.6×48.3) D.858–1896

Drawing room Bow. Part plans, elevations and section. Scale
$\frac{1}{2}$ *in*
$22\frac{1}{8} \times 16\frac{1}{4}$ (56.3×41.3) D.859–1896

As above. d. *Octr 1860*
Plate 74 from H. Laxton, *Examples of Building Construction*
$24\frac{1}{2} \times 21$ (61.7×53.2) D.866–1896

Elevation, section and details of windows below tower, south
front. Scale details $\frac{1}{2}$ *full size*
$22\frac{1}{8} \times 17\frac{1}{8}$ (56.1×43.6) D.862–1896

Porch. Plan, elevations, sections and details. Scale $\frac{1}{4}$ *in* and
$\frac{1}{4}$ *full size*
$13 \times 18\frac{3}{4}$ (33×47.7) D.863–1896

Sketches for glazed screen in archway. Scale *1 in*
$14\frac{5}{8} \times 19\frac{1}{2}$ (37.1 × 49.5) D.865–1896

Detail of dining room window and door including part plan, elevations, section and details. Scale $\frac{1}{2}$ *in* and $\frac{1}{4}$ *full size.* d. *Apl. 1858*
$12 \times 17\frac{3}{8}$ (30.5 × 44) D.860–1896

Design for ceilings in dining and drawg rms & vestibule. Scale $\frac{1}{8}$*th* and $\frac{1}{2}$ *in.* d. 24 [?] *Dec 1858*
$9\frac{3}{4} \times 11\frac{3}{4}$ (23.9 × 29.9) D.861–1896

Chimney by side of tower next old part of house. Scale $\frac{1}{2}$ *in*
$18\frac{7}{8} \times 10\frac{7}{8}$ (48 × 27.7) D.864–1896

Hattil Foll, father of the minor novelist of the same name, purchased Beckford Hall some time before 1863 from Walter Wakeman. It is not clear what the building consisted of at that time but it appears to have been a comparatively small Jacobean house on the foundations of an Augustinian priory founded in 1128. Some work may have been carried out in 1836 when the fabric was reported to be in poor condition. Foll, who died in 1881, sold the house in or before that year to Captain Henry Case who made various additions including a tower and wings, and a chapel designed by I. Price, and since much of this work, like Seddon's, was carried out in the existing style it is now difficult to work out what is what. The front, with seven even gables, for example, does not relate to Seddon's plan, and is presumably later. Seddon's gothic tower and bell turret do not appear to have been built.

Beckford Hall is now owned by the Salesian Society who purchased it in 1936.

N. Pevsner, *Worcestershire*, 1968, p.77
VCH, *Gloucestershire*, vol. VIII, pp.254-5
Picturesque Gloucestershire, 1928, pp.52-3

BETCHWORTH, Surrey. Church of St. Michael

Section of *old* roof. c. 1881
Insc. in ink *Betchworth Church Surrey* and with measurements
Pencil and water-colour
13 × 16 (33.1 × 40.8) D.1518–1896

St. Michael's, essentially 13th century but incorporating some earlier features, underwent several restorations in the 19th century particularly in 1851 (by E. C. Hakewill) and again in 1870. Seddon's work there appears to date from the early 1880s; he mentions the problems he had 'lately' encountered with the roof in 'On Sundry Working Drawings', and this date is further supported by a window in the south choir by Belham & Co inscribed 'H. S. Murray del 1881', and by Seddon's design for the pulpit, in RIBA of c.1885, one of the drawings he prepared for his illustrations of church fittings.

Because of the prohibitive cost of oak and contemporary dislike of tie rods Seddon explained in 'On Sundry Working Drawings' that at Betchworth 'I have introduced principals, at a moderate distance apart, in contradistinction to the treatment by the use of framed couples alone, which is peculiar for oak, and as I have had to place the collars high up, for the reason stated, I have made curved braces sustain these and connect them with the rafters thoroughly'.

N. Pevsner, I. Nairn and B. Cherry, *Surrey*, 1971, pp.108–110
RIBA *Catalogue*, p.34

BIRCHINGTON ON SEA, Kent

Plan of streets, houses, hotels, etc. Linear scale.
Insc. *Birchington-on-Sea* and with the names of the owners of some properties not owned by Seddon.
Pen and ink, and water-colour
24 × 32 (60.9 × 81.2) D.1404–1896
Exhib. '*Marble Halls*', no. 94.

Bungalows

Plans (5), elevations (5), and sections (2) of a large bungalow with tower and billiard room.
Pencil, and pen and ink.
$14\frac{5}{8} \times 21\frac{5}{8}$ (37.2 × 54.9) D.1473–1896

Proposed Bungalow Terrace, Office, and Cottages at Birchington-on-Sea, Isle of Thanet, Kent. Block and ground plans of two, three and four storey buildings. Linear scale. Insc. with names of rooms, etc. s. *John P. Seddon.* d. *June 1881* (?)
Pen and ink, and wash, on linen
31 × 22 (78.8 × 55.8) D.1405–1896

Semi-detached cottages

Semi-Detached Cottages at Birchington-on-Sea. Ground plan. First floor and attic plans. Front elevation. Back elevation. Section. Linear scale.
Insc. with measurements and names of rooms. On the back is a printed view of the Ecclesiastical Art Exhibition d. *1880.*
Pencil and water-colour
$13\frac{3}{8} \times 18\frac{3}{4}$ (34.1 × 47.7) D.1415–1896

Houses

Design for House at Birchington. Ground plan. First floor plan. Second floor plan. Roof plan. Section AB. Scale $\frac{1}{8}$" and linear
s. *J. P. Seddon Archt.* and insc. with measurements and names of rooms.
Pencil and water-colour
$21\frac{1}{4} \times 14\frac{1}{2}$ (53.8 × 36.7) D.1428 × 1896

Plans, elevations and sections (on 5 sheets) of a house for Major Seddon R.E.
Insc. in ink *House at Birchington for* and in pencil *Major Seddon R.E.* D.1416, 1420 insc. with names of rooms, and D.1416 with measurements.
Pencil and water-colour
D.1416–1420–1896

Ground floor and *1st floor* plans. Linear scale
$14 \times 20\frac{7}{8}$ (35.5 × 53) D.1416–1896

2nd floor and *roof* plans. Linear scale
$14 \times 20\frac{7}{8}$ (35.5 × 53) D.1420–1896

South and *east* elevations. Linear scale
$14 \times 20\frac{7}{8}$ (35.5 × 53) D.1417–1896

North and *west* elevations. Linear scale
$14 \times 20\frac{7}{8}$ (35.5 × 53) D.1418–1896

Section AB. Section CD. Linear scale. Wm. *1880*
$14 \times 20\frac{7}{8}$ (35.5 × 53) D.1419–1896

Plans, elevations and sections (on 5 sheets) of a house
Insc. *Design for House at Birchington.* s. *John P. Seddon Archt. 1 Queen Annes Gate Westminster.* d. *1880.* D.1411-3 insc. with names of rooms and measurements.
Pencil and water-colour
D.1410–1414–1896

Perspective view and elevation. Linear scale
$12\frac{7}{8} \times 18\frac{3}{4}$ (32.7 × 47.8) D.1410–1896

Basement plan. Ground floor plan. Linear scale
$12\frac{7}{8} \times 18\frac{3}{4}$ (32.7 × 47.8) D.1411–1896

1st floor plan. 2nd floor plan. Linear scale
$12\frac{7}{8} \times 18\frac{3}{4}$ (32.7 × 47.8) D.1412–1896

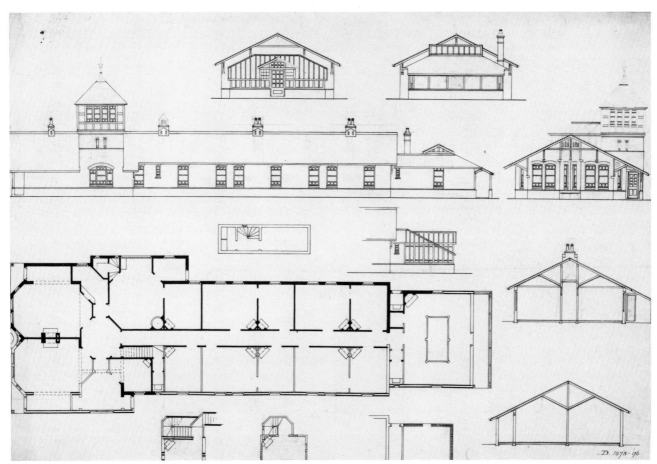

Birchington on Sea. Bungalow D.1473–1896

Attic plan. Section. Linear scale
$12\frac{7}{8} \times 18\frac{3}{4}$ (32.7 × 47.8) D.1413–1896

Two elevations. Linear scale
$12\frac{7}{8} \times 18\frac{3}{4}$ (32.7 × 47.8) D.1414–1896

Houses at Birchington for J. P. Seddon Esq. Ground, first and
second floor plans of two houses. Linear scale
Pencil
$13\frac{5}{8} \times 21$ (34.6 × 53.1) D.1427–1896

*Proposed design for house at Birchington. Basement, ground floor, 1st
floor* and *attic* plans. Two elevations and two sections. Linear
scale. s. *John P. Seddon.* d. *Oct. 78.* Insc. with measurements.
Pencil
$13\frac{3}{8} \times 16$ (34 × 40.5) On the back of D.1442–1896

*Design for Small Villa at Birchington. Ground plan. First floor plan.
Attic plan. End elevation. Back elevation. Front elevation. End
elevation. Cross section.* Scale $\frac{1}{8}$ and linear
s. *J. P. Seddon Archt.* d. *July 1880.* Insc. with measurements
and names of rooms.
Pencil and water-colour on tracing paper
$17\frac{1}{4} \times 23\frac{7}{8}$ (44 × 60.5) D.1422–1896

Design for a villa at Birchington. Four plans and two sections.
Linear scale. Wm. *1880*
Pen and ink
$24\frac{1}{2} \times 16\frac{5}{8}$ (62 × 42.2) D.1431–1896

Elevations and plans (on 5 sheets) of proposed terrace
D.1406, 1409 insc. *Proposed Terrace at Birchington-on-Sea* and s.
John P. Seddon Archt. d. *1882.* Insc. with measurements, and
D.1406, 1408, 1409, 1433 with names of rooms.
D.1406-9 pen and ink on linen. D.1433 pencil.
D.1406-9, 1433–1896

Elevation and composite plan showing all floors. Linear scale.
(2 copies)
$17\frac{1}{4} \times 24\frac{1}{2}$ (43.7 × 62.5) D.1406, 1408–1896

End elevation and plans of sub basements, basements, 1st and
2nd floors of *end house of Terrace* and *central houses* (D.1409)
(3 copies)
$17\frac{1}{4} \times 24\frac{1}{2}$ (43.7 × 62.5) D.1407, 1409–1896
$17 \times 24\frac{7}{8}$ (43 × 63) D.1433–1896

Hotels

Plans and elevations (on 3 sheets) of the Station (Bungalow)
Hotel, D.1402, 1420A insc. *Birchington.* D.1420A and B s. *John
P. Seddon*
D.1402 pen and ink on linen. D.1420A and B pencil and blue
print.
D.1402, 1420A and B—1896

Hotel, Stables etc. Ground plan, plan of *1st floor of Bar* and *1st
floor of stables. Elevation next Station. Front of cottages & stable yard.
Entrance. Back of coach house. Entrance. Front of Bar.* Scale *1/16th.*
Insc. with names of rooms in pencil.
$25\frac{1}{8} \times 38\frac{1}{4}$ (63.7 × 97) D.1402–1896

Hotel bar. Section AB
$8\frac{7}{8} \times 11\frac{1}{2}$ (22.5 × 29.3) D.1420A–1896

Hotel bar. *Front elevation.* Thumbnail sketch plan
$7\frac{7}{8} \times 11\frac{3}{8}$ (20 × 29) D.1420B–1896

Plans (on 2 sheets) probably preliminary designs for the Cliff
Hotel s. *John P. Seddon Archt. 1 Queen Anne's Gate SW.* Insc.
Design for an Hotel or Club and with measurements and names
of rooms.
Pencil, pen and ink, and water-colour
D.1429, 1430–1896

Ground plan. Linear scale. Alterations suggested in pencil
$17 \times 23\frac{3}{8}$ (43.2 × 59.2) D.1430–1896

First floor. Linear scale
$17 \times 23\frac{3}{8}$ (43.2 × 59.2) D.1429–1896

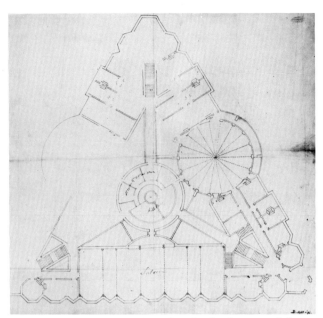

Birchington on Sea (possibly). Part plan of an hotel. D.1401–1896

BIRCHINGTON-ON-SEA, Kent. Possibly for

Part plan of a hotel
Insc. with names of some rooms
Pen and ink on linen
$25\frac{1}{2} \times 28$ (64.7 × 71) D.1401–1896

Plans, elevations and sections (on 2 sheets) of a detached house
Pencil
D.1425, 1426–1896

Three plans, elevation, and section. Thumbnail sketch plan
and elevations.
$20\frac{5}{8} \times 14\frac{1}{4}$ (52.3 × 36.4) D.1425–1896

Roof plan, three elevations and two sections
$18\frac{3}{8} \times 14\frac{1}{8}$ (46.6 × 35.8) D.1426–1896

*Design for a House by J. P. Seddon Archt. Basement plan. Ground
plan. First floor plan.* Thumbnail sketch elevation and plans
showing another arrangement. Scale $\frac{1}{8}$th and linear. d. *Jany
29th 1880*
Pencil and water-colour
$22 \times 15\frac{1}{4}$ (56 × 38.7) D.1424–1896

Elevation and three sections of a detached house
Pencil
$17\frac{1}{4} \times 24$ (43.8 × 61) D.1432–1896

The Isle of Thanet began to be developed as a resort in the late
1860s and early 1870s by John Taylor and C. N. Beazley. The
Building News in 1870 noted, for example, that between Margate
and Birchington: 'an estate of considerable extent has been laid
out . . . under the direction of Mr C. N. Beazley . . . a far better
character is observable in the few houses already built than is
usual among the speculative erections of the district'. At the same
time they were struck 'with another rather large group of buildings just erected near them by Mr John Taylor, architect, who is
well-known as the clever and scientific inventor of special
materials for almost every portion of a dwelling, and whose roofing tiles render this group of houses conspicuous from a distance . . . The site has nothing between it and the sea, and
nothing but sea between it and the North Pole, and must be as
bracing a spot as our island could supply. By the use of his patent
building blocks and tiles the first bungalow Mr Taylor built was
begun on the 14th August last year, was completely furnished
and dry within two months, and inhabited on the 14th October.
Since this he has built another, which was purchased by Mr
Erasmus Wilson, and four others afterwards, which have been
sold as soon as built'. These were apparently the first bungalows
—from the Indian word 'Bangla'—to be erected in the British
Isles.

Soon after beginning this development, which formed the
nucleus of what subsequently became Westgate, Taylor moved
one and a half miles along the coast to West Cliff, Birchington-
on-Sea, where he continued to build bungalows. These he sold
completely furnished 'even to a corkscrew, to gentlemen of position', and by 1879 he could claim to be able 'to export to any
country not a mere shell of a house, but a complete bungalow
residence, furnished with appropriate chair furniture, the whole
safely packed in a small compass'. Two of the bungalows he built
at Birchington, later called the 'Haun' and the 'Thor', were
illustrated and described at length by the *Building News* in 1873
and 1874 respectively, and versions of them still survive.

The precise nature of Seddon's involvement with Taylor is not
clear. Taylor's address as it appears on the 1873 and 1874 illustrations is 6, Whitehall, Seddon's old office, but by the time that
Seddon had become involved with Birchington, apparently in
about 1880, Taylor's name had been dropped. Indeed, Raffles
Davidson recorded in the *British Architect* that Seddon was in
partnership with a W. E. Martin, and a lithographed plan of the
scheme which appears on the back of D.1614 illustrates two of
Taylor's bungalows but indicates that Seddon was the architect.
Martin according to an advertisement in Mayhew, was the contractor for the works.

The plan on the back of D.1614, not noticed at the time D.1404
was exhibited in the 'Marble Halls' exhibition, does make the
story of the development clearer. Headed 'The Cliff Estate' it
shows how Seddon planned his roads and houses in a series of
terraces and crescents around the bungalows which Taylor had
already built. In fact, although the arrangement of the streets
closely follows that existing at Birchington, and many boundary
walls were apparently constructed, few of Seddon's houses
appear to have been erected. Raffles Davidson, who visited the
site in 1882, and drew the Station Hotel and tower bungalows,
noted that only the bungalows were complete, and even then he
was being optimistic because it would seem that only four of the
six blocks he shows were actually erected, certainly only four of
this group survive now (in Spencer Road). The terraces down to
the sea he depicted were certainly never constructed, the cliff
face being much higher than is shown. Indeed, all these particular 'rambling sketches' would have entailed his drawing while
either flying or swimming, and one presumes that he prepared
them from drawings supplied by Seddon.

The bungalows acquired a number of distinguished artists as
residents, Sir A. Gilbert, Simeon Solomon and Dante Gabriel
Rossetti.

BN, 16 September 1870, p.200; 16 August 1873, p.166 (illus);
16 February 1874, p.172 (illus); 28 March 1879, p.343.
A. Mayhew, *Birchington-on-Sea and its Bungalows*, 1881
A. D. King, 'The Bungalow: The Development and Diffusion
of a House-Type' in *Architectural Association Quarterly* Vol. 5,
1973, No. 3, pp.6–26
M. Darby, 'The First Bungalows', *Country Life*, 3 August 1978,
pp.306–309

BISHOPSBOURNE, Kent. Parsonage

Elevations and details (on 3 sheets) of fireplace and proposed
decorations of dining room for Rev. C. W. Sandford. 1871.
s. *John P. Seddon*. Insc. *Bishopsbourne Parsonage. Dining R.* or
similar, and with notes.
Pencil and water-colour
D.1651, 1652, 1940–1896

Part elevations of wall and ceiling. Scale $\frac{1}{2}$ inch. d. *1871*
$10\frac{1}{8} \times 12\frac{7}{8}$ (25.7 × 32.7) D.1651–1896

Part elevations of alternative designs for wall and ceiling.
Scale $\frac{1}{2}$ inch. d. *1871 Ma* (remainder cut off) and insc. *For the
Revd. C. W. Sandford*
$9\frac{7}{8} \times 13\frac{3}{8}$ (25.1 × 34) D.1652–1896

Front and *side* elevations, and details of fireplace. Scale *1 inch*.
d. *Nov 1871* and insc. *The Revd. Conningoney* [?] *Sandford* and
Mr Wilson, Builder, St. George's Rd. Canterbury
$10 \times 16\frac{1}{2}$ (25.5 × 42) D.1940–1896

The Tower Bungalows, Birchington, looking towards the sea. Sketch by Raffles Davidson reproduced in *British Architect*, 12 May 1882.

The Station Hotel, Birchington, later called the Bungalow Hotel. Sketch by Raffles Davidson reproduced in *British Architect*, 12 May 1882.

One of the 'Tower Bungalows', Birchington, as it appears today. Photograph courtesy of the Courtauld Institute of Art.

BRECON, Powys. Priory Church, now the Cathedral

Brecon Priory Church. Section of transept roof. Scale $\frac{1}{4}$ *inch to one foot* and *full size*. Insc. with measurements and notes
$13\frac{1}{4} \times 11\frac{1}{4}$ (33.6×28.5) D.1499–1896

Seddon's precise involvement with the church—if any—remains unclear. Sir Gilbert Scott (1862-75) and W. D. Caröe (1914-31) carried out most of the restoration. It became the Cathedral of the new Diocese of Swansea and Brecon in 1923.

Howell and Beazley, p.29

Christ College

Plans, elevations, sections and details (on 53 sheets). 1862-73. D.902-5, 907, 908, 910-2, 914, 916, 919, 921, 925-7, 931, 933, 934, 937-44, 946-9, 1310, 1515, 1542, 1543 insc. *Christ College, Brecon* or similar. D.902-5, 901, 911, 918, 919 insc. *Prichard & Seddon* etc. and D.912, 914, 916, 926, 927, 932-4, 948, 1543 s. or insc. *J. P. Seddon* or similar. D.906, 906A, 908, 909, 911, 913-5, 921, 922, 928, 941, 946, 1515 insc. with measurements, and D.911, 917, 918 with names of rooms. D.902, 910-2, 914, 922, 926, 929, 935 pen and ink, pencil and water-colour. D.903-7, 917, 918 pen and ink and water-colour. D.925, 927, 928, 930, 933, 934, 942, 947 pencil and water-colour. D.901, 906A, 908, 909, 913, 915, 938, 941, 943, 945, 948, 1310, 1542 pencil. D.920, 924, 936, 937, 940, 944, 946, 949, 1515 pen and ink. D.921, 931, 939 pencil, and pen and ink. D.916 pencil, crayon and water-colour. D.919 pencil, pen and ink, crayon and water-colour. D.923 crayon, and pen and ink. D.932 crayon, pen and ink, and wash. D.900 engraving.
D.901, 906, 911, 913, 915, 917, 918, 920, 935-8, 940, 944, 946, 949, 1515 in tracing paper. D.908, 909 on linen.
D.900-906, 906A, 907–949, 1310, 1515, 1542, 1543–1896

Perspective from the north west
$4\frac{1}{8} \times 6$ (10.6×15.2) D.900–1896
Cut from the *Illustrated London News*, 14 January 1865, p. 28

Sketch for above
$10\frac{3}{4} \times 15$ (27.2×38.2) D.901–1896

Ground plan. Scale *eight feet to an inch.* On a separate sheet pasted on, part elevation and section of *cloister.* Scale $\frac{1}{8}$ inch
22×36 (56×91) D.911–1896

One pair plan
$20\frac{1}{2} \times 16\frac{1}{2}$ (52×41.6) D.917–1896

Two pair plan. Attic plan
$20 \times 15\frac{3}{4}$ (50.7×40.1) D.918–1896

North elevation. Scale $\frac{1}{8}$th inch d. *Octr 1862*
$16 \times 22\frac{7}{8}$ (41×58) D.902–1896

South elevation. Scale $\frac{1}{8}$th inch d. *Octr 1862*
$15\frac{3}{4} \times 22\frac{3}{4}$ (40.1×57.9) D.903–1896

East elevation. Scale $\frac{1}{8}$th inch d. *Octr 1862*
$15\frac{1}{2} \times 22\frac{5}{8}$ (39.3×57.6) D.904–1896

West elevation. Scale $\frac{1}{8}$th inch d. *Octr 1862*
$16\frac{1}{4} \times 22\frac{3}{4}$ (41.4×57.9) D.905–1896

Chapel. Ground plan. North elevation. East elevation. Section. Section. Turret. s. *Wm. Williams.* Scale $\frac{1}{8}$th *in* and linear
$22\frac{1}{2} \times 15\frac{3}{8}$ (57.2×39) D.907–1896
Exhib. Plans and Prospects, 56a.

Chapel. Longitudinal section looking north. Longitudinal section looking south. Scale $\frac{1}{8}$th inch and linear
$22\frac{1}{4} \times 15$ (56.5×37.8) D.910–1896

Plan of chapel (?)
$19\frac{3}{4} \times 9\frac{1}{2}$ (50×24) D.948–1896

Detail of roof of chapel. *Elevations and details of chapel roof* Scale $\frac{1}{2}$ *in* and *full size* d. *Feb. 1863* and insc. *executed?*
$21\frac{5}{8} \times 28\frac{3}{4}$ (54.8×73) D.919–1896

Part elevation and plan of chapel roof timbers
$15\frac{5}{8} \times 11\frac{1}{4}$ (39.6×28.6) D.920–1896

Elevation and plan of chapel roof. Scale $\frac{1}{2}$ in. Insc. *This is the roof executed* and initialled *J.P.S.*
$19\frac{1}{8} \times 19\frac{3}{4}$ (48.6×50.1) D.921–1896

Elevations and details of chapel roof. Scale *full size* and linear. Insc. *not executed*
$22 \times 29\frac{7}{8}$ (56×75.8) D.922–1896

Part elevation and part section of chapel roof
$15 \times 17\frac{1}{4}$ (38×43.7) D.1515–1896

Details of Corbels to chapel roof. Scale $\frac{1}{4}$ *full size*
$17\frac{1}{2} \times 11\frac{3}{4}$ (44.5×30) D.930–1896

Detail of bell-turret including elevations and section. Scale $\frac{1}{2}$ inch. Torn
$13\frac{1}{4} \times 12\frac{1}{4}$ (33.5×31.5) D.906–1896

Chapel. Detail of cross on roof including elevations, section and details. Scale $\frac{1}{4}$ *full size* and larger. d. *Septr 9th 1863* and initialled *R.C.J.*
$18\frac{3}{4} \times 13$ (47.5×33) D.932–1896
Exhib. Plans and Prospects, no. 56b

Sedilia; sketch of details
$12\frac{1}{2} \times 10\frac{5}{8}$ (31.6×27.1) D.908–1896

Sketches of details of sanctuary wall opposite sedilia
$12\frac{1}{4} \times 8\frac{1}{2}$ (31.2×21.6) D.909–1896

Sedilia; elevation. d. *1863.* Scale *inch*
$15\frac{1}{8} \times 22\frac{1}{8}$ (38.3×56.3) D.912–1896

Detail of Sedilia. Plan. Elevation. Section. Scale *inch*
$15\frac{1}{2} \times 24$ (39.5×60.8) D.914–1896

Details of Sedilia. Scale *full size*
$16\frac{1}{2} \times 22\frac{1}{2}$ (42×57) D.916–1896

Sketch of tile pattern for sedilia. On the back sketches of tiles
$16\frac{5}{8} \times 35\frac{1}{4}$ (42.2×89.3) D.942–1896

Part plan of chapel showing seating. Scale $\frac{1}{8}$th *of an inch to one foot*
$17 \times 12\frac{1}{2}$ (43×32) D.924–1896

Details of stalls to chapel including plans, elevations and sections. Scale linear and *full size*
$23\frac{7}{8} \times 16$ (60.5×40.5) D.925–1896

Canopied stalls and seats. Front and end elevations. Scale *inch.* d. *Nov 1863.* Initialled *RCJ*
$13 \times 19\frac{1}{4}$ (33×48.8) D.926–1896

Elevations of ends of stalls including Chancellor's stall
$18\frac{1}{2} \times 14\frac{3}{4}$ (47×37.5) D.923–1896

West Stalls. Plans, elevations, sections and details. Scale *inch*, $\frac{1}{4}$ *full size* and *full size*
$26\frac{3}{8} \times 19\frac{1}{4}$ (67×48.6) D.931–1896

Elevation of side of chapel with pulpit and stalls
$23\frac{5}{8} \times 35\frac{1}{2}$ (60.1×90.3) D.1310–1896

Plans, elevations, sections and details of pulpit. Scale linear and *full size*
$23\frac{1}{2} \times 16\frac{1}{2}$ (59.7×41.8) D.928–1896

Altar table and *Lectern.* Plans, elevations, sections and details. Scale *inch, half full size* and *full size.* d. *Jany 63*
$23\frac{3}{4} \times 16\frac{1}{2}$ (60.3×42) –1896
A similar design is in the RIBA

Sketch of tile patterns in chapel. Scale $1\frac{1}{2}$ *inch*
$14\frac{3}{8} \times 35\frac{3}{4}$ (36.5×91) D.943–1896

Sketch of tile patterns in chapel. Scale $\frac{1}{2}$ *inch*
$7\frac{1}{4} \times 15\frac{1}{2}$ (18.5×39.3) D.947–1896

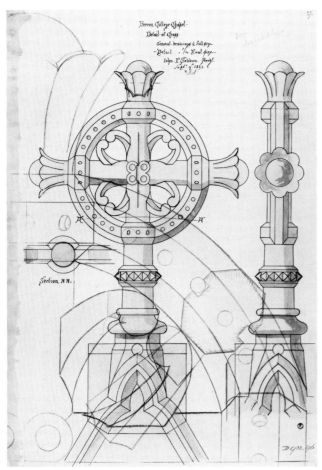

Brecon. Christ College D.932–1896

Part plan of chancel floor and part elevation of east wall showing arrangements of tiles
$20\frac{1}{2} \times 15\frac{3}{8}$ (51.8 × 39.1) D.929–1896

Chapel porch. Detail of roof. Scale *inch* and *full size.* d. *Aug. 1866*
$17\frac{3}{4} \times 24\frac{1}{4}$ (45.2 × 61.6) D.934–1896

Plan, elevation and section of chapel porch. Alterations suggested in pencil.
$22\frac{1}{4} \times 16\frac{1}{2}$ (56.5 × 41.8) D.935–1896

Chapel. Details of porch window including plan, elevations, and section. Scale $\frac{1}{2}$ *inch* and *full size.* d. *Aug. 1866*
$17\frac{1}{4} \times 23\frac{1}{4}$ (43.7 × 59.1) D.933–1896

East window, detail of moulding. Fragment
3×4 (7.7 × 10) D.906A–1896

Detail of door between chapel yard & cloisters with a thumbnail sketch of another door. Scale $\frac{3}{4}$
$12 \times 7\frac{1}{4}$ (30.6 × 18.5) D.1542–1896

Detail of dining hall and dais window. Scale $\frac{1}{2}$ *inch* (2 sheets joined)
$17\frac{1}{8} \times 22\frac{1}{8}$ (43.5 × 56.2) D.936, 937–1896

Detail of bay window. Scale $\frac{1}{2}$ *inch*
$17\frac{1}{2} \times 12\frac{3}{8}$ (44.5 × 31.4) D.940–1896

Elevations and sections of windows. Scale $\frac{1}{2}$ *inch*
$24\frac{5}{8} \times 19\frac{3}{4}$ (62.6 × 50) D.946–1896

Sketch of dining hall roof. d. (?) *1875*
$9\frac{7}{8} \times 8$ (25.1 × 20.3) D.941–1896

Detail of roof over dining hall. Scale $\frac{1}{2}$ *inch*
$15 \times 19\frac{3}{4}$ (38 × 50) D.949–1896

Lib[rar]y. Detail of *cornice* including *fragment of old oak cornice*
9×7 (22.9 × 17.7) D.913–1896

Sketch elevations of two chimneys. Scale $\frac{1}{2}$ *inch*
$15\frac{1}{8} \times 12$ (38.3 × 30.3) D.938–1896

Plans and elevations of two chimneys. Scale $\frac{1}{2}$ *inch*
$13 \times 20\frac{1}{8}$ (33 × 51) D.939–1896

Detail of chimney. Scale $\frac{1}{2}$ *inch*
$14\frac{1}{2} \times 17\frac{1}{8}$ (37 × 43.5) D.944–1896

Detail of moulding
$11 \times 7\frac{1}{4}$ (28.1 × 18.7) D.915–1896

Design for cupboards. Plan, elevation, section and details. Scale *inch to a foot.* d. *March 20 1873*
15×15 (38 × 38) D.1543–1896

Large size desk for schoolroom. Plans and elevations. Scale *2 inch* and linear
$14\frac{3}{8} \times 17\frac{7}{8}$ (36.6 × 45.3) D.945–1896

Prichard and Seddon won a competition for the reconstruction of Christ College in 1859. The College had been founded in 1541 when Henry VIII transferred the College of Abergwili to the Priory of the Friars Preachers at Brecon. By 1837, however, only seven boys attended and the Charity Commissioners arranged the 'Christ College of Brecknock Act' by which a new governing body was appointed and a scheme for rebuilding the school formulated. Prichard and Seddon's designs involved the restoration of part of the 12–14th century ruins of the Friary, particularly the chancel, which they converted into the College chapel, and some decanal buildings, which they converted into school rooms. The *Ecclesiologist* noticed that the design involved 'large and highly decorative' additions. 'The schools and residences seem very judiciously planned: and we note a very satisfactory development of ornate work in statuary and constructional polychrome, with multitudes of turrets, and cappings, and many-windowed oriels, and high roofs and ridge crestings. An arcaded covered playground is a good thought for a large school'. At the same time they thought that this design would 'probably be much modified in execution'.

The *Builder* noticed on 6 July 1861 that the buildings were 'just being commenced'—the foundation stone was laid by Dr Thirwall—and also reported that the headmaster had been obliged to ask for additional funds. The work, which cost £10,000 was carried out by Messrs Williams under the superintendence of Walter Brecon, and was completed, except for the tower roof and the cloister which linked the school buildings with the chapel, by 21 June 1864 when the new school was opened. It would appear that much remained to be done in the chapel too, and as late as 1885 the *British Architect* illustrated a scheme for decorating the walls drawn up by a Mr Rossiter under Seddon's guidance which they noticed still remained to be carried out. The first headmaster was the Rev. J. D. Williams, but he was replaced after only one year by the Rev. Lewis Lloyd.

The *Illustrated London News* reported that the buildings, which included besides the chapel, a master's residence, octagonal kitchen library and accommodation and class rooms for forty boys, were designed by John Prichard, but the drawings indicate that Seddon played a major part particularly in the restoration of the chapel. Indeed, one wonders, since the completed designs appear to differ from that described in the *Ecclesiologist* which was almost certainly mainly the work of Prichard, and since there are elevations apparently in Seddon's hand among the V & A drawings of the school buildings dated October 1862 after the partnership had broken up, whether he did not play an integral part in their design too.

The school remains one of the most important in Wales.

Ecc, xx, 1859, p.209; xxi, 1860, p.329
Br, 6 July 1861, p.469; 3 September 1864, p.657; 13 May 1871, p.359
ILN, 14 January 1865, pp.33, 34
BA, 23 October 1885
St. James Budget, 1 June 1894, pp.18–21
Eastlake Appendix p.[112]
Howell and Beazley, p.29
RIBA *Catalogue*, p.34
Haslam, pp.293–296

BRIDGEND, Glamorgan. School

Plans, elevations, sections and details (on 11 sheets) depicting three different schemes. 1859–1860.
Insc. *Prichard and Seddon* etc. D.997–1006 insc. *Bridgend Schools Glamorganshire*, D.997–1000 with names of rooms, and D.997-9 with measurements.
D.997–1001, 1005, 1007 pencil, pen and ink, and water-colour. D.1002-4 pen and ink, and water-colour. D.1006 pencil and water-colour. D.1003-6 on tracing paper.
D.997–1007–1896

Ground plan. Principal front—South. Scale $\frac{1}{8}$*th inch.* Insc. *Accommodation Boy's school 78 [Boys] Classroom 32 Girl's school 84 Infant's school 57 total 251.* Some alterations in pencil
$22\frac{1}{4} \times 16\frac{1}{4}$ (56.3×41.1) D.997–1896

Site plan. *Chamber plan. East elevation.* Scale $\frac{1}{8}$*th inch*
$21\frac{1}{8} \times 15\frac{7}{8}$ (53.6×40.3) D.998–1896

Ground plan. South elevation. Scale $\frac{1}{8}$*th inch.* d. *Septr. 1859*
Alterations suggested in pencil
$19\frac{5}{8} \times 14\frac{5}{8}$ (49.8×37.1) D.999–1896

Site plan. *Chamber plan. End elevation.* Scale $\frac{1}{8}$*th inch.* Wm. *1857*
$19\frac{1}{2} \times 14\frac{5}{8}$ (49.6×37) D.1000–1896

Transverse section. Longitudinal section. Scale $\frac{1}{8}$*th inch.* d. *Septr. 1859*
$19\frac{1}{2} \times 14\frac{5}{8}$ (49.6×37.1) D.1001–1896

Back elevation. End elevation. Scale $\frac{1}{8}$*th inch*
$19\frac{5}{8} \times 14\frac{5}{8}$ (49.7×37.1) D.1002–1896

North elevation. Section thro CD. Section thro IT. Masters house—bedroom plan. Scale $\frac{1}{8}$*th of an inch to a foot.* d. *Nov. 59*
$22 \times 14\frac{3}{4}$ (55.8×37.6) D.1003–1896

West elevation. East elevation. Section thro AB. Scale $\frac{1}{8}$*th of an inch to a foot.* d. *Nov. 1859*
$21\frac{3}{8} \times 15\frac{1}{2}$ (54.3×39.5) D.1004–1896

Elevations, sections and details of doors and windows. Scale *half inch* and *full size.* d. *Decr. 1859*
$29\frac{1}{2} \times 20$ (75×51) D.1005–1896

Elevations and sections of windows. Scale *half inch.* d. *Decr. 1859*
$22\frac{5}{8} \times 20$ (57.5×50.8) D.1006–1896

The 4 Dormers in front. Plan, elevations, section and details. Scale $\frac{1}{2}$ *in* and *full size.* d. *21 June 1860*
$19 \times 14\frac{1}{2}$ (48×37) D.1007–1896

BRISTOL, Avon. Assize Courts

Competition designs (on 4 sheets). 1866
D.897 lettered *Justitia fiat et* (the rest is missing), and with names of rooms.
Pen and ink, and water-colour
D.736, 897–899–1896

Ground plan
$25\frac{5}{8} \times 20\frac{3}{4}$ (65.2×52.7) D.897–1896

Front elevation
$12\frac{1}{8} \times 20\frac{3}{8}$ (30.9×51.6) D.736–1896

Longitudinal section through court rooms. The bottom part of the design including the cellars has been cut off.
$8\frac{7}{8} \times 20\frac{1}{2}$ (22.5×52) D.898–1896

Transverse section through court room
10×12 (25.5×30.3) D.899–1896

Bristol. Assize Courts D.736–1896

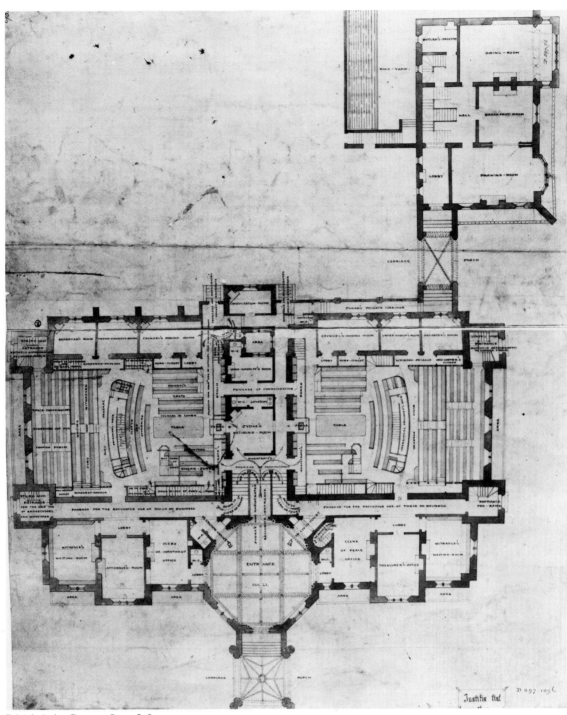

Bristol. Assize Courts D.897–1896

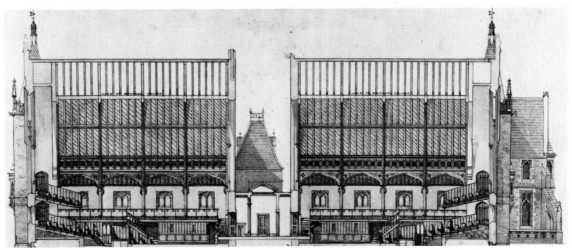

Bristol. Assize Courts D.898–1896

A competition for 'plans and estimates for altering the present guildhall and erecting a second court, etc., in rear of same; and also for the erection of two assize courts in Queen's Square' was announced in the Bristol press early in 1866. The conditions laid down that no design was guaranteed to be accepted and that no premium was to be offered. When coupled with the fact that the Corporation were rumoured not to have settled officially on a site for the new buildings, this prompted a group of local architects to write to the Editors of the *Builder* and *Building News* pressing for a new competition with better conditions. When only one design was received, from Messrs Pope and Bindon, the Council agreed, and a new competition with prizes of 100, 50 and 25 guineas was announced, and Alfred Waterhouse asked to judge the entries.

By June some thirteen entries had been received and Godwin and Crisp were declared the winners of all three prizes. It quickly became known that their designs were the only ones to adhere strictly to the plan provided in the instructions, and that the ten others had been discounted for including a piece of land not in the possession of the Council. Subsequently the Council saw the desirability of obtaining this land, and after considerable protest from amongst others the Council of the Royal Institute of British Architects which included Seddon himself, they announced yet another competition in 1868. G. E. Street was appointed to adjudicate and he declared Pope and Bindon the winners, Godwin and Crisp the runners up, and Hansom and Sons third. By January 1869 work had begun on Pope and Bindon's building and it was completed in the following year.

Seddon's designs, apparently submitted to the first competition, do not appear to have been mentioned in the National press.

Br, 27 January 1866, p.70; 10 March 1866, p.173; 4 August 1866, p.583; 29 September 1866, p.728

BN, 12 January 1866, p.30; 22 June 1866, p.421; 27 July 1866, p.502; 10 August 1866, p.533; 24 August 1866, p.566; 28 September 1866, pp.648, 649; 16 November 1866, p.767; 15 January 1869, p.50.

BRITON FERRY, Glamorgan.
Church of St. Mary

Design for 3 windows for Briton Ferry Church
Initialled *J.P.S.* d. *1890*. Insc. *Seddon and Carter Architects* and with measurements.
Pencil, pen and ink, and water-colour
$13\frac{7}{8} \times 22\frac{1}{2}$ (35.2×57) D.1749–1896

Seddon and Carter demolished the 18th century church except for the tower in the south west corner, part of which dated from the 13th century, and replaced it with a simple barn-like structure capable of seating 346 people. The walls were built of a local stone with brick dressings and the whole was plastered internally. The cost was estimated in 1891, at which time the church was about to be commenced, to be £1,100.

J. Coates Carter showed a drawing of the church at the Royal Academy in 1891, and one assumes that he was primarily responsible for its design.

BN, 26 June 1891, pp. 874, 890, 891; including illustration of Carter's RA drawing.

BROADSTAIRS, Kent. Church of St. Peter

Plans, elevations and details (on 3 sheets) of boundary walls, gates and lamps. 1874-75
Insc. or s. *John P. Seddon*. D.1561 addressed *1 Queen Anne's Gate, Westminster*. D.1950, 1966 insc. *S. Peter's Isle of Thanet* or similar.
Pencil and water-colour, some inscriptions in ink. D.1966 on tracing paper
D.1561, 1950, 1966–1896

Design for boundary wall including *plan* and elevation of *entrance gate* and *side gate*; and *plan* and elevation of *main piers* and *side piers*. Insc. *Entire length of wall about 120ft* and with notes and measurements. d. *Oct 26 1874*
$12\frac{3}{4} \times 18\frac{1}{2}$ (32.3×47.1) D.1561–1896

Sketch showing proposed lamps. Scale $\frac{1}{4}$ *of an inch to a foot. Detail of lamp*. Scale *inch to a foot*. Insc. *own sketch stem to be shorter*. d. *April 1875*
$9\frac{3}{8} \times 12\frac{1}{2}$ (23.7×31.7) D.1950–1896

Detail of lamp. Scale *inch to a foot*. d. *April 75*. Tracing of part of D.1950
$8\frac{3}{8} \times 6\frac{1}{8}$ (21.4×15.6) D.1966–1896

Church of St. Peter (possibly for)

Design for a panel of Gothick ornament
Insc. *Gothick pattern No. 2—as arranged for Thanet. 6 ins sqre.*
Pen and ink, and ink wash on tracing paper
$8 \times 9\frac{3}{8}$ (20.4×23.8) D.1965–1896

Newman says of the church: 'One of the big, flint, basically Norman churches of Thanet, over-restored like all the rest'. He notices that Joseph Clarke provided all the tracery in 1852 and 1859 and a new chancel arch, but mentions no work by Seddon.

J. Newman, *North East and East Kent*, 1969, pp.155, 156

St. Peter's Orphanage

Elevations of chimneypieces. c.1867.
Insc. *St Peter's Orphanage Broadstairs, bedrooms, L. Pugh Pugh Esq.* and with measurements.
Pencil
$19\frac{1}{8} \times 13\frac{1}{4}$ (48.6×33.6) D.1616–1896

The orphanage was built on a site at Stonehouse on the road from Broadstairs to Margate, given by the Archbishop of Canterbury, who owned the land. The funds to build it were raised by Mrs Tait who had previously opened a home at Fulham for orphan girls left destitute in the east of London after the cholera epidemic of 1866. In 1867, after the Archbishop moved from the See of London to that of Canterbury, he determined to allow Mrs Tait to raise funds for an institute of a more permanent character, and Seddon was employed as architect. The principal portion of his design provided accommodation for one hundred orphan girls from London and Canterbury, but a part of the building was also devoted to convalescent children requiring care and sea air but not hospital treatment. The cost of the work which was completed by April 1873 was estimated to be £16,000. The General Contractor was Thomas Williams of Cardiff, the heating arrangements were made by Messrs Nelson of Leeds and John Barber of Broadstairs, the gas fittings by Mr Hammond, and the furniture made to Seddon's designs by Collmann of George Street. The grounds were laid out under the direction of Lucius Spooner.

The orphanage has now been demolished.

It is not clear why the design should be inscribed with the name of Lewis Pugh Pugh for whom Seddon built Abermad near Aberystwyth.

BN, 18 April 1873, p.448 (including description of the arrangement of the rooms, etc.) and pp.449, 451 (illustrations)

BRONCROFT CASTLE, Nr Tugford, Shropshire

Broncroft Castle, Salop. Design for alterations, etc. Ground plan. Front elevation. Photograph *View of Present Front*. Scale *eight feet to an inch*. c.1868
Insc. *J. P. Seddon, Architect, 12 Park Street, Westminster*
Pencil, water-colour, and an attached photograph
$20\frac{1}{4} \times 17\frac{1}{2}$ (51.5×44.4) D.1377–1896

Possibly exhib. Architectural Exhibition 1868, no. 163.

Pevsner, *Shropshire* 1958, p.86.

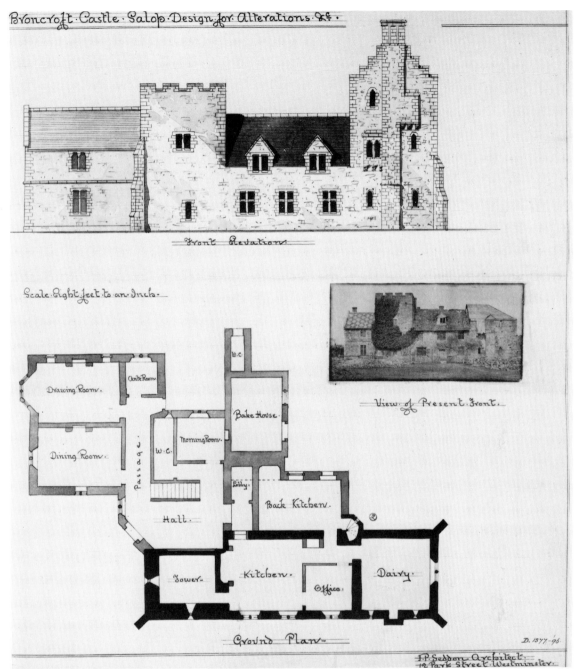

Broncroft Castle D.1377–1896

Broncroft Castle. Photograph view of front before restoration D.1377–1896

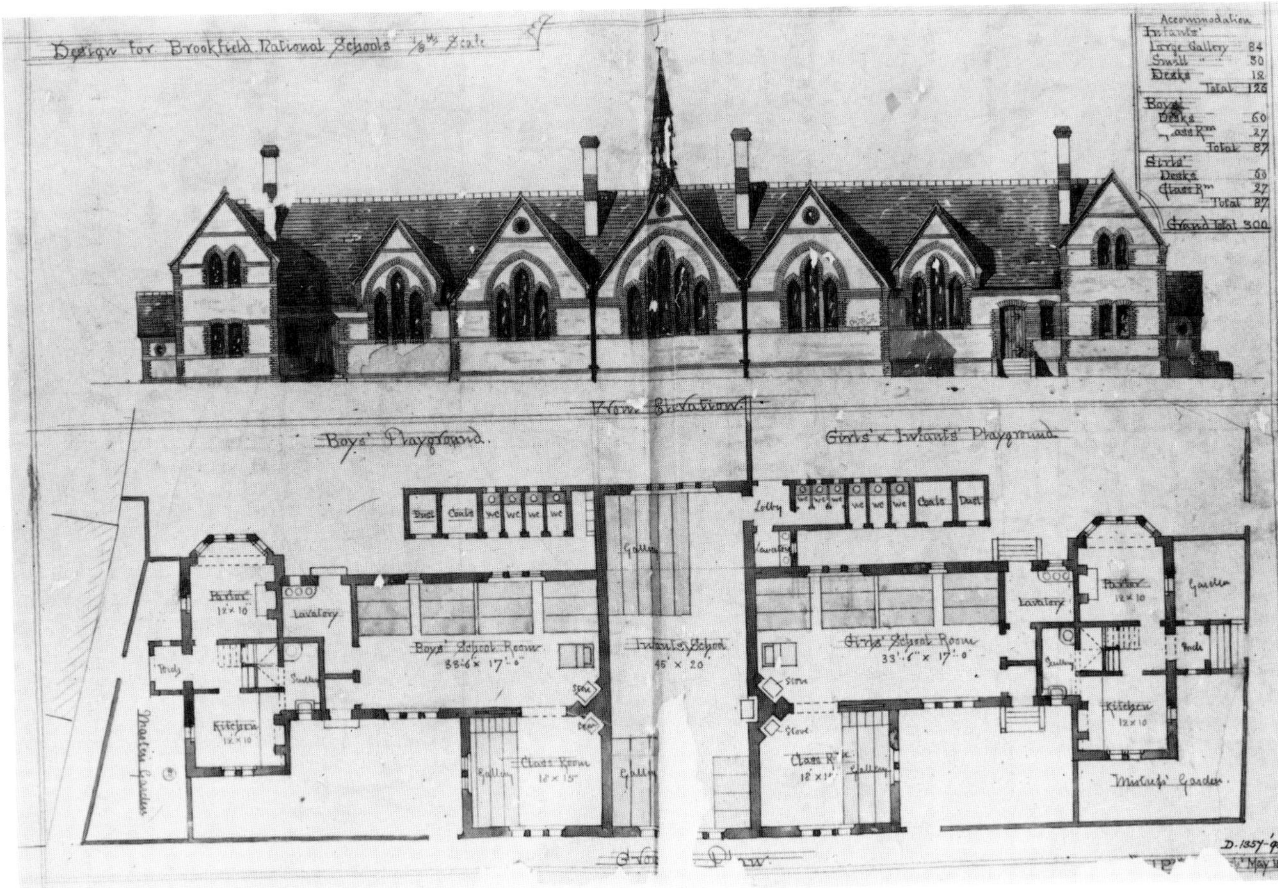

Brookfield. National Schools D.1357–1896

BROOKFIELD. National schools

Plan, elevation and detail (on 2 sheets)
Insc. *Brookfield National Schools* and with measurements. D.1516
s. *John P. Seddon Archt. 12 Park St. Westr.*
Pencil and water-colour on tracing paper
D.1357, 1516–1896

Ground plan. Front elevation. Scale $\frac{1}{8}$*th.* Insc. with details of the *accommodation* including *grand total 300.* d. *May 1870.* Torn
$15\times22\frac{1}{2}$ (37.9×57) D.1357–1896

Detail of school roofs including part sections and part elevation. Scale $\frac{1}{2}$ *inch.* Insc. *This was the roof of Highgate* (the next word is unreadable) *schools which everyone cites. See if it be too expensive or is it possible to reduce the cost of it. The spans will be 18 feet.* d. *July '70*
$14\frac{3}{4}\times16\frac{1}{4}$ (37.5×41.2) D.1516–1896

It is not clear whether this is the Brookfield in London, Worcestershire or Sussex.

CAERLEON, Gwent. Parsonage

Plans, elevations, sections and details (on 14 sheets) depicting two different schemes. c.1860
D.1024, 1088–1095, 1143-7 insc. *Caerleon Parsonage* or similar. D.1024, 1088-92, 1143-7 stamped *Prichard and Seddon*, etc. D.1088, 1090, 1143, 1144 insc. with names of rooms. D.1088, 1090-2, 1143, 1146 insc. with measurements.
Pencil, pen and ink, and water-colour except D.1094, 1095 pencil and water-colour
D.1024, 1088–1095, 1143–1147–1896

Ground plan. Section ab. Scale $\frac{1}{8}$ *inch to a foot. Drawing No. 1*
$18\frac{1}{4}\times12\frac{3}{8}$ (46.4×31.5) D.1143–1896

Basement plan. Chamber plan. Attic plan. Scale $\frac{1}{8}$ *inch to a foot. Drawing No. 2.* On the back a sketch of a dormer window.
$18\frac{1}{4}\times12\frac{3}{8}$ (46.4×31.5) D.1144–1896

South elevation. West elevation. Scale $\frac{1}{8}$ *inch to a foot. Drawing No. 3*
$16\frac{5}{8}\times12\frac{1}{2}$ (42.3×31.7) D.1145–1896

East elevation. Transverse section on line cd. Scale $\frac{1}{8}$ *inch to a foot. Drawing No. 4.* Wm. *1860*
$18\frac{1}{8}\times12\frac{1}{4}$ (46×31.2) D.1146–1896

Roof plan. Roof plan showing timbers. Scale $\frac{1}{8}$ *inch to a foot. Drawing No. 5*
$18\frac{1}{8}\times12\frac{3}{8}$ (46.1×31.5) D.1147–1896

Block *plan shewing drains. North elevation.* Scale $\frac{1}{8}$ *inch to a foot. Drawing No. 6*
$16\frac{5}{8}\times13\frac{1}{4}$ (42.3×33.6) D.1024–1896

Ground plan. Chamber plan. Scale $\frac{1}{8}$
$16\frac{1}{2}\times11\frac{5}{8}$ (42×29.5) D.1090–1896

Attic plan. East elevation. Scale $\frac{1}{8}$ *inch to a foot.* Insc. with notes
$17\frac{1}{8}\times11\frac{5}{8}$ (43.6×29.5) D.1088–1896

Block plan. Section on line CD. Scale $\frac{1}{8}$ *inch to a foot*
$17\frac{1}{8}\times11\frac{5}{8}$ (43.6×29.5) D.1092–1896

Front elevn. West elevation. Scale $\frac{1}{8}$
$16\frac{1}{2}\times11\frac{5}{8}$ (42×29.5) D.1089–1896

North elevation. Section on line AB. Scale $\frac{1}{8}$ *inch to a foot*
$17\frac{1}{8}\times11\frac{5}{8}$ (43.6×29.5) D.1091–1896

Details of front door, porch window above. Plans, elevations and sections. Scale *inch.* On the back sketch of cresting to roof
$21\frac{3}{4}\times17\frac{1}{4}$ (55.4×44) D.1093–1896

Elevation and section of dormer. On the back elevation and section of a door
$16\frac{1}{2}\times11\frac{3}{4}$ (42×29.8) D.1094–1896

Elevations of stairs. Scale *inch.* Wm. *1860*
$17\frac{1}{4}\times23\frac{5}{8}$ (43.8×60) D.1095–1896

D.1088–1095 show the parsonage as built, although the tower and porch on the entrance front, and the circular tower at the back were omitted.

Church of St. Cadoc

Chancel Caerleon Church. Elevation showing decoration.
Pencil
17×46 (43.1×117) D.1660–1896

Caerleon Church. Plan of tile floor. An alternative design for part is pasted on.
Insc. *Prichard and Seddon* etc. and with notes
Pencil, pen and ink, and water-colour
14×20⅜ (35.9×51.8) D.2078–1896

Caerleon gates. Sketch elevation and section of gate and pier.
Scale ½ in. Insc. in ink with measurements
Pencil
10⅝×15⅞ (27×40.3) D.1580–1896

Seddon's involvement with Caerleon appears to have begun around 1862 when the *Monmouthshire Merlin* reported that he had built the vicarage there. One presumes that D.2078, the plan for the tile floor, is of this date or perhaps a little earlier. In 1867-68 the *Church Builder* noted that Seddon had enlarged the church and that 60 additional seatings had been gained as a result of this. Whether the two remaining drawings are of this date or earlier is not clear. A stone pulpit was given at this time by Mrs Jenkins and an oak lentern by Miss Jones, the daughter of the late vicar. The enlargement cost £2,400. In 1890 Seddon, in partnership with Carter, carried out further work but it is not clear what this was. Most of Seddon's fittings were swept away in 1935 by W. D. Caröe when he extended the chancel and added the Lady Chapel.

There is a drawing for a lectern at the RIBA. (Illus. RIBA, *Transactions*, ns. VI, 1890, p.175.)

Basil Clark notes that the church was restored in 1874 but this appears to be an error.

CB, 1867-68, p.40
BN, 17 January 1890, p.115
Howell and Beazley, p.209
RIBA *Catalogue*, p.34

CAMROSE, Dyfed. Church

Designs for three stained glass windows. Scale 1½
Insc. *Camrose Ch. design for Glazing* and *Cathedrals*. s. *John P. Seddon*. d. *Mar. 1883*
Pencil and water-colour
13×12¼ (33×31) D.1694–1896

CARDIFF, Glamorgan.
Church of Eglwys Dewi Sant
(previously St. Andrews)

Plans, elevations, sections and details (on 54 sheets) depicting various designs, and some working drawings. From 1859.
D.737 insc. in ink *S–Church Cardiff*. *Andrews* added in pencil, D.739-48, 779 insc. *S–Church Cardiff*. D.749, 750, 754, 757-62, 764, 773-7, 780, 782, 783, 785 insc. *Cardiff Church*. D.778, 784, 790 insc. *St. Andrew's Church, Cardiff*. D.737, 740-9, 751, 754, 757-61, 764, 767, 770, 772-4, 778-80, 783, 790 lettered, insc. or stamped *Prichard and Seddon* etc. D.744, 746-8 s. *A. Llandaff*. D.744, 746-9 with the seal of the *Incorporated Church Building Society* D.761, 766, 773 insc. with measurements. D.761, 765 insc. with notes.
D.737, 738, 742, 744, 746-56, 762, 763, 766, 767, 769, 773, 778-80, 782, 783, 790 pencil, pen and ink, and water-colour. D.739, 740, 743 pen and ink, and wash. D.741, 745, 784 pen and ink, and water-colour. D.786 pencil and wash. D.757-60 pencil, and pen and ink. D.761, 764, 765, 768, 771, 772, 774-7, 785, 787-9 pencil and water-colour. D.770 pencil. D.737-42 on linen. D.786 on tracing paper.
D.737–790–1896.

Perspective from the south west
23¼×16½ (59.2×42) D.738–1896

Perspective of interior
20¾×13⅛ (53×35.5) D.781–1896
Exhib. *Plans and Prospects*, no. 77

Cardiff. Church of Eglwys Dewi Sant D.738–1896

Cardiff. Church of Eglwys Dewi Sant D.781–1896

Ground plan. Scale ⅛. Insc. with details of the *Accommodation* including *Total adults 918 children 106*
16¾ × 23⅞ (42.7 × 60.6) D.737–1896

West elevation. Scale ⅛
24 × 16¾ (61 × 42.6) D.739–1896

South elevation. Scale ⅛
16¾ × 24 (42.5 × 61) D.740–1896

Longitudinal section. Scale ⅛
17 × 24 (61 × 43.2) D.741–1896

Transverse section. Scale ⅛. Faint perspective sketch of a church with a large central tower and spine.
24 × 17 (61 × 43.2) D.742–1896

Part *South elevation.* Scale ⅛
24⅛ × 16⅞ (61.1 × 42.8) D.743–1896

Part *Longitudinal section.* Scale ⅛
16⅝ × 23⅞ (42.2 × 60.5) D.745–1896

Ground *plan.* Scale ⅛*th.* Sketch site plan. Insc. with details of the *Accommodation* including *Total 583.* d. *18 April 1859* by seal.
16¾ × 24 (42.5 × 61) D.744–1896

East elevation. West elevation. Scale ⅛*th inch.* d. *18 April 1869* by seal. Insc. *as executed*
16⅝ × 23¾ (42.3 × 60.4) D.746–1896

South elevation. Scale ⅛*th inch.* d. *18 April 1859* by seal. Insc. *as executed*
16½ × 23⅞ (42 × 60.6) D.747–1896

Longitudinal section. d. *18 April 1859* by seal
16⅜ × 23¾ (41.6 × 60.4) D.748–1896

Details of Nave. Transverse section. Part *Longitudinal section.* Part *exterior* elevation. Scale ¼ *inch.* d. *18 April 1859* by seal
16⅞ × 24 (42.8 × 61) D.749–1896

Plan of *foundations* and sketch details. Scale *3/16.* d. *24 April 60*
16¾ × 24⅛ (42.6 × 61.3) D.761–1896

Vestry window. Plan, elevation, section and details. Scale *inch* and *full size.* d. *June 1860*
19 × 12⅞ (48.2 × 32.7) D.764–1896

South elevation
16¾ × 23⅞ (42.6 × 60.7) D.750–1896

East elevation. *West elevation*
16¾ × 23¼ (42.5 × 59) D.751–1896

Longitudinal section. Wm. *1859*
16¾ × 24⅛ (42.5 × 61.2) D.752–1896

Elevation of vestry. Transverse section of nave. Section of Chancel. Wm. *1859*
16⅞ × 24¼ (43 × 61.8) D.753–1896

West elevation. Scale ⅛*th inch.* Wm. *1859*
23¾ × 16½ (60.2 × 42) D.757–1896

North elevation. Scale ⅛*th inch.* Wm. *1859*
16⅛ × 24½ (41 × 62.5) D.758–1896

South elevation. Scale ⅛*th inch.* Wm. *1859*
15¾ × 24⅛ (39.9 × 61.2) D.759–1896

East elevation. Section of nave. Section of Chancel. Scale ⅛*th inch*
16¾ × 24 (42.5 × 61) D.760–1896

Part elevations of east window
19⅝ × 14⅜ (49.8 × 36.6) D.755–1896

Window in chancel. Plan. Outside. Inside. Section. Details same as west window. Scale ½″. Wm. *1859*
18⅝ × 12⅝ (47.4 × 32.2) D.754–1896

[*Cha*]*ncel arch.* Elevations and details
19½ × 14½ (49.7 × 37) D.756–1896

Elevations and details of porch and door. Scale ½″ and *full size*
17¼ × 13⅞ (43.8 × 35.2) D.762–1896

Part *inside* and outside elevations of nave. *Section of door. Plan of window.* Torn
18½ × 31⅝ (47.2 × 80.2) D.766–1896

Vestry door. Vestry window. Tower staircase door. Elevations, section and details
21⅛ × 13⅛ (53.8 × 33.2) D.767–1896

Part elevation of clerestory. Torn
16½ × 21½ (42 × 54.7) D.768–1896

Elevation of west window. Plan of exterior. Interior. Section. Details
19⅝ × 14½ (49.9 × 36.7) D.769–1896

Sill of aisle window, section. Scale *full size.* d. *June 1860.* On the back section through a detail *to be carved*
18⅞ × 12⅜ (47.9 × 31.4) D.770–1896

Details of *small windows, vestry chimney piece* and *fender.* Scale *inch* and ½ *inch*
12⅜ × 19⅛ (31.5 × 48.6) D.771–1896

Credence Recep[tacle]. Part elevations, section and details. d. *June 1860*
18⅝ × 12¾ (47.3 × 32.4) D.772–1896

Details of various mouldings. Scale *full size*
22½ × 49 (57.2 × 124.4) D.773–1896

Details of *moldings* [sic] *of upper arcade.* Scale *full size*
23⅛ × 15½ (57.7 × 39.2) D.776–1896

East window. Details of mouldings. Scale *full size*
22 × 14⅛ (55.8 × 35.8) D.777–1896

Clerestory windows. Section of mullion
22⅝ × 15¼ (57.4 × 38.9) D.775–1896

Detail of *jamb of aisle windows.* Scale *full size.* d. *June 1860*
21½ × 14¼ (54.8 × 36.3) D.774–1896

Study for West elevation
18⅝ × 13½ (47.4 × 34.2) D.786–1896

West elevation. Scale *4 feet to one inch.* Wm. *1860.* Insc. in pencil *shewing manner of completion as intended by Mr S*
24 × 16⅛ (61 × 41) D.778–1896

East elevation. Scale *4 feet to one inch*
22¼ × 17⅝ (56.7 × 44.8) D.784–1896

Design for nave roof. Half transverse section. Half transverse section. Part of longitudinal section. Scale ½ *inch to a foot.* Wm. *1860.* Insc. with details of sizes of *Scantlings*
16¾ × 23⅞ (42.5 × 60.7) D.790–1896

Section and *elevation of chancel arch. Elevation* and *plan of screen.* Scale *inch to a foot.* Wm. *1860*
23⅝ × 16¾ (60 × 42.4) D.779–1896

Details of *West gable.* Scale ½ *inch to a foot* and ½ *full size*
24 × 16⅞ (61 × 42.7) D.780–1896

West Window. Plan. *External elevation. Section.* Wm. *1860.* Scale ½ *inch to a foot*
24½ × 19⅜ (64.8 × 49.2) D.782–1896

Internal elevation of west end. Scale [½] *inch to a foot*
26⅞ × 17⅝ (68.2 × 44.7) D.783–1896

Sections showing east window
14⅛ × 19⅝ (36.1 × 49.7) D.787–1896

Part elevation showing clerestory windows
14⅛ × 19½ (36 × 49.5) D.788–1896

Part elevation and section showing another treatment of clerestory windows
13 × 19 (33 × 48.2) D.789–1896

Study for clerestory. Part elevations and section. Insc. with notes of cost
14¼ × 19½ (36.2 × 49.5) D.785–1896

Elevation and section of part of west end. Insc. *18 feet height of 2nd contract*
14⅛ × 19½ (36 × 49.5) D.765–1896

Plans, sections and elevations of a door and a window
11¼ × 16¾ (28.7 × 42.5) D.763–1896

D.737-42 a set with tower.

D.743, 745 show slight alterations to preceding.

D.744, 746-9 a set, submitted to the Incorporated Church Building Society.

D.750-3, 757-60 two sets for the same design, with a tower.

The *Ecclesiologist* explained in 1859 that 'a design by Messrs Prichard and Seddon, of some architectural pretensions and with some remarkable features, was accepted for a new church at Cardiff, but afterwards materially modified through want of funds'. These alterations included reducing the length, and omitting the central tower and spire. In fact, further alterations were necessary because by the time building reached the eaves the funds ran out, and Colonel Roos, Architect to the Bute Trustees, completed the work in a less elaborate manner. The church was consecrated in March 1863. The reconsecration, as Eglwys Dewi Sant, took place after the Second World War.

Prichard and Seddon's original design, as stated by the *Ecclesiologist*, did include a number of unusual features. The nave, spanned by great brick arches and lit by five bays of huge clerestory windows, was very wide; wider, in fact, than the tower, so that it was contracted at the crossing and the entrance to the transepts set on the diagonal. This width meant that seating was unnecessary in the aisles which are really no more than ambulatories separated from it by pairs of coupled columns. Thus the Tractarian ideal of seating the large congregation with un-impeded views of the chancel was achieved. Howell and Beazley note that this appears to be the first use of 'passage aisles' which were taken up a few years later by G. E. Street at All Saints, Clifton, and then became increasingly common. Externally the nave was not intended to be roofed with a sharp pointed gable but with a sort of hipped gable. The *Ecclesiologist* remarked about the design: 'The central tower and its spire were well treated; and the whole design showed skill and power and fertility of resources'.

In 1884-6 William Butterfield added the transepts and vestries, and choir stools and tiled floor to Roos's plain chancel.

Ecc, XX, 1859, p.208
Plans and Prospects, p.90
CB, 1864, p.33
Howell and Beazley, pp.236-7

CARDIFF (Canton), Glamorgan. School

Canton Schools. Ground plan. Front elevation. Scale 8 feet to an inch.
c.1885. Insc. *Prichard and Seddon* etc. and with names of rooms
Pen and ink and water-colour
$20\frac{3}{4} \times 13$ (52.5 × 33.2) D.956–1896

Prichard and Seddon showed a design for the church of St. John, St. John's Crescent, Canton at the Architectural Exhibition in 1854-55 (nos. 310, 312, 314) and this was apparently almost completed by 1856 when it was described in the *Ecclesiologist* (XVII, 1856, p.310) although work went on until 1902. The school followed immediately afterwards and was complete by 1857 when it was also described by the *Ecclesiologist* 'The design is picturesque, and an effect of height and dignity well obtained. The style is Pointed, of a modified character: the material a bluish stone with quoins enlivened by bands and patterns of red brick. The staircase to the girl's school-room is very well treated with a rising open arcade. The bell gable is pretty, but might perhaps have been better placed'. The arrangement of the school allowed for girls' class rooms on the first floor, boys on the ground floor, and a master's house attached.

The school has now been demolished.

Ecc, XVIII, 1857, p.259

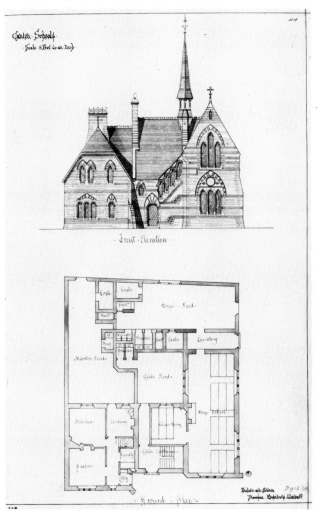

Cardiff. Canton School D.956–1896

CARDIFF, (Grangetown), Glamorgan.
Church of St. Paul

Plan, elevations, section and a perspective sketch of the interior (on 9 sheets) c.1888
D.1271, 1273-7 insc. *Church, Grangetown Cardiff*
D.1271-3, 1275-7 pen and ink. D.1274 pen and ink, and pencil.
D.1278, 1314 pencil
D.1271–1278, 1314–1896

Plan. Scale linear. Insc. with notes about the accommodation and the cost.
$13 \times 19\frac{3}{4}$ (33.1 × 50.3) D.1273–1896

East elevation. West elevation. Scale linear
$13 \times 20\frac{1}{8}$ (33 × 51.1) D.1271–1896

South elevation
$13\frac{1}{4} \times 19\frac{3}{4}$ (33.7 × 50.1) D.1272–1896

Sketch of south elevation
$13\frac{3}{8} \times 20\frac{1}{4}$ (34 × 51.3) D.1314–1896

Longitudinal section through aisle. Wm. 1886
$13 \times 19\frac{5}{8}$ (33 × 49.7) D.1274–1896

Section through nave looking east. Scale linear
$19\frac{1}{2} \times 12\frac{1}{2}$ (49.6 × 31.8) D.1275–1896

Section through nave & elevation of west end. Section through chancel & elevation of east end. Wm. 1886
$12\frac{7}{8} \times 19\frac{3}{4}$ (32.7 × 51) D.1276–1896

Longitudinal section through nave and chancel
$13\frac{1}{8} \times 19\frac{3}{4}$ (33.2 × 50) D.1277–1896

Perspective sketch of the interior. Insc. *Mr Voisey called*
$13\frac{1}{8} \times 19\frac{3}{4}$ (33.5 × 51) D.1278–1896

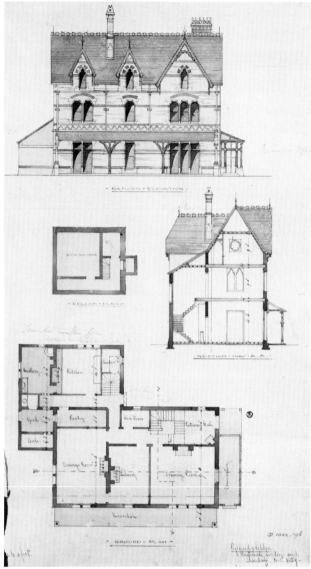

Cardiff. St. Fagans (possibly). Rectory D.1032–1896

The church, which still survives, was built for Lord Windsor in what was a poor, but rapidly expanding district of Cardiff. The materials used were local limestone with Penkridge stone and cast concrete details for the walls, and red deal and red Broseley tiles for the roof.

These drawings show slight differences from the perspective and plan by Coates Carter published in the *Builder* in 1890, when the church was in course of erection. As completed, the spire and sculpture at the West end were omitted.

Br, 25 Jan 1890, p.62

CARDIFF (St. Fagans), Glamorgan. Rectory, possibly

Plans, elevations and a section (on 4 sheets). 1859
D.1032, 1033 insc. *Prichard and Seddon* etc. and D.1032–34 with names of rooms.
Pencil, pen and ink, and water-colour
D.1032–1035–1896

Cellar plan. Ground plan. Garden elevation. Section thro' AA. d. *Decr 1859.* Insc. with notes about alterations and with measurements.
$21\frac{1}{8} \times 20\frac{1}{2}$ (54.1 × 31.7) D.1032–1896

Attic plan. Roof plan. Entrance elevation
$21\frac{1}{2} \times 12\frac{1}{4}$ (54.5 × 31.1) D.1033–1896

First floor plan. Front elevation
$19\frac{7}{8} \times 12\frac{1}{4}$ (50.5 × 31.2) D.1034–1896

Section. Side elevation
$18\frac{3}{8} \times 12\frac{1}{4}$ (46.6 × 31.1) D.1035–1896

As built there are many modifications to these drawings but nevertheless they do seem to be for the rectory. The inscription 'No windows to floor' supports this because as completed the windows under the verandah do not give access to the garden. The Rectory was built of local limestone with Bathstone dressings by Thomas Williams for £1,400. The *Building News* remarked that it was by Prichard alone and since much of the detailing is similar to Eatington one wonders whether he undertook the alterations to Seddon's first proposals after the partnership broke up.

Ecc, XIX, 1858, p.71
BN, 10 August 1866, p.530 (illus)

CHALFONT, Buckinghamshire. House (probably 'Roughwood')

Dining room & drawing room chimney piece. Half front elevation. Dining room and half front elevation *drawing room. Side elevation* and details. Scale *inch* and *full size.* c.1885
Insc. *J. G. Robinson Esq., Chalfont, Bucks.* and with notes of colours
$13\frac{3}{8} \times 17\frac{1}{4}$ (34 × 43.6) D.1614–1896

On the back is a printed plan of Birchington

BN, 17 January 1890, p.115
See SPECIFIC CLIENTS. G. Robinson

CHARLTON. Parsonage

Plans and elevations (on 2 sheets). 1864
Insc. *John P. Seddon Archt. 12 Park St. Westr.* and initialled *R.C.J.* Insc. *Design for Parsonage. Charlton* and with the names of the rooms
D.1176 pen and ink, and water-colour. D.1177 pencil, pen and ink, and water-colour
D.1176, 1177–1896

Side elevation. Garden front. Basement and *attic floor* plans. Scale $\frac{1}{8}$th. d. *Oct. 1864*
$18\frac{1}{2} \times 12\frac{1}{2}$ (47 × 31.8) D.1176–1896

Side elevation. Entrance front. Ground floor and *chamber floor* plans. Scale $\frac{1}{8}$th. d. *Oct. 1864.* Some alterations in pencil. On the back there is a sketch elevation of one wall of a room
$18\frac{1}{2} \times 12\frac{1}{2}$ (47 × 31.8) D.1177–1896

It is not clear which Charlton this is.

CHEPSTOW, Gwent. Church of St. Mary

Church of St. Mary, Chepstow. Elevation of *the pulpit* and sketch *plan of groining.* Scale $\frac{1}{2}$ inch
Insc. *Seddon and Carter Archts Cardiff.* d. *1890*
Pencil, pen and ink, and wash on tracing paper
$11 \times 10\frac{1}{2}$ (28 × 26.8) D.1630–1896

The church was 'restored' in the 17th century, and again in 1838-41 by Wyatt and Brandon. The *Building News* said of the latter: 'under their direction the eastern bay of the nave, together with two of the pieces of the central tower, and probably one of the arches also, though of this there is some uncertainty, were destroyed, and the most fearful chancel and transepts with galleries were erected in the lank, attenuated 'Norman' of that period, and a large gallery was also erected in the nave, the walls of which were plastered. The floor also . . . was again raised to a height of 3ft. 9in. above the original level, and the aisles were totally destroyed'. Seddon and Carter's work, carried out between 1890–1904, involved rectifying these 'injustices': lowering

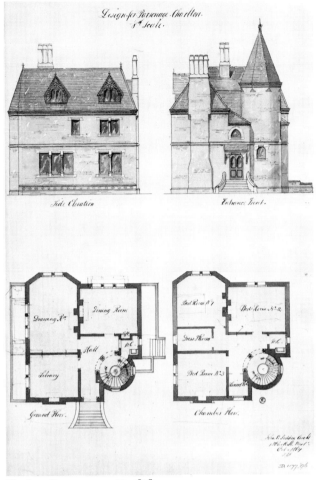

Charlton. Parsonage D.1177–1896

the floor, removing the plaster, re-building the aisles and entire eastern end, opening up the 17th century tower arch, etc.

CB, 1891, pp.77–82
BN, 17 January 1890, p.115; 26 June 1891 (including illustration of Carter's perspective and plan)
Howell and Beazley, p.190

CHESTER, Cheshire. Church of St. Mary on the Hill

Designs for two stained glass windows. Scale *3 ins*
Insc. *ary Chester* (the rest cut off)
Pencil and water-colour
$21\frac{5}{8} \times 13\frac{3}{8}$ (55 × 34) On the back of D.1261–1896 of drawings for the porch of St. Margaret's Westminster.

Seddon restored the church, which is of Norman foundation, in 1890-91.

N. Pevsner and E. Hubbard, *Cheshire*, 1971, p.151 (no mention of glass)

CHIGWELL ROW, Essex. Church of All Saints

Perspective, elevations and sections (on 6 sheets). c.1865
D.721-5 insc. *S–Church, Chigwell* and *John P. Seddon Archt. 12, Park St. Westminster*
D.720 pencil and water-colour. Rest pencil, pen and ink, and water-colour
D.720–725–1896

Perspective. Pasted to a sheet Wm. *1864*
$19\frac{3}{8} \times 13\frac{3}{4}$ (49.3 × 35) D.720–1896

Ground plan. Scale ⅛*th.* Insc. with details of the accommodation including *Total 419*
$16\frac{1}{4} \times 22\frac{1}{2}$ (41 × 57.5) D.721–1896

South elevation. Scale ⅛*th*
$16\frac{1}{4} \times 22\frac{1}{2}$ (41 × 57.5) D.722–1896

West elevation. East elevation. Scale ⅛*th*
$16\frac{1}{4} \times 22\frac{1}{2}$ (41 × 57.5) D.723–1896

Transverse section thro' nave. Transverse section thro' chancel. Scale ⅛*th*
$16\frac{1}{4} \times 22\frac{1}{2}$ (41 × 57.5) D.724–1896

Longitudinal section. Scale ⅛*th*
$16\frac{1}{4} \times 22\frac{1}{2}$ (41 × 57.5) D.725–1896

Perspective, plan, elevations and sections (on 7 sheets). c.1865
D.727–729, 731, 732 insc. *S–Church* and *John P. Seddon Archt. 12 Park St. Westminster*
D.726 pencil and water-colour. D.727 pen and ink, and water-colour
Rest pencil, pen and ink, and water-colour
D.726–729, 731–733–1896

Perspective
20 × $14\frac{3}{4}$ (50.7 × 37.6) D.726–1896

Ground plan. Insc. with details of the *accom*modation including *Total 426.* Scale ⅛*th*
$16\frac{1}{4} \times 22\frac{1}{2}$ (41.4 × 57.2) D.727–1896

West elevation. Scale ⅛*th*
$22\frac{1}{2} \times 16\frac{1}{4}$ (57.2 × 41.4) D.728–1896

South elevation. Scale ⅛*th*
$16\frac{1}{4} \times 22\frac{1}{2}$ (41.4 × 57.2) D.729–1896

East elevation. Scale ⅛*th*
$22\frac{1}{2} \times 16\frac{1}{4}$ (57.2 × 41.4) D.731–1896

Transverse section thro' nave. Transverse section thro' chancel. Scale ⅛*th*
$16\frac{1}{4} \times 22\frac{1}{2}$ (41.4 × 57.2) D.732–1896

Chigwell Row. Church of All Saints D.726–1896

Chigwell Row. Parsonage D.1178–1896

Longitudinal section. Scale ⅛th
16¼ × 22½ (41.4 × 57.2) D.733–1896

The church is listed by Eastlake. It was completed, except for the tower and spire, by October 1867 at which time the cost was estimated to be £8,000. The builder was Thomas Williams of Canton, the carving was carried out by E. Clarke and Son, and the stained glass provided by Clayton and Bell. The fabric is brick faced with Godalming stone and Bath stone dressings and the plan designed to accommodate 300 persons.

The Church was built to a revised version of the second of these two schemes. The main differences are that the tower—the spire was never built—was moved to the south side of the west front, and the west cloister, reminiscent of that at Hoarwithy, was simplified and includes the west entrance, the porch being omitted. The tower is buttressed to the ground. The west window was changed to a wheel form.

Eastlake, Appendix, p.127
Br, 5 October 1867, p.738
Pevsner and Radcliffe, *Essex*, 1965, pp.122-3

Parsonage

Perspective, plans, elevations and sections (on 5 sheets). c.1865
D.1179-82 insc. *Parsonage, Chigwell Row* and s. *John P. Seddon Archt. 12 Park Street, Westminster*
D.1178 pencil and water-colour. D.1179-82 pencil, pen and ink, and water-colour on tracing paper mounted on linen
D.1178–1182–1896

Perspective
12⅝ × 18¾ (32 × 47.7) D.1178–1896

Cellar plan. Ground plan. First floor plan. Alternative design for arrangement of entrance hall & staircase. Scale 8 feet to one inch. Insc. with names of rooms and measurements
17⅝ × 24¼ (44.9 × 61.5) D.1179–1896

Back elevation. Garden elevation. Scale 8 feet to one inch
17 × 24¼ (43 × 61.5) D.1180–1896

Entrance elevation. End elevation. Section AB. Section CD. Section EF. Scale 8 feet to one inch
17⅝ × 24¼ (44.9 × 61.5) D.1181–1896

Elevation of stables. Back elevation of stables. Second floor plan. Roof plan. Scale 8 feet to one inch. Insc. with details of the *scantlings*
17⅝ × 24¼ (44.7 × 61.5) D.1182–1896

The parsonage, which still survives, cost £2,300 and was completed, to a slightly modified version of this scheme, at the same time as All Saints church. If the stabling was ever built it has now been demolished.

Br, 5 October 1867, p.738

CORK, Ireland. Cathedral of St. Finn Barr

Perspective, plans, elevations and sections (on 15 sheets) including the original competition drawings. 1862.
D.791 s. *J. P. Seddon* and insc. *Comptn drawing Cork Cathdl* and *to be mounted on large she*[et]. D.792-6 stamped *Prichard and Seddon* etc. and insc. '*Most heartily I do beseech the Court to give the judgement*' and *Cathedral of S Finn Barr, Cork.* D.797, 798, 800–803, 805, insc. *Cork Cathedral*
D.791 pencil and wash. D.792-6 pen and ink and wash.
D.797–803, 805 pencil and water-colour. D.804 pencil.
D.792-6 mounted on linen
D.791–805–1896

Sketch perspective and thumbnail sketch plan. d. [18] *62*
14½ × 11 (37 × 28) D.791–1896

Ground plan
14 × 22½ (35.6 × 57.1) D.804–1896

Ground plan. Insc. with names of areas and measurements
23¾ × 30¼ (60.5 × 76.6) D.792–1896
Exhibited Architectural Exhibition 1863, no. 3

North elevation
28⅝ × 30 (57.6 × 76.2) D.793–1896
Exhibited Architectural Exhibition 1863, no. 4

West elevation
30 × 22⅞ (76.3 × 58) D.794–1896
Exhibited Architectural Exhibition 1863, no. 5

East elevation
29⅞ × 22⅝ (75.8 × 57.5) D.795–1896
Exhibited Architectural Exhibition 1863, no. 1

Transverse section looking west. Longitudinal section
22⅞ × 30 (58 × 76.2) D.796–1896
Exhibited Architectural Exhibition 1863, no. 2

Plan. Section and elevation of bay of nave. Scale half inch
49½ × 23⅞ (125 × 60.5) D.797–1896

Cork. Cathedral of St. Finn Barr D.791–1896

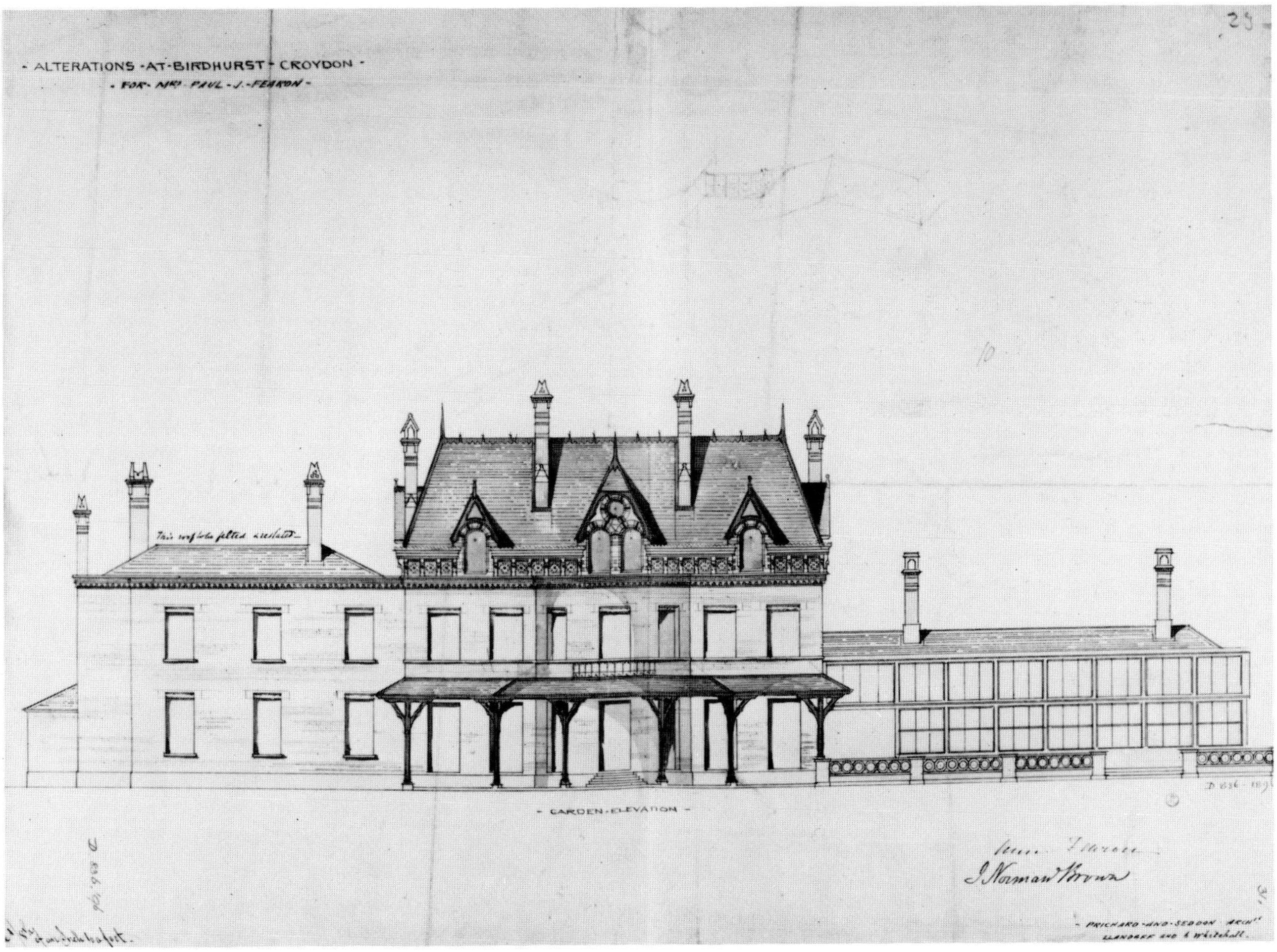

Croydon. Birdhurst D.836–1896

Part *elevation of east end.* Scale *half inch*
$39.5 \times 23\frac{1}{2}$ (100×59.7) D.798–1896

Part *west elevation*
$42\frac{3}{4} \times 25\frac{3}{4}$ (108.5×57.9) D.799–1896

Part *section looking west.* Scale *half inch*
$41 \times 23\frac{3}{4}$ (104.2×60.4) D.800–1896

Chapterhouse. Half *plan thro' columns.* Half *plan thro' windows. Half section. Half elevation.* Scale *half inch*
$42 \times 23\frac{3}{8}$ (106.7×59.9) D.801–1896

Tower. Part *east and west elevations* and part *north and south elevations.* Scale *half inch*
$48\frac{7}{8} \times 23\frac{1}{2}$ (124×59.7) D.802–1896

Half elevations of transept. North transept. South transept. Scale *half inch*
$42\frac{1}{2} \times 23\frac{1}{2}$ (108×59.5) D.803–1896

Part *section looking east.* Scale *half inch*
$42\frac{1}{2} \times 23\frac{5}{8}$ (108×60) D.805–1896

A competition for the Cathedral was announced in April 1862 and by October sixty eight sets of designs had been received and were exhibited in Cork Athanaeum.

The *Building News* said of Seddon's design that it was 'probably, the finest design among the ten or twelve illustrated. The nave is of five bays, with side aisles; at the crossing of nave and transepts, there is a massive tower with a low conical roof; east of this there is one more bay in the choir, which there receives an apsidal termination with the aisle running round it. The transepts show on the ground plan as projections, though the lower part of them would not enlarge the space on the floor of the church. The style chosen is extremely severe and simple, yet the effect is rich as well as dignified. This is especially the case in the interior, which, as shown in the somewhat obscure internal perspective, leaves an impression of great size and breadth. A band of mosaics or paintings running round the nave, at the level where the triforium would occur, were there such a feature, adds much to the beauty of the design, the least satisfactory feature of which, is perhaps the centre tower and its roof'. But although the *Building News* found it the finest the judges did not, and the result was given in favour of William Burges.

C. Handley Read, 'St. Fin Barre's Cathedral', *AR*, CXLI, 1967, pp.422-30
BN, 1 May 1863, p.329

CROYDON, Surrey. Birdhurst

Perspective, plans, elevations, sections and details (on 12 sheets) for alterations for Mrs Paul J. Fearon. 1859-60.
D.830, 831, 833, 835–838, 1606, 1990 insc. *Alterations at Birdhurst, Croydon for Mrs Paul J. Fearon* or similar. D.830, 831, 836–838, 1990, 1606 insc. *Prichard and Seddon* etc. D.836–838 s. *Ann Fearon* and *J. Norman Brown.* D.830, 832–834, 838, 1606 insc. with measurements.
D.806, 831, 1990 pencil and water-colour. Rest pencil, pen and ink, and water-colour. D.1606 on tracing paper
D.806, 830–838, 1606, 1990–1896

Perspective of entrance front
$14\frac{3}{4} \times 16\frac{7}{8}$ (37.4×43) D.806–1896

Basement plan. Ground plan. d. *Oct 1859* (Cut off)
$22\frac{1}{8} \times 16\frac{3}{8}$ (56×41.5) D.838–1896

Attic plan. First floor plan. Scale $\frac{1}{8}$ *of an inch to a foot.* d. *Oct 1859*
$22\frac{1}{4} \times 16\frac{3}{8}$ (56.6×41.7) D.837–1896

Garden elevation. Scale $\frac{1}{8}$*th of an inch to a foot.* d. *Oct 1859*
$16\frac{1}{4} \times 22\frac{1}{2}$ (41.4×57.2) D.836–1896

Side elevations. Scale $\frac{1}{8}$*th of an inch to a foot*
$13\frac{1}{4} \times 19\frac{1}{2}$ (33.6×49.5) D.835–1896

Section and *elevation of upper part of entrance front* with sketch of central dormer on garden front. Scale $\frac{1}{2}$ *inch to the foot*. d. *Oct 1859*
$15\frac{1}{4} \times 21\frac{5}{8}$ (38.6 × 55) D.833–1896

Detail of verandah including elevations and sections. Scale $\frac{1}{2}$ *inch* and $\frac{1}{4}$ *full size*. d. *1859*
$12\frac{3}{4} \times 18\frac{1}{2}$ (32.3 × 46.9) D.831–1896

Elevation of ground floor windows on the entrance front, with plan and section
$15\frac{1}{2} \times 22\frac{1}{8}$ (39.5 × 56.1) D.832–1896

Details of roof & chimnies including section and elevation of a dormer. Scale $\frac{1}{2}$ *inch* and *full size*
$22 \times 16\frac{5}{8}$ (56 × 42.2) D.834–1896

Elevations, sections and details of entrance porch and corridor. Scale $\frac{1}{2}$ *an inch to a foot* and *full size*. d. *Jan. 1860*
$20\frac{7}{8} \times 29$ (53.2 × 73.5) D.830–1896

Elevation of *gates* and pallisading. Scale $\frac{1}{8}$ *inch*
$5\frac{3}{8} \times 21\frac{1}{4}$ (13.7 × 53.9) D.1606–1896

Detail of ironwk to corridor. Scale *full size*. d. *1859*. Insc. with notes
$28 \times 40\frac{1}{8}$ (71 × 101.8) D.1990–1896

D.835–838 form a set.

Birdhurst was demolished several years ago and a modern estate built on the site. Seddon's alterations were carried out as indicated in the drawings.

CWMAFAN (near Port Talbot), Glamorgan. Church of All Saints

Plans, elevations, sections and details (on 11 sheets) depicting two different schemes, and the organ screen. 1853.
Insc. *Prichard and Seddon* etc. D.703–712, 1572 insc. *Cwm Avon Church* or similar.
D.704, 705, 707, 708, 712 pen and ink, and water-colour. D.1572 pencil, pen and ink, and wash. Rest pencil, pen and ink, and water-colour. D.703–708 mounted on linen. D.1572 on tracing paper.
D.703–712, 1572–1896

Ground plan. Scale $\frac{1}{8}$. d. *May 1853*. Insc. with details of the *accommodation* including *total 558*.
Alterations indicated in pencil
$14\frac{1}{4} \times 19\frac{1}{2}$ (36.2 × 49.7) D.709–1896

West elevation. Scale $\frac{1}{8}$. d. *May 1853*
$19\frac{1}{2} \times 14$ (49.7 × 35.5) D.710–1896

East elevation. Scale $\frac{1}{8}$. d. *May 1853*
$20 \times 13\frac{3}{4}$ (51 × 35) D.711–1896

Transverse section. Scale $\frac{1}{8}$. d. *May 1853*. Insc. with measurements of the spire *134′6″*
$19\frac{1}{2} \times 14\frac{1}{4}$ (49.5 × 36) D.712–1896

Doorway in screen of organ chapel. Plan, elevation and section. Scale *inch*
$12\frac{7}{8} \times 16\frac{3}{8}$ (32.7 × 41.7) D.1572–1896

Plan. Scale $\frac{1}{8}$. d. *July 1853*. Insc. with details of the *accommodation* including *total 427*. Numbered *1*
$20 \times 15\frac{3}{4}$ (50.5 × 40) D.703–1896

West elevation. Scale $\frac{1}{8}$. d. *July 1853*. Numbered *2*
$20 \times 15\frac{3}{4}$ (50.5 × 40) D.704–1896

East elevation. Scale $\frac{1}{8}$. d. *July 1853*. Numbered *3*
$20 \times 15\frac{3}{4}$ (50.5 × 40) D.705–1896

North elevation. Scale $\frac{1}{8}$. d. *July 1853*. Numbered *4*
Alterations indicated in pencil
$20 \times 15\frac{3}{4}$ (50.5 × 40) D.706–1896

Longitudinal section. Scale $\frac{1}{8}$. d. *July 1853*. Numbered *5*
$20 \times 15\frac{3}{4}$ (50.5 × 40) D.707–1896

Section through chancel. Section through nave. Scale $\frac{1}{8}$. d. *July 1853*. Numbered *6*
$20 \times 15\frac{3}{4}$ (50.5 × 40) D.708–1896

D.703–708 form one scheme and D.709–712 another.

As built various alterations were made to the first of these schemes including the omission of the transepts and the inclusion of lean-to aisles. The *Building News* noted in August 1860 that it had been built 'a short time since, at the sole cost of the Governor and Company of Copper Miners in England, William Gilbertson Esq., being . . . the local manager of the vast works belonging to the Company'.

The materials used were hammer-dressed sandstone for the walls, alternating with courses of random pebble work, and the dressings were of Combe Down Bath stone. All the ornamental shafts were of polished serpentine but these were removed shortly after the church had been completed because the stone was found to be faulty. The timber was of Memel or pitch pine, and the doors of oak. The paving was of Minton's tiles, and the total cost in excess of £5,000. The foundation stone was laid 15 May 1855. Howell and Beazley record that the church is notable for its very tall nave, a west window of unusual design and its tall and slender spire of unusual outline.

See also TYNANT, Glamorganshire
BN, 24 August 1860, pp.656, 661 (illus)
Br, 2 June 1855, p.261; 28 June 1856, p.356
Howell and Beazley, p.267

CWM BRAN see PONTNEWYDD, Gwent

CYNWYL GAIO (Conwil), Dyfed. Church

Details of roofs, west and aisle doors, and stained glass windows. 1859–1876.
Conwil Church, Caermarthenshire. Detail of chancel roof. Half section of principal and rib. Half section of common rafter and rib. Longitudinal section of one bay and details. Scale *half inch* and $\frac{1}{2}$ *real size*
Insc. *Prichard and Seddon*, etc. and d. *Oct 1859*. The drawing bears the wax seal of the *Society for enlarging, building, and repairing churches and chapels. Incorporated 1828*. This stamp is d. *Feb 16′63*
Pen and ink and water-colour
$12 \times 17\frac{1}{2}$ (30.5 × 44.5) D.1502–1896

Conwil Church, Caermarthenshire. Detail of Nave Roof including section, part elevation and details. Scale *half inch*
Lettered *Prichard and Seddon* etc. and d. *Augst 18* (the rest is torn off). Insc. *Drawing to shew the description of new roofs in case the old ones prove too decayed to restore* and *The Aisle roof will be similar*, and with measurements.
Pen and ink and water-colour on tracing paper
$14\frac{1}{2} \times 19\frac{3}{4}$ (37 × 50) D.1503–1896

Conwil Church. Aisle door, elevations and detail. Scale linear and *3″*. s. *J. P. Seddon Archt*. d. 9/11/76
Pencil and wash
$12\frac{3}{4} \times 18\frac{5}{8}$ (32.4 × 47.3) D.1549–1896

Details of door furniture for *west door* and *aisle door Conwil church*. Scale linear $\frac{1}{3}$ *full size* and *full size*. Insc. *J.O*[sic] *Seddon Archt* and with a note about the nails. d. *17/11/76*
Pencil and wash
$18\frac{5}{8} \times 12\frac{5}{8}$ (47.3 × 32.1) D.1988–1896

Conwil Church, Caermarthenshire. Designs for stained glass windows. Scale *1½″ to a foot*. s. *J. P. Seddon Architect, 1, Queen Anne's Gate, Westminster*. Insc. with measurements·
Pencil and water-colour
$12\frac{1}{4} \times 21\frac{3}{4}$ (31.2 × 55.2) D.1747–1896

The *Ecclesiologist* reported in 1860: 'This church is to be restored at the cost of £700 by Messrs Prichard and Seddon. The new arrangement is good, except that there is no chancel screen. A vestry is screened off at the east end of the north chancel aisle. We cannot admire the western bell cote. It is heavy and ugly, and the whole church is very uninteresting'.

Ecc, XXI, 1860, pp.52–53

DINGESTOW, Gwent. Dingestow Court

Perspectives, plans, elevations, sections and details (on 12 sheets) for alterations and additions, 1859.
D.885, 888–896 insc. *Dingestow Court. Design for alterations* or similar, and *Prichard and Seddon* etc. D.885, 888–891, 894 insc. with measurements, and D.885, 888, 889, 894 with names of rooms.
D.886, 887 pencil. D.890, 891 pencil and water-colour. D.892, 893 pen and ink, and pencil. D.894–896 pen and ink, and water-colour on tracing paper. D.885, 888, 889 pencil, pen and ink, and water-colour.
D.885–896–1896

Perspectives (2) of back facade showing different designs for re-modelling
$11\frac{3}{4} \times 15\frac{1}{2}$ (29.7×39.6) D.886, 887–1896

Ground plan. Front elevation. Scale $\frac{1}{8}$*th inch.* d. *Sep 1859*
$19\frac{1}{2} \times 14\frac{1}{8}$ (49.6×36) D.885–1896

Ground plan as altered. Front elevation as altered. Section thro' GH. Section thro' JK. Scale $\frac{1}{8}$*th of an inch to a foot.* d. *Nov 1859*
$22 \times 14\frac{1}{2}$ (55.8×37) D.889–1896

First floor plan as altered. Attic plan as altered. Plan of roof timbers. Section thro LM. Plan of covered roof. Scale $\frac{1}{8}$*th of an inch to a foot.* d. *1859*
$22\frac{1}{4} \times 15$ (56.5×38) D.888–1896

Details of new windows; plans, elevations and details. Scale $\frac{1}{2}$ *in* and *full size.* d. *Dec. 1859*
22×30 (55.8×76) D.890–1896

Plans, elevations and details of chimneys. Scale $\frac{1}{2}$ *in* and *full size.* d. *Dec 59*
22×30 (55.8×76.2) D.891–1896

Plan of dining room ceiling. Scale $\frac{1}{2}$ *inch.* Insc. *Taken from one in an old inn in Monmouth*
$14\frac{3}{4} \times 16\frac{3}{4}$ (37.5×42.5) D.892–1896

Sections of dining room showing woodwork. Scale $\frac{1}{2}$ *inch*
$10 \times 15\frac{3}{4}$ (25.6×39.9) D.893–1896

Design for stables. Ground plan
$8\frac{7}{8} \times 13\frac{3}{8}$ (22.7×34.1) D.894–1896

Design for stables. Front elevation. Scale $\frac{1}{8}$
$9\frac{3}{4} \times 14\frac{1}{2}$ (25×36.8) D.895–1896

Design for stables, side elevation. Scale $\frac{1}{8}$*th inch*
$8\frac{3}{4} \times 13$ (22.3×32.9) D.896–1896

The original house was designed by Lewis Vulliamy for S. Bosanquet in 1845. Seddon's alterations to the dining room, passage and kitchen, and rooms above are in the same Elizabethan style.

Howell and Beazley, p.180

DIXTON, Gwent. Church

Perspective, plans, elevations and sections (on 6 sheets) for two lych gates and an organ.
D.1637 insc. *Dixton Ch. Monmouth* and D.1555, 1556 *Dixton Church Yard Lych Gate* or similar. D.1593 s. *John P. Seddon.* D.1556 lettered *J. P. Seddon Archt. 12 Park St. Westminster.*
D.1554, 1595, 1637 pencil. D.1593 pencil and water-colour. D.1555, 1556 pen and ink, and water-colour
D.1554–1556, 1593, 1595, 1637–1896

Sketch elevations of lych gate
$13\frac{1}{4} \times 15\frac{1}{4}$ (33.8×38.7) D.1554–1896

Plan. Elevation. Section. Scale $\frac{1}{2}$ *inch*
$12\frac{5}{8} \times 18\frac{3}{8}$ (32×46.7) D.1556–1896

Plan. Elevation. Section. Scale *inch.* d. *1868* and insc. with measurements
$19\frac{3}{4} \times 25\frac{1}{2}$ (50.2×65) D.1593–1896

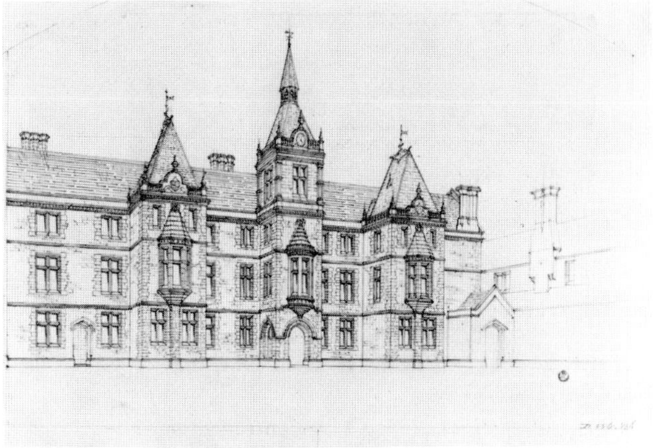

Dingestow Court D.886 1896

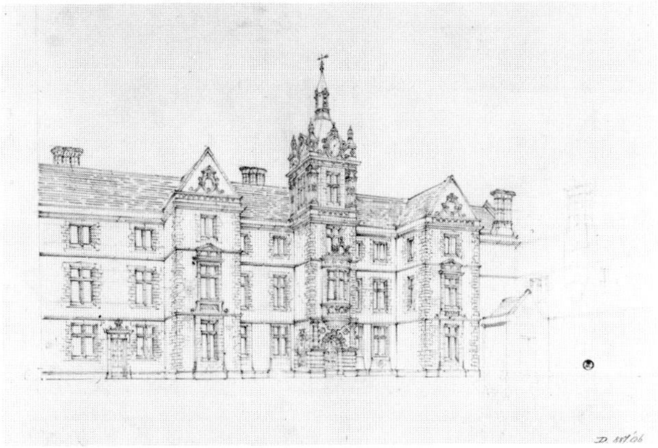

Dingestow Court D.887–1896

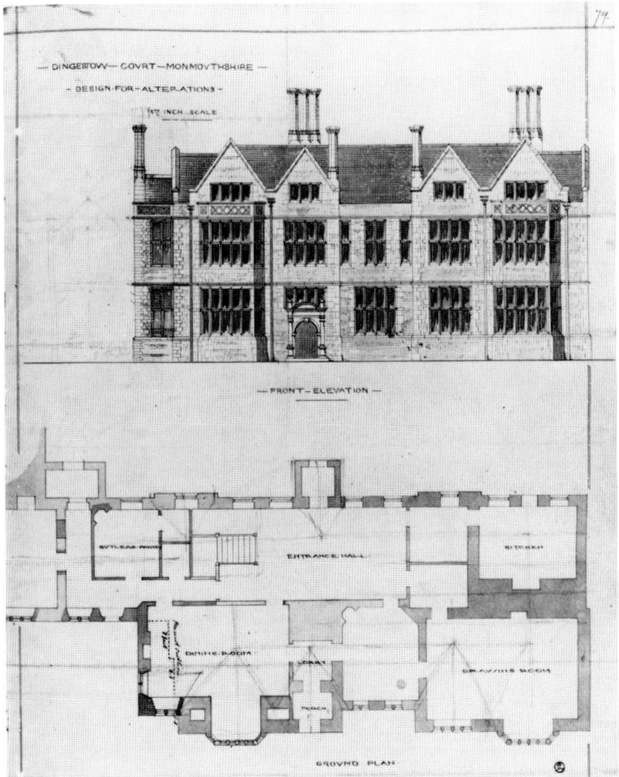

Dingestow Court D.885–1896

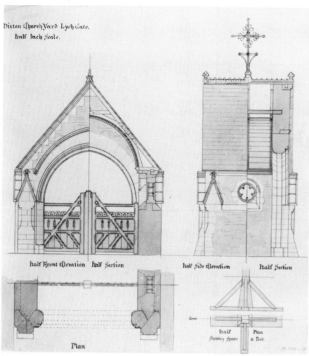

Dixton. Church D.1555–1896

DYTCHLEY, Oxfordshire. Cottages

Design for triple cottage for the Right Hon. Lord Dillon.
Ground plan. Plan of upper floor. Front elevation. Scale $\frac{1}{8}$
Insc. *J. P. Seddon, Archt. 12 Park St. Westmr.* and with
measurements and names of rooms.
Pen and ink and water-colour on tracing paper
$16\frac{7}{8} \times 11\frac{5}{8}$ (42.8 × 29.5) D.1444–1896

Double cottage for the Right Hon. Lord Dillon at Dytchley Park.
Ground plan. Chamber plan. Front elevation. Section at AA. Scale
eight feet to an inch. s. *John P. Seddon, Archt. 12, Park St., Westmr.*
Insc. with notes, measurements and names of rooms.
Pencil and water-colour
$18\frac{1}{4} \times 12\frac{5}{8}$ (46.3 × 32.1) D.1463–1896

Seddon showed a 'design for Park Lodge, Labourers Cottages,
etc. at Dytchley, Oxon for the Rt. Hon. Lord Dillon' at the Architectural Exhibition in 1868 (no. 68), and the *Building News*
noted on 26 June in the same year 'A block of workmen's cottages
is about to be built at Dytchley Oxon for Lord Dillon, J. P.
Seddon Architect'.

BN, 26 June 1868, p.438

EATINGTON PARK, Warwickshire

Eatington Park, Warwickshire. Detail of skeleton tables. Side. End.
Plan looking down. Scale inch.
Insc. *Prichard and Seddon* etc. and with measurements. d. *1861*
Pen and ink
$12\frac{3}{4} \times 18\frac{3}{4}$ (32.6 × 47.5) D.1882–1896

Probably for

Design for picture frames for drawings for E. P. Shirley Esqre.
Scale full size
Stamped *Prichard and Seddon* etc. and insc. with notes
Pencil and water-colour
$11\frac{3}{8} \times 14\frac{3}{4}$ (28.9 × 37.5) D.1852–1896

Seddon's precise involvement with the design of Eatington is not
clear but he seems to have carried out minor work only. In a
short article about the house which he wrote to accompany
reproductions of Axel Haig's illustrations in the *Building News* in
February 1869 Seddon stated: 'Mr John Prichard ... was ... consulted, and under his direction the Palladian portico and sundry
pseudo-classical excrescences were removed, and an entirely new
casing to the mansion was put in in accordance with the designs
of that architect'.

The house was designed and erected between 1856–1863.
Thomas Williams of Cardiff was the builder, and Edward Clarke
of Llandaff did the carving including panels designed by H. H.
Armstead. The house is now a hotel.

Ecc, xx, 1859, p.193
Br, 1859, p.322
BN, 19 February 1869, pp.158–160; 25 June 1869, pp.576–578
Eastlake, pp.304–306 and Appendix No. 169, p.102
M. Girouard, *The Victorian Country House*, 1971, pp.36-7, 180
and pl.34

EGTHORNE. Church

Plan of tile pavement for Egthorne church. Scale $\frac{3}{4}$ *in*
Lettered *John P. Seddon Esqre Architect 12 Park St. London* and
insc. in pencil *not too bright*. Blind stamped *Maw & Co Estimate*
No. 25/132. A printed label of instructions to the designer, is
attached.
Pen and ink, and water-colour
$15\frac{1}{2} \times 14$ (39.4 × 35.6) D.2067–1896

It is not clear where Egthorne is. Is this perhaps a misspelling for
Eythorne in Kent where Seddon restored the Church (*BN*, 17
Jan 1890, p.115, RIBA *Catalogue*, p.35)?

Perspective sketch of lych gate
$18\frac{5}{8} \times 12\frac{1}{2}$ (47.3 × 31.8) D.1595–1896

Plan. Half front elevation. Half section. Half side elevation. Half
section. Half plan shewing spurs to post. Scale half inch
$17 \times 15\frac{1}{4}$ (43.2 × 39) D.1555–1896

Design for organ. Front elevation. Side elevation. Scale $\frac{3}{4}$ *inch*
$12\frac{1}{2} \times 9\frac{7}{8}$ (31.7 × 25.1) D.1637–1896

Neither Lych gate was built. Prichard and Seddon also designed
a stained glass window for the church, made by Lavars and
Barraud at the cost of J. E. Powles, as early as March 1862 (*Br*,
15 March 1862, p.190).

DONNINGTON PRIORY, Newbury, Berkshire. Cottage

John Hughes Esq. Donnington Priory, Newbury, Berks. Design for
Cottage. Ground plan. One pair plan. Front elevation. Back elevation.
End elevation. Section on line AB. Scale $\frac{1}{8}$*th.*
Insc. *Prichard and Seddon* etc., and with measurements and
names of rooms. d. *August 1853*
Pencil, pen and ink, and water-colour
$16\frac{1}{8} \times 21\frac{5}{8}$ (41 × 55) D.1477–1896

DROITWICH, Worcestershire. St. Peter's Parsonage

Parsonage, S. Peters Droitwich. Part plan. Part front el[evation].
Entrance elevation. Section AB. Section CD. Scale 8 *feet to one inch.*
Initialled in the brickwork *WL* and d. *1861*. Insc. with notes,
measurements and names of rooms.
Pencil, pen and ink, and water-colour. The sheet has been cut
so that part of the design is missing.
$18\frac{1}{8} \times 12\frac{1}{4}$ (46.2 × 31) D.1120–1896

Seddon's designs are for an addition including a dining room,
porch, and lobby, to an earlier building.

EPSOM, Surrey. A street

Plans, elevations and sections (on 5 sheets) of various buildings forming a street, for G. White. c.1884.
D.1493 s. *J. P. Seddon Archt. 1 Queen Anne's Gate, SW.* D.1492, 1494-6 insc. with measurements. D.1493 pencil, pen and ink, and water-colour on linen. Rest pencil and water-colour
D.1492–1496–1896

Cottages at Epsom for G. White Esq. Block plan showing arrangement of houses, shop, public house, estate office and hall. Scale linear
$17\frac{1}{4} \times 24\frac{1}{2}$ (43.8 × 62.2) D.1493–1896

Plans (3), elevations (6) and sections (2) of a pair of houses and a block of four houses.
$17 \times 24\frac{7}{8}$ (43 × 63.1) D.1492–1896

Plans (4), elevations (5) and section (3) of a block of three houses and outbuildings. Wm. *1884*
$17 \times 24\frac{7}{8}$ (43 × 63.2) D.1494–1896

Plans (4), elevations (4) and sections (2) of public house. Scale $\frac{1}{8}''$
$17 \times 24\frac{7}{8}$ (43 × 63.2) D.1495–1896

Shop. *Ground floor plan.* First floor plan. *Front elevation. Back elevation.* Side elevation. *Section.* Insc. *G. White Esq.* and with names of rooms. Scale linear
$10\frac{1}{2} \times 23\frac{7}{8}$ (26.6 × 60.6) D.1496–1896

FISHPONDS, Bristol. Parsonage

Plans, elevations, sections and details (on 6 sheets) for the Rev. A. B. Day. 1871-73.
D.1323-6 insc. *Fishponds, Bristol, Parsonage* or similar. D.1326, 1327 insc. *For the Reverend A. B. Day.* D.1324 s. *John P. Seddon* and D.1326, 1328 insc. *John P. Seddon, 12, Park St., Westminster & Henry Crisp, Bristol Architects.* D.1324, 1325, 1327 insc. with names of rooms, and D.1324, 1327 with measurements. D.1323, 1325, 1328 pencil. D.1324 pencil and water-colour. D.1326, 1327 pen and ink. D.1326–1328 are on tracing paper.
D.1323–1328–1896

Ground plan. Scale $\frac{1}{8}$*th*. d. *2 Feb 1871*
$8\frac{3}{4} \times 11\frac{3}{8}$ (22.2 × 29) D.1324–1896

Sketch ground plans. Scale $\frac{1}{8}$*th*
$12 \times 17\frac{5}{8}$ (30.5 × 44.7) D.1325–1896

Sketch front elevation. Scale $\frac{1}{8}$*th*
$7\frac{7}{8} \times 11\frac{3}{4}$ (20 × 30) D.1323–1896

Block plan of site. Plan of foundations. Linear scales. d. *Jan 73*
$24\frac{3}{4} \times 16\frac{7}{8}$ (60.2 × 42.8) D.1326–1896

First floor plan. Roof plan. Section on Line. Section on line EF. Section on line CD. Section on line KC. Section on line AB. Scale *8 feet to an inch* and linear
$24\frac{1}{4} \times 16\frac{5}{8}$ (61.5 × 42.3) D.1327–1896

Roof plan. East elevation. Scale linear
$21 \times 14\frac{3}{8}$ (53.5 × 36.4) D.1328–1896

Seddon had earlier built the church at Fishponds which he mentions in a discussion following Papworth's paper 'On the Fall of the Dome of the Kaltovskoie Church at St. Petersburgh' at the RIBA in 1871 (*Trans*, 1871-2, p.140).

GELLIGAER, Glamorgan. Parsonage

Plans, elevations, sections and a detail (on 4 sheets). 1860. Insc. *Gelly Gaer* or similar. D.1126, 1127 insc. *Prichard and Seddon* etc. D.1126-8 insc. with measurements and D.1126, 1127 with names of rooms.
Pen and ink, and water-colour
D.1126–1129–1896

Plan of cellar. Ground plan. East elevation. Section AB. Scale $\frac{1}{8}$*th* d. *Feby. 1860*. Numbered in red *13*
$17\frac{3}{8} \times 11\frac{5}{8}$ (44 × 29.5) D.1126–1896

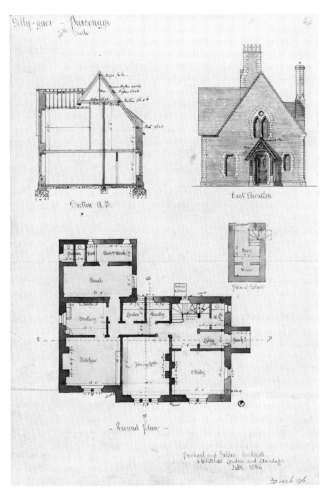

Gelligaer. Parsonage D.1126–1896

First floor plan. South elevation. Scale $\frac{1}{8}$*th*. d. *Feby. 1860.* Numbered in red *14*
$17\frac{3}{8} \times 11\frac{5}{8}$ (44 × 29.5) D.1127–1896

North elevation. West elevation. Section CD. Scale $\frac{1}{8}$*th*. Numbered in red *15*. Wm. *1857*
$17\frac{3}{8} \times 11\frac{5}{8}$ (44 × 29.5) D.1128–1896

Detail of roofs etc. Includes part elevations, and section of part of south facade with part plan of one window. Scale *half inch*
$17\frac{3}{8} \times 12$ (44.1 × 30.4) D.1129–1896

The *Ecclesiologist* noted that the parsonage 'is of very small dimensions, and the study (in the absence of a drawing room) is the largest of the apartments. The windows in the upper floor are of two trefoiled lights with an unpierced quatrefoil above'.

Howell and Beazley notice an extension of 1863 to the Old Rectory.

Ecc, XXII, 1861, p.201
Howell and Beazley, p.228

GREAT KIMBLE, Buckinghamshire. Church of St. Nicholas

Design for a window for Gt Kimble Church with two lights. Scale $1\frac{1}{2}$. s. *John P. Seddon* and d. *1879*
Pencil and water-colour
$8\frac{1}{4} \times 5\frac{3}{8}$ (21 × 13.6) D.1707–1896

A drawing by Seddon of 1874 of the exterior, in connection with proposed restoration, survives at the church, (I am grateful to John Physick for pointing this out to me) and Seddon mentions in 'On Sundry Working Drawings' that he replaced the roof to the chancel. He explains that he encountered at Great Kimble 'the worst example of walls having been thrust outwards by the spreading of roofs that I have met with; but I was able there to restore them bodily to their proper upright position without having them rebuilt, by the simple expedient of hauling them up with ropes by windlasses, after having disengaged the bases of the columns of the arcades, which were subsequently underpinned'. He also notes that in 1882 the church authorities were considering cutting out and dispensing with the tie beam and king posts of the roof 'because it happens to cross from some points of view, part of the eastern window'.

BA, 29 December 1882, p.621

See also LACEY GREEN, Buckinghamshire. Church of St. John Evangelist

GREAT YARMOUTH, Norfolk.
Church of St. James

Section and detail of roof. Linear scale. c.1870-78.
Lettered *S. James Church Gt. Yarmouth*. The lettering has been crossed through with a blue crayon.
Pen and ink on tracing paper
19¾ × 20⅝ (50.2 × 52.5) D.1514–1896

The church was built by Seddon c.1870-78 and survives in Queen's Road. There is a design for the altar in the RIBA.

N. Pevsner, *NE Norfolk*, 1962, p.147
RIBA *Catalogue*

Church of St. Nicholas

Design for arrangement of floor-tiles.
Insc. *S. Nicholas Yarmouth*
Pencil and water-colour
6¾ × 14 (17.2 × 35.3) D.2037–1896

The restoration of the Church of St. Nicholas, one of the largest parish churches in the country, was among Seddon's most important commissions. In an article on the work written in 1864 he recalled how he was first approached in 1862 by a committee including among its members Rev. H. R. Neville and Charles J. Palmer, which had been specially formed for the purpose of undertaking a complete restoration of the church. He found that a great deal needed doing; a poor spire had been built by Wilkins in 1807 to replace one damaged by lightning in 1683; many pinnacles had been removed; the whole of the exterior had been 'hacked' so as to provide a keying for cement rendering; huge buttresses had been added against the West front in 1811 which in Seddon's opinion were 'useless'; and the tower had been 'swaddled up with bands of cast iron!' The 'notorious James Wyatt', Seddon recalled, had even submitted plans for a new church on a different site, intending that the old one should be allowed to fall into ruin.

Some more 'sensitive' work had been done in 1845 by J. H. Hakewill who, under the direction of the Rev. H. Mackenzie, had replaced the pews and galleries with 'proper' oak benches.

Seddon's own work was extensive. He replaced all the roofs including those of the 40′ wide aisles, without ties; stripped plaster from the walls; concreted in the whole area of the chancel which was honeycombed with vaults; rebuilt the south pier of the chancel arch and made good that to the north; repaired the exterior walls; replaced the cornice and parapet with new work; and designed elaborate new choir stalls. The designs for the last, now in the RIBA, he exhibited at the Royal Academy in 1873, and they were illustrated in the *Building News*.

The interior of the church was gutted when it was bombed during the Second World War but photographs survive in the NMR of the pre-war state.

Ecc, xxv, 1864, pp.29–34 (illus); 124–125; 376–377
BN, 26 December 1873, p.721 (illus)
BA, 8 December 1882, p.623
RIBA *Transactions* n.s. vi, 1890, p.181

Church of St. Nicholas, possibly for

Section of an iron roof.
Insc. *St. Nicholas. More expensive than in wood*. Stamped *W & T Phillips Iron & Steel 29 & 30 Coal Exchange EC*
Pen and ink, and water-colour on tracing paper. Torn
12 × 11⅝ (30.5 × 29.6) D.1505 1896

GROSMONT, Gwent. Church of St. Nicholas

Perspective for illustration.
Initialled *J.P.S.* Insc. *reduce AB to ac or one half*, and in pencil *Grosmont Ch.*
Pen and ink
6½ × 8¾ (16.5 × 21.2) D.1305–1896

Seddon's work at Grosmont was among the most important and technically difficult of the restorative commissions he carried out. By 1858 the church had become much too large for a dwindling parish and, with Prichard, he re-arranged the seats removing many from the nave and aisles, and installing stalls in the chancel. At the same time he proposed to add a spiral staircase to the belfry in the angle between the north transept and the chancel, but there was some opposition to this, the *Ecclesiologist* persuasively pointing out that it would alter the contour of the church, and it was not carried out. Seddon probably conceived this staircase as a relieving buttress because the great weight of the impressive tower and spire had forced the crux arches to buckle and twist out of shape, and this pressure had been transmitted north, south and west with the result that the end walls of the transepts and the West wall leaned outwards. Ten years later the problem had worsened and he was called back again to undertake more major work. He began on the chancel and Eleanor Chapel—the richest parts of the church—which although less badly affected structurally than other parts, were taken almost entirely down and rebuilt between 1869-70. The shoring of the tower and spire, a very complex and difficult operation, followed immediately afterwards and was complete by 1873, when Seddon lectured at the RIBA on the techniques he had used.

Most noticeable of the fittings which Seddon added to the church is the large wooden screen separating the chancel, 'Queen Eleanor's Chapel' (now the Vestry), and transepts from the nave, which is glazed with plain glass in geometric shapes.

There is a design for shoring the tower in the RIBA.

Ecc, xix, 1858, p.278
CEAJ, 1 January 1864, p.7 and pl.2
BN, 7 February 1873, pp.149-51 (reprint of his RIBA lecture 'On the Shoring of Grosmont Church Tower')
Ecclesiastical Art Review, March 1878, p.45
C. E. Stock, *A Treatise on Shoring and Underpinning and Generally Dealing with Ruinous and Dangerous Structures*, 1882, pp.32–44
Howell and Beazley, p.165
Rev. A. A. McAdam, *The Church of St. Nicholas, Grosmont*. [1971]
RIBA *Catalogue*, p.35

GUERNSEY, Possibly

Plans, elevations, sections and details (on 9 sheets) for alterations and additions to house including a new studio, for Paul Naftel. 1864.
D.1114, 1115, 1117, 1118 insc. *Studio for P. Naftel Esq.* D.1118A *Mr Naftel's Studio*. D.1112 *Proposed alterations to house for P. Naftel Esq.*, and D.1603 *P. J. Naftel*. D.1114-1117, 1118A
s. *J. P. Seddon Archt. 12 Park St. Westr.* D.1115, 1117, 1118A
initialled *R.C.J.* Most inscribed with measurements.
D.1112, 1113, 1603 pencil. D.1117, 1118A pencil and water-colour. D.1114–1116, 1118 pencil, pen and ink, and water-colour.
D.1112–1118A, 1603–1896

Front and back elevations. Scale ⅛
17⅜ × 12⅛ (44.1 × 31) D.1113–1896

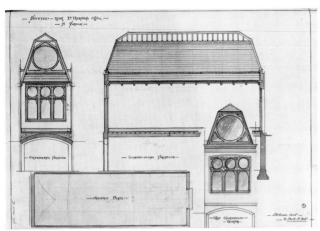

Guernsey (possibly). Studio for P. Naftel D.1114–1896

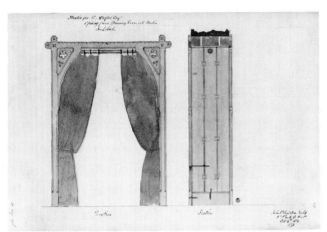

Guernsey (possibly). Studio for P. Naftel D.1117–1896

Front and back elevations. Scale ⅛
16⅝ × 11 (42.3 × 28) D.1112–1896

*Studio. Ground plan. End elevation north. Longitudinal section.
Transverse section.* Scale ¼
12⅝ × 18⅝ (31.9 × 37.2) D.1114–1896

Studio. Details of roof and windows. Scale *inch* and *full size.*
d. *March 11th 1864*
16¾ × 22¾ (42.5 × 58) D.1115–1896

Door to studio. Plan. ½ *exterior,* ½ *interior* elevations. *Section.* Wm.
1863
16⅝ × 12 (42.3 × 30.3) D.1116–1896

Opening from drawing room into studio. Elevation. Section. Scale
inch. d. *Oct. 6th 1864*
12½ × 18½ (31.9 × 46.8) D.1117–1896

Studio. Detail of north window
19 × 13 (48 × 33.1) D.1118–1896

Studio. Details of windows and plasterwork. Scale *full size.*
d. *March 11th 64*
19 × 26⅝ (48.5 × 62) D.1118A–1896

Plans, elevations, sections and details of woodwork
21½ × 25⅞ (54.5 × 65.7) D.1603–1896

Seddon appears to have known Paul Jacob Naftel (1817–1891),
the painter, since his youth for D.962–1896 (catalogued under
Topographical Drawings) is inscribed 'P. Naftel, Conway
Castle' and is dated August 1849. Naftel was born in Guernsey
and apparently did not move to England until 1870.

HENTLAND, Herefordshire.
Church of St. Dubricius

*Design for Lichgate. Hentland Church Yard. Plan. Elevation near road
Side elevation. Section thro' AB. Section thro' CD.* Scale ½ *inch*
Insc. *J. P. Seddon Archt. 12 Park St. Westminster,* and with
measurements.
Pencil and water-colour on tracing paper. Inscriptions in ink.
17 × 13 (43.1 × 33) D.1573–1896

Possibly for

Elevation of east (?) wall showing decoration including a band
insc. 'I am the Good Shepherd'.
Insc. *Hen* (the rest has been cut off)
Pencil and water-colour on tracing paper
13¼ × 8½ (33.7 × 21.5) D.1659–1896

Seddon restored the church in 1853

Parsonage

Photograph, plans, elevations, sections and details (on 14
sheets) depicting three schemes, the last for the Reverend W.
Poole. 1858-64.
D.1066-70, 1072, 1151-4, 1613 insc. *Hentland Parsonage* or
similar, and D.1071, 1072 *Rev'd W. Poole.* D.1066, 1067, 1071
s. *J* or *John P. Seddon Archt.* D.1070, 1072, 1151–1154 lettered
or insc. *Prichard and Seddon* etc.
Pencil, pen and ink, and water-colour, except D.1613 pencil
and water-colour
D.1065–1072, 1150–1154, 1613–1896

Ground plan. East elevation. Scale ⅛ *inch.* Wm. *1857*
18¾ × 12 (47.5 × 30.3) D.1153–1896

*Bedroom floor plan. Transverse section on line AB. Transverse section
on line CD.* Scale ⅛ *inch*
18¾ × 12 (47.5 × 30.3) D.1154–1896

South elevation. West elevation. Scale ⅛ *inch.* Wm. *1858*
18¾ × 12⅜ (47.5 × 31.4) D.1152–1896

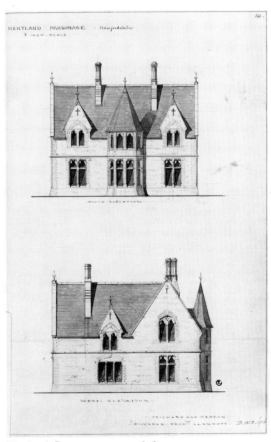

Hentland. Parsonage D.1152–1896

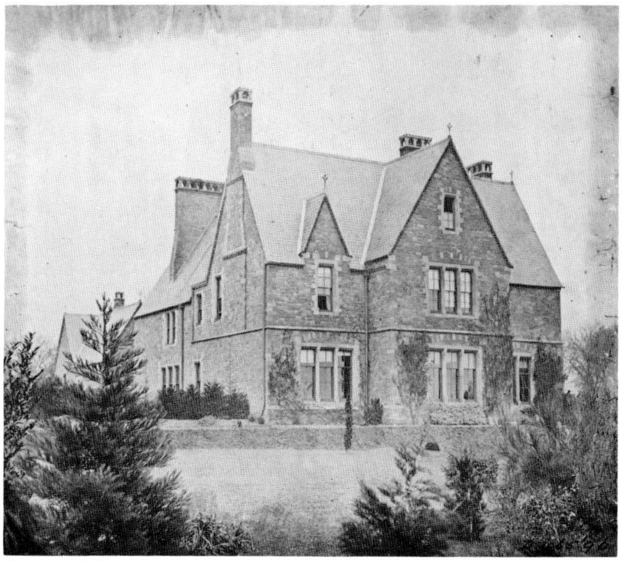

Hentland. Parsonage D.1065–1896

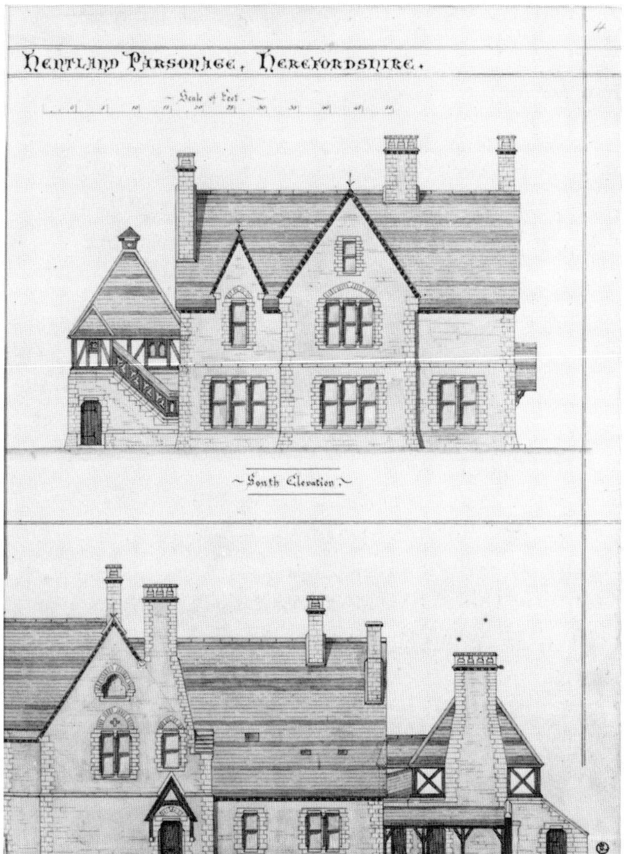

Hentland. Parsonage D.1068–1896

Cellar plan. *Plan of ground floor. Plan of bedroom floor. Plan of attic. Section on line CD. Section on line EF. Section on line AB.* Part *Longitudinal section of roof over hall.* Scale $\frac{1}{8}$
$15\frac{1}{4} \times 21\frac{1}{4}$ (38.8×54) D.1151–1896

East elevation. South elevation. North and west elevations. Insc. in a later hand *?St Fagans*
$15\frac{1}{4} \times 21\frac{1}{4}$ (38.8×54) D.1150–1896

Photograph of completed building
$9 \times 10\frac{1}{4}$ (22.6×26) D.1065–1896

Ground plan. Linear scale. Insc. with measurements and names of rooms
$12\frac{1}{4} \times 18\frac{5}{8}$ (31.1×47.4) D.1066–1896

South elevation. East elevation. Linear scale. Part has been cut off
$12\frac{1}{2} \times 16\frac{5}{8}$ (31.7×42.3) D.1068–1896

West elevation. Longitudinal section. Transverse section through library. Linear scale
$18\frac{1}{2} \times 12\frac{1}{2}$ (47×31.7) D.1067–1896

Parlor windows. Part plans, elevations, section and details. Scale $\frac{1}{2}$ *inch* and *full size.* Numbered in red *26*
$11\frac{5}{8} \times 17\frac{1}{8}$ (29.5×43.5) D.1069–1896

Part elevations of *Porch.* Scale *inch.* d. *May 1860.* Insc. with notes about slates and measurements
$12\frac{5}{8} \times 10\frac{1}{8}$ (32×25.6) D.1070–1896

Garden steps. Plan. Half elevation. Half section. Transverse section. Scale $\frac{1}{2}$ *inch.* d. *Feb 19th 64.* Initialled *R.C.J.*
$12\frac{1}{4} \times 18\frac{5}{8}$ (31.2×47.3) D.1071–1896

Plan of stabling. Plans, front and side elevations. Scale $\frac{1}{8}$*th.* d. *1858.* Insc. with names of rooms. Numbered in red *21.* On the back is a sketch of a chimney
$11\frac{1}{2} \times 17\frac{1}{8}$ (29.1×43.4) D.1072–1896

Fireplaces; plan, elevations and details. Insc. with measurements
$18\frac{3}{8} \times 12\frac{3}{8}$ (46.6×31.4) D.1613–1896

D.1152–1154 comprise the first scheme, D.1150, 1151 the second, and the remainder the third. The *Ecclesiologist* thought the porch 'almost too ecclesiastical', though they liked the French gabled roof over the attic 'which gives a picturesque exterior', the verandah on the south side supported by stone shafts which 'is a good thought, well worked out', and the general arrangement.

Plans, sections and elevations (on tracing paper); a specification and an affidavit dated March 1859; and a bond dated July 1859 are in the Hereford Record Office.

Raffles Davison drew a part of the parsonage for the *British Architect* in 1885.

Ecc, xx, 1859, p.74
BA, 17 July 1885, p.30

School

Photograph, plans, elevations, sections and details (on 14 sheets) depicting various schemes. c.1859.
D.971, 973, 977, 979–985 insc. *Hentland Schools, Herefordshire* or similar. D.971, 977, 980–983, 985 stamped or insc. *Prichard and Seddon* etc. D.971, 973, 979 insc. with measurements and names of rooms, and D.972, 977, 983 with measurements.
D.978 photograph. D.974, 977, 981, 982 pen and ink, and water-colour. D.976 pencil and water-colour. Remainder pencil, pen and ink, and water-colour. D.972–974 are on tracing paper.
D.971–974, 976–985–1896

Photograph of completed building
$7\frac{1}{8} \times 8\frac{5}{8}$ (18.2×22) D.978–1896

Plan, front and side elevations, and a section. Wm. *1859.* Insc. with names of rooms
$12\frac{7}{8} \times 17\frac{3}{4}$ (32.7×45.3) D.976–1896

Site plan. *Back elevation. Longitudinal section BB. Section AA.* Details of a window. Linear scale
$16\frac{1}{8} \times 22\frac{3}{4}$ (40.8×57.9) D.977–1896

Ground plan. Chamber plan. Elevation to road. Elevation towards garden. Elevation to road. Elevations of *Bell turret.* Scale $\frac{1}{8}$ *inch to a foot* and $\frac{1}{2}$ *inch*
$15\frac{5}{8} \times 22\frac{1}{2}$ (39.6×57.3) D.971–1896

Ground plan. Scale $\frac{1}{8}$*th*
$11\frac{5}{8} \times 15$ (29.6×38) D.973–1896

South elevation. Transverse section. Scale $\frac{1}{8}$ *inch.* d. *July* (the rest has been cut off)
$16\frac{1}{8} \times 11\frac{1}{2}$ (41×29.2) D.972–1896

Ground plan. Scale $\frac{1}{4}$. Alterations indicated in pencil
$19\frac{1}{2} \times 27\frac{1}{4}$ (49.5×69.2) D.979–1896

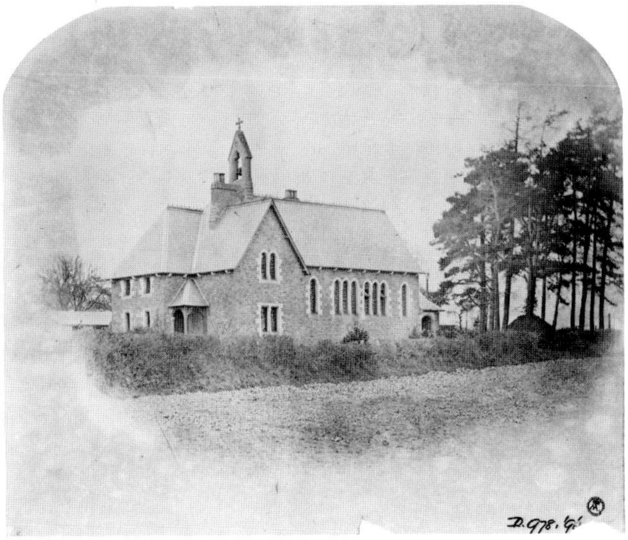

Hentland. School D.978–1896

Front elevation. Scale $\frac{1}{4}$ *inch to a foot.* Alterations indicated in pencil
$16 \times 22\frac{3}{4}$ (40.6×57.7) D.980–1896

Back elevation. Scale $\frac{1}{4}$ *inch to a foot*
$16 \times 22\frac{3}{4}$ (40.7×57.8) D.982–1896

West elevation. Section on line CD. Scale $\frac{1}{4}$ *inch to a foot.* Alterations suggested in pencil
$15\frac{7}{8} \times 22\frac{5}{8}$ (40.2×57.5) D.983–1896

East elevation. Details of windows in school room. Scale $\frac{1}{4}$ *inch to a foot* and $\frac{1}{2}$ *inch to a foot*
$15\frac{1}{2} \times 22\frac{3}{4}$ (39.4×57.7) D.981–1896

Section thro' school rm and part of front elevn. Scale $\frac{1}{2}$ *inch*
$16\frac{3}{8} \times 24\frac{3}{8}$ (42×61.5) D.984–1896

Tracing of above
$17\frac{5}{8} \times 25\frac{1}{4}$ (44.7×64) D.974–1896

Plans, elevations and sections of windows and doors. Scale $\frac{1}{2}$ *inch* and $\frac{1}{8}$ *real size*
$22\frac{1}{2} \times 21\frac{1}{4}$ (57.2×54.2) D.985–1896

D.971 and 977 form part of a set, as do D.972 and 973.

The *Ecclesiologist* found the architectural detailing 'good' but did not see much advantage in 'the unusual arrangement of the surrounding corridor'.

Ecc, XXI, 1860, p.49

HEREFORD, Cathedral

Three designs (on 3 sheets) for west front. c. 1890–1900.
Insc. in pencil *Hereford Cathl*
D.2159 pencil, pen and ink. D.2160 pen and ink. D.2161 pencil
D.2159–2161–1896

Plan. Elevation. Scale linear
$19\frac{1}{2} \times 13\frac{5}{8}$ (49.5×34.7) D.2159–1896

Plan. Elevation. Scale linear
$20\frac{1}{2} \times 14\frac{1}{8}$ (52×35.8) D.2160–1896

Elevation. Wm. *1886.* Another version of D.2160
$20\frac{3}{8} \times 14\frac{1}{4}$ (54.2×36.2) D.2161–1896

On the 17 April 1786 the west tower of Hereford Cathedral collapsed destroying not just the west end but a large proportion of the Norman nave and aisle too. James Wyatt was called in and proposed sweeping away all that was left of the nave and erecting a new one to his own Gothic design. He was not permitted to do this but did nevertheless destroy a large amount of the original work in his restoration which involved shortening the nave by one bay of 15 feet and erecting a new west front on a 'neat Gothic pattern'. In the first six decades of the 19th century various architects, particularly Cottingham, and Sir Gilbert Scott undertook more serious restoration work but it was not until the end of the century that Wyatt's west end was pulled down and a new one put up to the design of John Oldrid Scott. This was completed by 1908 and cost £16,000.

It is not clear how Seddon came to be involved nor when these designs, which are more elaborate than Scott's, were prepared.

G. Marshall, *Hereford Cathedral Its Evolution and Growth*, n.d. (c.1951)
J. W. Leigh, *Hereford Cathedral Church, Record of Work Done*, 1910
N. Pevsner, *Herefordshire*, 1963, pp.146–174
CEAJ, September 1859, pp.296-97

HERNE, Ridgeway, Kent. Double Cottage

Plans, elevations, sections and details (on 4 sheets). 1870.
s. *John P. Seddon* and D.1457, 1475 addressed *12 Park St. Westm. SW.* D.1445, 1457, 1589 insc. with measurements. D.1445, 1457 insc. with names of rooms.
D.1445 pencil and water-colour. D.1457 pencil. D.1475 pen and ink, pencil and water-colour. D.1589 pencil and water-colour
D.1445, 1475, 1589–1896

Design for double cottage at Ridgeway Herne, Kent for George Dering Esqre. Ground plan. First floor plan. Front elevation. Back elevation. Side elevation. Transverse section. Scale $\frac{1}{8}$*th in.*
$12\frac{3}{4} \times 18\frac{1}{2}$ (32.5×47) D.1457–1896

Cottage at Ridgeway nr Herne Kent, for G. Dering Esq. Ground plan. First floor plans. Front elevation. Back elevation. Side elevation. Transverse section. Details. Scale $\frac{1}{8}$*th.*
A sketch of a door has been pasted on. Insc. with notes and measurements and *This is the plan referred to in our contract of date 7th of June 1870* and s. *J. Adams*
$16\frac{3}{8} \times 24\frac{1}{2}$ (41.7×61.7) D.1475–1896

Plan, elevations and details of *doors.* Scale *inch* and $\frac{1}{2}$ *full size.* d. *June 1870.* Insc. *Cottage at Herne for G. Deering* (sic) *Esq.* and with instructions to the joiner including *all of oak.*
$13\frac{5}{8} \times 17$ (34.6×43.1) D.1589–1896

Design for a double cottage. Ground plan. First floor plan. *Front elevn. Side* elevation. Scale $\frac{1}{2}$ *in.* Insc. *1st suggested for Mr Deering but found too expensive. Provides for 4 or 5 bedrooms*
$16\frac{3}{8} \times 12$ (41.5×30.6) D.1445–1896

HOARWITHY, Herefordshire. Church of St. Catherine

Plans, elevations and details of West door and designs for stained glass windows (on 5 sheets). 1874. 1890.
D.1568, 1569, 1695–1697 insc. *Hoarwithy Church* or similar.
D.1569 insc. *John P. Seddon Architect, 1 Queen Anne's Gate, Westminster.*
D.1568 pencil, D.1569 pencil and water-colour. D.1695-7 pen and ink and water-colour. D.1569 is on tracing paper.
D.1568, 1569, 1695–1697–1896

West door; plan, elevation and details. Scale $1\frac{1}{2}''$
$17 \times 25\frac{7}{8}$ (43.3×65.7) D.1568–1896

Detail of west door. Plan. Outside and *Inside* elevations. Scale $1\frac{1}{2}$ *to a foot.* d. *November 74.* Insc. *Panels stained or of darker kind of wood*
$19\frac{1}{4} \times 11\frac{1}{2}$ (49×29.3) D.1569–1896

Series of windows as executed on west front. Insc. with names of some saints
$11\frac{5}{8} \times 16\frac{3}{4}$ (29.5×42.5) D.1695–1896

Design for stained glass window. Scale $1\frac{1}{2}$ *inch.* d. *1890.* s. *H. G. Murray* and lettered *S. Belham & Co. Stained Glass and Mosaic Works, 155 Buckingham Palace Road, London.* Insc. with measurements
$14\frac{3}{4} \times 9\frac{1}{4}$ (37.6×23.3) D.1696–1896

Two stained glass windows *Centre* and *Side.* Scale $\frac{1}{8}$ *full size*
$13\frac{3}{8} \times 15\frac{3}{4}$ (34×40) D.1697–1896

Hoarwithy. School and residence D.1011–1896

The parsonage, Hoarwithy, as it was built. Photograph courtesy of Clive Wainwright.

School and residence

Hoarwithy Herefordshire. Design for altering old house into school and residence. Ground plan. First floor plan. Front elevation. Back elevation. End elevation. Side elevation. Scale ⅛
Lettered *John P. Seddon Archt. 12 Park St. Westminster.* Wm. *1868.* Insc. with measurements and names of rooms
Pencil and water-colour
19⅜ × 26 (49.2 × 66) D.1011–1896

Possibly exhibited at the Architectural Exhibition 1868, no. 76

The church is one of Seddon's best known buildings and unusual in being in the Romanesque style. This might be accounted for by the fact that 'the neat modern brick building' of 1843 which Seddon encased was also in that style. The work was paid for by the Rev. Poole of Hentland, and the woodwork was cut from trees on his land. The building was apparently 'still far from complete' in 1885. The prayer desk was carved by Harry Hems to Seddon's design and the stained glass windows inserted in 1906 in memory of Rev. Poole.

There is a design for the choir stalls in the RIBA.

The school and house as built were somewhat altered from the design shown in these drawings. Seddon retained the two school rooms in the existing house, but moved the sitting room with its bay to the front—perhaps because the view from there is much better—and added a central gable above the doors.

Br, 5 July 1884, p.12; 10 February 1906, p.150
B.N, 22 June 1883, p.886
N. Pevsner, *Herefordshire,* 1963, p.192

HOLDGATE, Shropshire. Parsonage

Perspective, plans, elevations, sections and details (on 28 sheets) depicting several schemes. 1862-64.
D.1155-7, 1161, 1162, 1165 lettered *Holgate* and D.1074-82, 1084-87, 1160, 1163, 1164, 1166-9 *Holgate.* D.1077-82, 1084-7 s. *John P. Seddon, 12 Park St. Westminster.* D.1077, 1078, 1082, 1085, 1087 initialled *R.C.J.* D.1155-7, 1166-9 stamped *Prichard and Seddon* etc. and D.1155-7, D.1165 lettered *Prichard and Seddon* etc. Most insc. with measurements and names of rooms.
D.1167-9 pen and ink, and water-colour. Rest pencil, pen and ink, and water-colour.
D.1073–1087, 1155–1157, 1160–1169–1896

Ground plan. Front elevation. Scale ⅛ inch to a foot. Insc. *Drawing no. 1.* Alterations suggested in pencil
15¼ × 20¾ (38.7 × 52.6) D.1166–1896

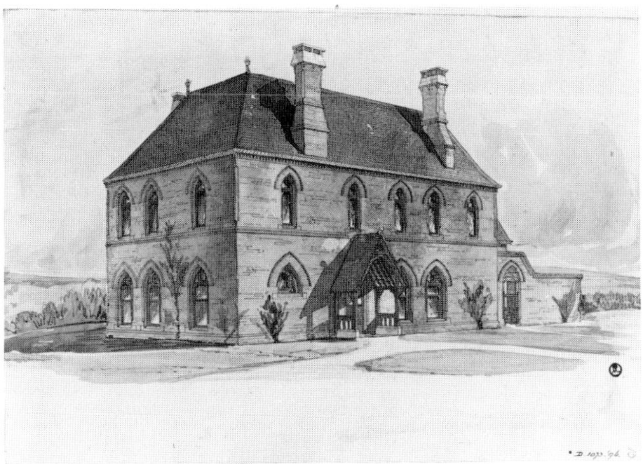

Holdgate. Parsonage D.1073–1896

Chamber plan. Back elevation. End elevation. Scale *8 inch to a foot.* Insc. *Drawing no. 2*
$15\frac{1}{4} \times 20\frac{3}{4}$ (38.7 × 52.6) D.1167–1896

End elevation. Section on line bb. Section on line cc. Elevation of stables. Scale $\frac{1}{8}$ *inch to a foot.* Insc. *Drawing no. 3*
$15\frac{1}{4} \times 20\frac{3}{4}$ (38.7 × 52.6) D.1168–1896

Roof plan. Section on line aa. Scale $\frac{1}{8}$ *inch to a foot.* Insc. *Drawing no. 4.* Wm. *1859*
$15\frac{1}{4} \times 20\frac{3}{4}$ (38.7 × 52.6) D.1169–1896

Cellar plan. Ground plan. Chamber plan. Front elevation. Scale $\frac{1}{8}$*th*
Alterations suggested in pencil
$18\frac{5}{8} \times 12\frac{1}{2}$ (47.2 × 31.8) D.1161–1896

Plan of roofs. Side elevation. Back elevation. Section. Scale $\frac{1}{8}$ *in to 1 foot*
$18\frac{5}{8} \times 12\frac{1}{2}$ (47.2 × 31.8) D.1162–1896

Block plan. Cellar Plan. Side Elevn. Section through cellar. Scale $\frac{1}{8}$*th*
$18\frac{3}{4} \times 12\frac{1}{2}$ (47.6 × 31.7) D.1164–1896

Ground plan. Front elevation. Section thr' AA. Scale $\frac{1}{8}$. Wm. *1860.*
Slight alteration suggested in pencil
$18\frac{3}{4} \times 12\frac{5}{8}$ (47.6 × 32) D.1160–1896

Chamber plan. Back elevn. Yard elevn. Section BB. Scale $\frac{1}{8}$*th*
Alterations suggested in pencil
$18\frac{3}{4} \times 12\frac{5}{8}$ (47.6 × 32) D.1163–1896

Ground plan. Front elevation. Scale *8 feet to an inch.* Numbered *1* and d. *1862.* Alterations suggested in pencil
$18\frac{3}{4} \times 12\frac{3}{8}$ (47.5 × 31.5) D.1155–1896

Copy of above but position of door between larder and boot room changed. Wm. *1861*
$18\frac{1}{8} \times 12\frac{3}{8}$ (46 × 31.5) D.1165–1896

One pair plan. End elevation. Scale *8 feet to an inch.* Numbered *11.* Alterations suggested in pencil
$18\frac{3}{4} \times 12\frac{3}{8}$ (47.5 × 31.5) D.1156–1896

End elevation. Back elevation. Section AA. Scale *8 feet to an inch.* Numbered *111.* Wm. *1862*
$18\frac{3}{4} \times 12\frac{3}{8}$ (47.5 × 31.5) D.1157–1896

Perspective. The house has been cut from another sheet and pasted onto the landscape
$8\frac{1}{4} \times 12\frac{1}{4}$ (21.2 × 31.1) D.1073–1896

Ground plan. Chamber plan. Front elevation. Scale $\frac{1}{8}$*th.* Alterations suggested in pencil
$18\frac{5}{8} \times 12\frac{1}{2}$ (47.3 × 31.8) D.1074–1896

Back elevation. End elevation. Section AB. Section CD. Scale $\frac{1}{8}$*th*
$18\frac{5}{8} \times 12\frac{1}{2}$ (47.3 × 31.8) D.1075–1896

Roof plan. Cellar plan. Side elevation. End elevn of offices. Scale $\frac{1}{8}$*th*
$18\frac{5}{8} \times 12\frac{1}{2}$ (47.3 × 31.8) D.1076–1896

Details of chimnies. Plans, elevations and a section. Scale $\frac{1}{2}$ *inch.* d. *March 14th 64.* Initialled *R.C.J.* and insc. with notes
$12\frac{5}{8} \times 18\frac{3}{4}$ (32 × 47.6) D.1077–1896

Plans, elevations and sections of *library window, window to servant's bed-room* and *larder window.* Scale *inch.* Initialled *R.C.J.* and d. *Feby 18th 1864*
$19 \times 12\frac{5}{8}$ (48.3 × 32) D.1078–1896

Detail of dining room window. Plan. Half outside and *half inside* elevations. *Section.* Scale *inch*
$18\frac{1}{2} \times 12\frac{1}{4}$ (46.8 × 31.1) D.1079–1896

Details of windows. Scale *full size.* d. *Feby 1st 1864*
$26\frac{1}{4} \times 18\frac{7}{8}$ (67 × 48.1) D.1080–1896

Details of windows. Scale *full size.* d. *Feby 19th 1864.* Initialled *R.C.J.*
$26\frac{1}{4} \times 18\frac{7}{8}$ (66.5 × 48.1) D.1082–1896

Chamber floor windows and *staircase window.* Plans, elevations and sections. Scale *inch.* d. *Feb 15th 1864*
$17\frac{1}{4} \times 22\frac{3}{4}$ (43.9 × 57.8) D.1081–1896

Plans, elevations and sections of windows to *kitchen, scullery* and dining room. Scale *inch*
$18\frac{7}{8} \times 12\frac{1}{2}$ (47.9 × 31.7) D.1083–1896

Back door and *yard door.* Plans, elevations and a section. Scale *inch*
$12\frac{3}{8} \times 18\frac{5}{8}$ (31.5 × 47.3) D.1084–1896

Details of chamber floor windows. Scale *full size.* d. *Feby 13th 1864*
$26\frac{1}{4} \times 18\frac{7}{8}$ (67 × 48.1) D.1085–1896

Detail of yard gate. Plan and elevation. *Detail of plaster cornices* to *study, dining room* and *drawing room.* Scale *inch* and *full size*
$12\frac{1}{4} \times 19\frac{1}{8}$ (31.7 × 48.5) D.1086–1896

Stables *Plan, south elevation, west elevation* section AA and details of brackets. *Elevation of WC.* Scale $\frac{1}{8}$*th inch.* Initialled *R.C.J.* and d. *Feb 27th 1864*
$18\frac{5}{8} \times 12\frac{1}{2}$ (47.4 × 32) D.1087–1896

The parsonage was apparently completed in 1864 when the *Ecclesiologist* noted that it was 'cheap and good' and 'treated with much originality'.

Plans, sections and elevations; an affidavit; a certificate; bonds and a specification dating from December 1863 and January 1864 are in the Hereford Record Office.

Ecc, XXV, 1864, p.52

HOLMBURY ST. MARY, Surrey. Joldwynds

Perspective, plans, elevations, sections and details (on 21 sheets) for additions for Champion Wetton. 1859–1860.
D.807, 811–823, 2158 insc. *Additions to Joldwynds, Surrey. For Champion Wetton Esq* or similar (D.816 *Jordens.* D.817 *Jordens* r crossed out and *l* substituted in pencil. D.822, 823 *Joldens* D.2157 insc. *Champion Wetton Esq.* D.807–809, 811–814, 817–821, 824 insc. *Prichard and Seddon* etc. and D.2158 s. *John P. Seddon Archt.* D.807, 821, 823, 824 insc. with names of rooms, and D.807, 812, 815, 819, 821, 823, 824, 2157 with measurements.
D.810 pencil. D.811, 816, 817, 825, 2157, 2158 pencil and water-colour. D.812 pen and ink, and water-colour. Rest pencil, pen and ink, and water-colour. D.2158 is on tracing paper.
D.807–825, 2157, 2158–1896

Ground plan. East elevation depicting existing house. Scale $\frac{1}{8}$*th of an inch to a foot.* Alterations indicated in pencil
$16\frac{1}{2} \times 22\frac{1}{2}$ (41.9 × 57) D.824–1896

North elevation etc. *South elevation. West elevation. Elevation of stable.* Scale $\frac{1}{8}$*th an inch to a foot*
$21 \times 15\frac{1}{8}$ (53.4 × 38.3) D.822–1896

Roof plan. First floor plan. Section thro' AB. Section thro' CD. Alterations indicated in pencil
$21\frac{1}{2} \times 15\frac{1}{8}$ (54.6 × 38.2) D.823–1896

East *elevation of dining room* with part plan, section and interior elevation. Scale $\frac{1}{2}$ *in.* d. *Nov 185* (the rest has been cut off)
$22\frac{5}{8} \times 16\frac{1}{4}$ (57.5 × 41.5) D.817–1896

Bow window in south front. *Section* and detail of *parapet to bay window in entrance front.* Elevations of front and *side of bay.* Scale $\frac{1}{2}$ *in*
$22\frac{5}{8} \times 16\frac{3}{8}$ (57.5 × 41.4) D.816–1896

Perspective from the south west
$17\frac{1}{8} \times 14\frac{7}{8}$ (43.6 × 37.9) D.825–1896
Possibly exhib. Architectural Exhibition 1863, no. 252.

Ground plan. Scale $\frac{1}{4}$ *of an inch to a foot.* Wm. *1859.* Alterations (?) indicated in pencil
$15\frac{1}{4} \times 22\frac{1}{8}$ (38.7 × 56.2) D.821–1896

South elevation. Scale $\frac{1}{4}$. d. *Jan. 1860*
$22\frac{1}{4} \times 14\frac{3}{4}$ (56.4 × 37.5) D.820–1896

North elevation. d. *Jan. 1860*
$21\frac{1}{2} \times 14\frac{1}{8}$ (54.8 × 36) D.814–1896

East elevation. Scale $\frac{1}{4}$. d. *Jan. 1860.* An alternative design for the bay window is indicated in pencil
$22\frac{1}{4} \times 15\frac{1}{8}$ (56.3 × 38.4) D.819–1896

West elevation. Scale $\frac{1}{4}$. d. *Jan. 1860*
$22\frac{1}{2} \times 16$ (57.3 × 40.8) D.818–1896

Stable. *Ground plan, west elevation.* Scale $\frac{1}{4}$. d. *Jan. 1860.* Alterations indicated in pencil
$22\frac{5}{8} \times 16$ (57.6 × 40.8) D.807–1896

Section on the line BB. Scale $\frac{1}{4}$ *inch.* d. *Jany. 1860*
$22\frac{1}{4} \times 16\frac{1}{2}$ (56.7 × 42.1) D.813–1896

Section on the line AA. Scale $\frac{1}{4}$ *inch.* d. *Jan. 1860*
$19\frac{3}{8} \times 14\frac{7}{8}$ (49 × 37.7) D.812–1896

Details of oriel window. Plan, section, elevation, and *side elevation.* Scale $\frac{1}{2}$ *inch* and $\frac{1}{2}$ *full size*
$22 \times 16\frac{1}{4}$ (55.7 × 41.3) D.815–1896

Ground floor window in tower. Plan, elevation, and *details.* Scale *1 in* and $\frac{1}{2}$ *full size.* d. *Feby 1860*
$19\frac{3}{8} \times 12\frac{1}{2}$ (49.3 × 31.7) D.808–1896

Fireplace in dining room. *Plan, elevation,* and *section.* Insc. *The whole of the stonework inside dining room must be in Hopton Wood stone.* A piece has been cut from the sheet
$16\frac{1}{8} \times 22\frac{5}{8}$ (41 × 57.6) D.811–1896

Elevation showing another treatment of the dining room fireplace
$14\frac{5}{8} \times 19\frac{7}{8}$ (37.1 × 50.6) D.810–1896

Internal doors ground floor and *internal doors first floor.* Elevations, sections and details. Scale *1 inch* and *full size*
$16 \times 22\frac{5}{8}$ (40.5 × 57.5) D.809–1896

Elevations, part plan and details of dining room wood-work. Scale *inch*
$17\frac{3}{8} \times 26\frac{1}{2}$ (44 × 67.5) D.2157–1896

Tracing of above. *Design for fitting side of dining room at Joldwynds.* Scale *inch.* Insc. with notes and d. *Feb. 62*
$16\frac{3}{8} \times 27\frac{1}{8}$ (41.5 × 69) D.2158–1896

This appears to be a previously unknown scheme for a house on the site (?) of that built by Philip Webb and subsequently demolished for the present building of 1934 by Oliver Hill.

Details of the ground and first floor windows were illustrated in *Examples of Building Construction*, 1859-60, plate 77.

N. Pevsner & I. Nairn, *Surrey*, 1962, p.271.

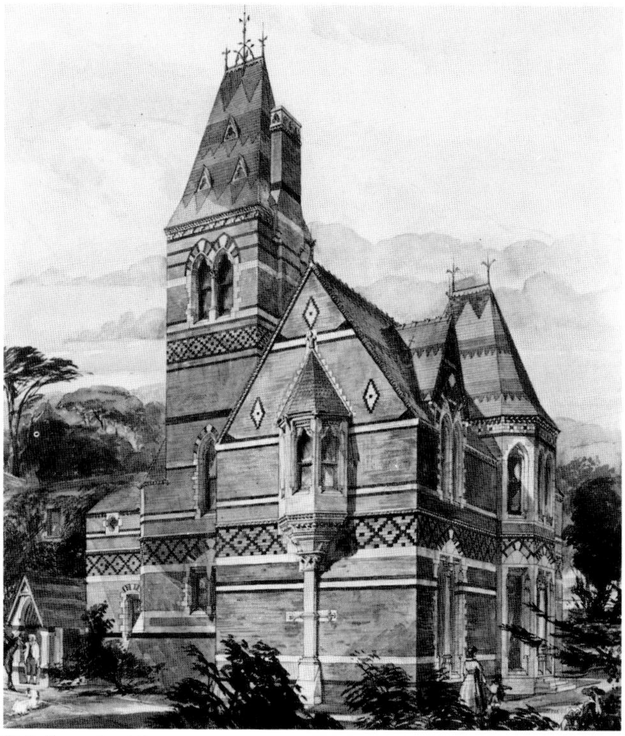

Holmbury St. Mary. Joldwynds D.825–1896

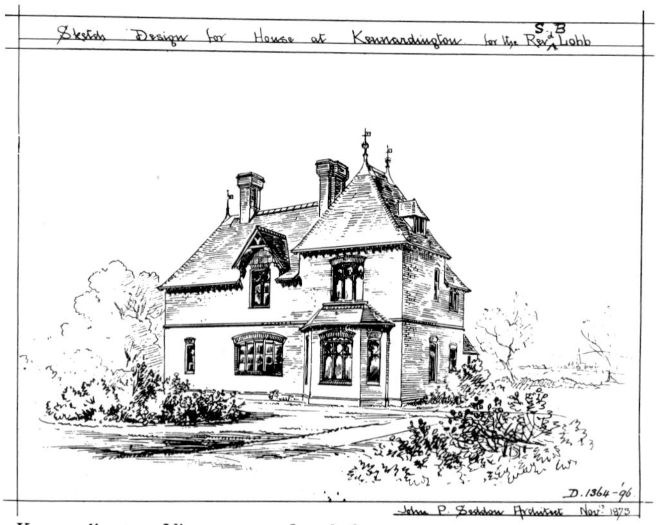

Kennardington. Vicarage D.1364–1896

INGHAM, Norfolk. Church of the Holy Trinity

Ingham Church. Porch door. Plan, elevations and details. Scale *2" to foot; 2½" to foot; 3" to foot* and *4" to foot.* c.1876. Insc. *I. P. Seddon Architect*
Pencil and water-colour
$12\frac{7}{8} \times 18\frac{5}{8}$ (32.6 × 47.3) D.1550–1896

Designs (on 2 sheets) for circular stained glass windows. Scale *1½".* D.1750 insc. *Ingham*
Pencil and water-colour on tracing paper
D.1750 $22\frac{5}{8} \times 32\frac{1}{2}$ (57.5 × 82)   D.1756 $16\frac{3}{4} \times 25\frac{1}{8}$ (42.6 × 63.8)
D.1750, 1756–1896

Seddon added a south aisle and clerestory to the 14th century church in 1876, and also designed the lectern and screen.

Designs for the restoration of the chancel and for various fittings are in the RIBA and include a perspective of the east end by H. Gaye which was exhibited at the Royal Academy in 1877 (1156) and in the Paris Exhibition of 1878 where it won a prize medal.

N. Pevsner, *North East Norfolk and Norwich*, 1962, pp.176–178.
RIBA *Catalogue*, p.35

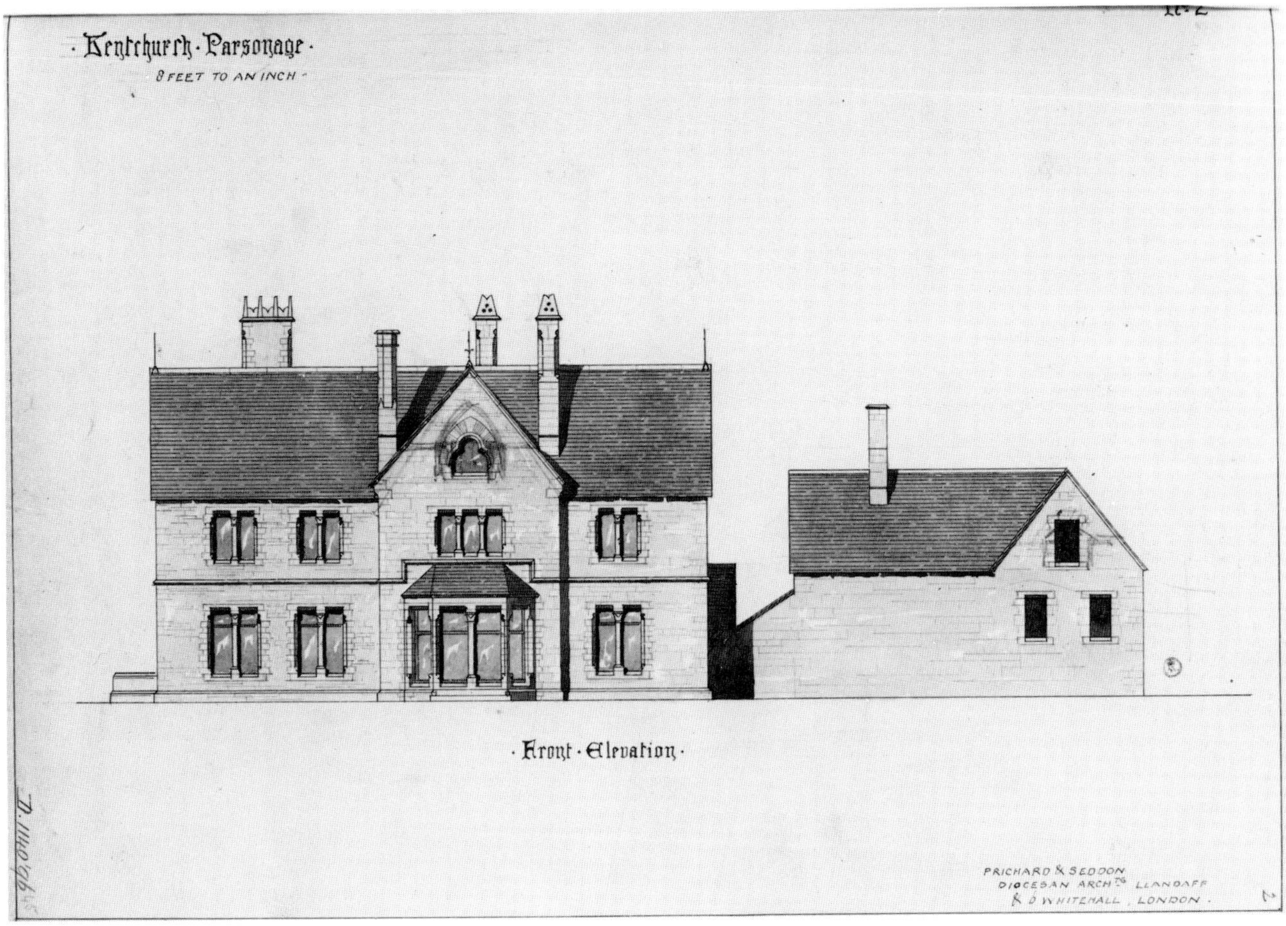
Kentchurch · Parsonage ·
8 FEET TO AN INCH
· Front · Elevation ·
PRICHARD & SEDDON
DIOCESAN ARCHTS LLANDAFF
& 6 WHITEHALL, LONDON.

Kentchurch. Parsonage D.1140–1896

KENNARDINGTON. Vicarage

Perspective view and plans, elevations, sections and details of windows, doors, etc. (on 9 sheets) for Reverend S. B. Lobb. 1873.
D.1329, 1331-5, 1364, 1562 insc. *Kennardington Vicarage* or similar and D.1334, 1364 *For the Revd Lobb.* D.1330, 1332-5, 1364 s. *John P. Seddon* and D.1332 addressed *12 Park St. Westminster.* D.1330, 1332-5 insc. with measurements.
D.1329-35, 1562 pencil and water-colour. Rest pencil, pen and ink, and water-colour. D.1364 pencil, pen and ink on tracing paper.
D.1329–1335, 1364, 1562–1896

Perspective. d. *Nov. 13 1873*
$8\frac{1}{2} \times 10\frac{3}{4}$ (21.4×27.2) D.1364–1896

Detail of staircase. Scale *inch to a foot*
$9\frac{7}{8} \times 28$ (25.1×71) D.1329–1896

Plan, elevation and details of a window
$29 \times 10\frac{5}{8}$ (73.8×26.9) D.1330–1896

Details of windows; plans, elevations, sections. Scale *inch to a foot.* d. *December 1873*
$21\frac{7}{8} \times 29\frac{1}{2}$ (55.5×75) D.1335–1896

Details of dormers; plans, elevations and sections. Scale *inch to a foot* and *full size.* d. *Dec. 8 1873*
$21\frac{1}{2} \times 29\frac{3}{4}$ (54.6×75.6) D.1332–1896

Detail of French casement in drawing rm. Plan, *elevation, section* and details. Scale *inch to a foot*
$21\frac{1}{8} \times 29\frac{7}{8}$ (53.7×75.8) D.1331–1896

Plans, elevations, sections and details of *dormer in attic* and chimneys. Scale *inch to a foot* and *full size.* d. *Dec. 73*
$21\frac{3}{4} \times 29\frac{7}{8}$ (55.3×75.8) D.1333–1896

Details of roofs. Scale $\frac{1}{2}''$. d. *December 1873*
$21\frac{3}{8} \times 29\frac{3}{4}$ (54.3×75.7) D.1334–1896

Details of doors. Back door; elevation. *Bedroom doors*; details. Section of a roof. Scale *inch*
$14\frac{1}{2} \times 21$ (36.1×53.2) D.1562–1896

It is not clear where Kennardington is.

KENTCHURCH, Herefordshire. Parsonage

Plans, elevations and a section (on 4 sheets), c.1860.
Lettered *Kentchurch Parsonage* and *Prichard and Seddon* etc.
D.1139, 1140 insc. with names of rooms and measurements.
Alterations are suggested in pencil on all the sheets.
Pencil, pen and ink, and water-colour
D.1139–1142–1896

Basement plan. Ground plan. Section thro' basement. Scale *8 feet to an inch.* Wm. *1860.* Numbered *1*
$11\frac{1}{2} \times 17$ (29.2×43.3) D.1139–1896

Front elevation. Scale *8 feet to an inch.* Numbered *2*
$11\frac{1}{2} \times 17$ (29.2×43.3) D.1140–1896

Chamber plan. Entrance front elevation. *Section through coach house.* Scale *8 feet to an inch.* Numbered *3*
$11\frac{1}{2} \times 17$ (29.1×43.3) D.1141–1896

Back elevation. Scale *8 feet to an inch.* Wm. *1860.* Numbered *4*
$11\frac{3}{4} \times 16\frac{1}{2}$ (30×41.9) D.1142–1896

Prichard and Seddon rebuilt the church of St. Mary at Kentchurch around 1858 (*Ecclesiologist*, XIX, 1858, p.203. *Br*, 12 June 1858, p.416) and the parsonage apparently followed shortly afterwards. The *Ecclesiologist* noted that the 'design is of extreme simplicity, and we much like it . . . As usual we complain of an insufficiently large "study"'.

As executed the parsonage is much smaller than shown in these plans and lacks any gothic detailing.

Plans, a section, elevations, a specification and other documents dating from October 1864, referring to alterations are in the Hereford Record Office.

Ecc, XXII, 1861, p.201

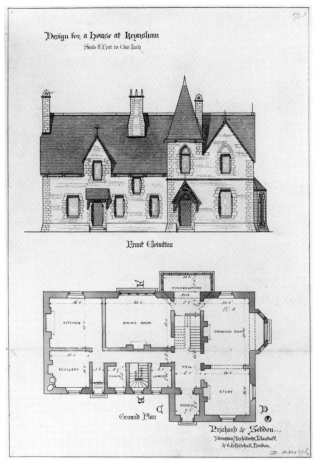

Keynsham. House D.1134–1896

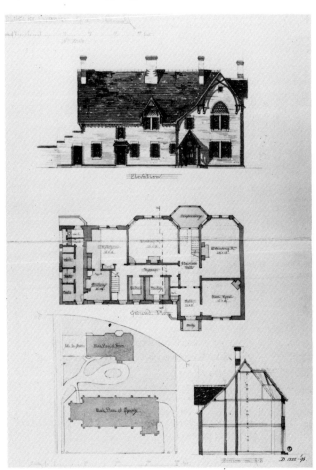

Kingston Hill. Parsonage D.1322–1896

KEYNSHAM, Somerset. House

Plans and elevations (on 2 sheets). c.1856.
Insc. *Design for a house at Keynsham* and stamped *Prichard and Seddon* etc. Insc. with names of rooms and D.1134 with measurements
Pencil, pen and ink, and water-colour
D.1134, 1135–1896

Ground plan. Front elevation. Scale *8 feet to one inch*
17¼ × 11¾ (43.7 × 30) D.1134–1896

Chamber plan. Back elevation. Scale *8 feet to one inch*
16½ × 11¾ (42.1 × 30) D.1135–1896

KILPECK, Herefordshire. Parsonage

Kilpeck Parsonage. Cellar plan. Ground plan. First floor plan.
Insc. with notes and measurements
Pencil
17½ × 12 (44.6 × 30.6) D.1319–1896

Not executed. Seddon also designed a porch for the church at Kilpeck (illustrated in the *BA*, 10 February 1882, p.64) which was not carried out either.

KINGSTON HILL, Kingston, Surrey. Parsonage

Plans, elevation and section (on 2 sheets). 1870.
Insc. with measurements and names of rooms. D.1138 s. *John P. Seddon*
Pencil and water-colour. D.1138 on tracing paper
D.1138, 1322–1896

Design for parsonage at Kingston Hill. Ground plan. Scale ⅛.
d. *7 June 1870*
8¼ × 13 (21.1 × 32.7) D.1138–1896

Site plan including *block plan of house, site for stables,* and *block plan of church. Ground plan.* Front *elevation. Section on AB.* Scale ⅛*th* and linear.
22⅜ × 15½ (56.7 × 39.5) D.1322–1896

LACEY GREEN, Buckinghamshire. Church of St. John Evangelist

Details of door. Plan, *outside elevation, inside elevation* and detail.
s. *J. P. Seddon Archt.* and d. *August 21 1871.* Insc. *Lacy Green Church. The chancel aisle door and frame for Kimble Church can be taken from this and made to fit.*
Pencil and water-colour
17⅛ × 13¼ (43.4 × 33.6) D.1548–1896

Seddon added a chancel in 1871 to J. Chadley's church of 1826. N. Pevsner, *Buckinghamshire,* 2nd ed. 1973

LITTLE DEWCHURCH, Herefordshire. Parsonage

Plans (on 2 sheets). Insc. *Proposed new parsonage house, Little Dewchurch, Herefordshire* and with measurements and names of rooms.
D.1188 pen and ink, and wash on tracing paper. D.1189 pencil, pen and ink, and wash on tracing paper.
D.1188, 1189–1896

Basement plan. Ground plan. Scale ⅛*th in to a foot*
12⅜ × 17⅞ (31.5 × 45.4) D.1189–1896

Chamber plan. Attic plan. Scale linear
12⅜ × 17⅞ (31.5 × 45.4) D.1188–1896

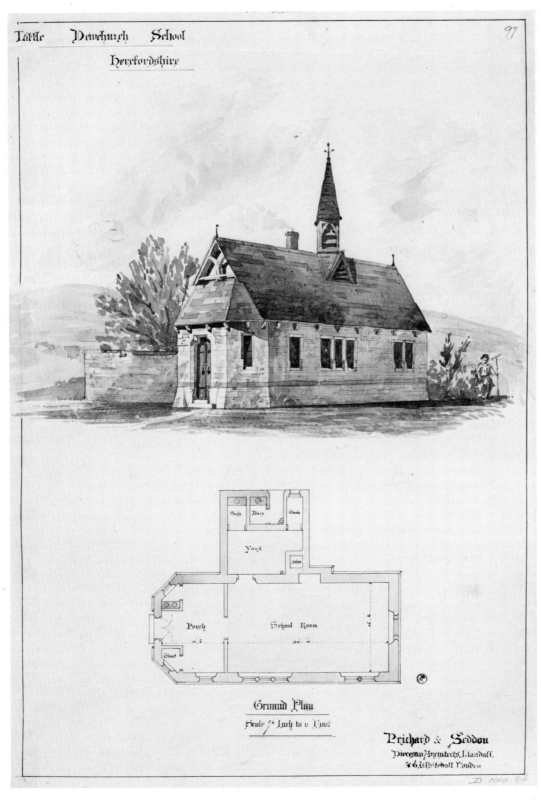

Little Dewchurch. School
D.1010–1896

School

Perspective, plans, elevations and sections (on 2 sheets) c.1861.
Insc. *Little Dewchurch School, Herefordshire. Not executed* and with
measurements. Stamped *Prichard and Seddon* etc.
Pencil, pen and ink, and water-colour
D.1009, 1010–1896

Perspective view. *Ground plan*. Scale ⅛ inch to a foot
18⅜ × 12¾ (46.6 × 32.3) D.1010–1896

*Ground plan. North elevation. South elevation. West elevation.
Transverse section. Longitudinal section.* Scale ⅛ inch to a foot
18¼ × 13 (46.5 × 33) D.1009–1896

Although these designs are inscribed 'not executed' the *Ecclesiologist* implied in 1861 that the school was built: 'This new school
is a small room, 30ft by 16ft by Messrs Prichard and Seddon,
with a porch at one end in the shape of a small apse. We cannot
admire this unusual and unnecessary arrangement. A small
quadrangular bell-turret, set angle-wise rises from the middle of
the roof'. It is possible, of course, that they might have been re-
viewing Seddon's drawings rather than the building itself.

Ecc, XXII, 1861, p.201

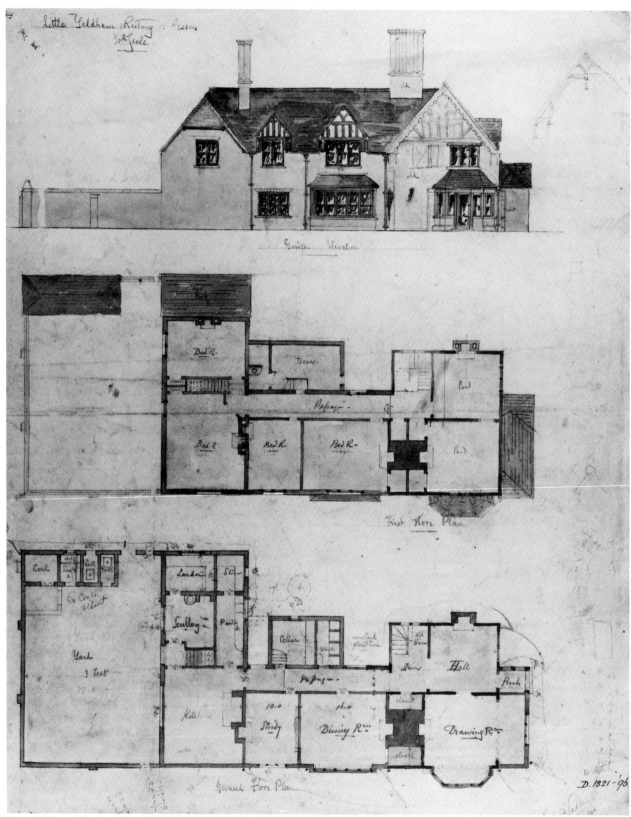

Little Yeldham. Rectory D.1321–1896

LITTLE YELDHAM, Essex. Rectory

Little Yeldham rectory, Essex. Ground floor plan. First floor plan.
Garden elevation. Scale ⅛th. s. [J.] P. Seddon and d. '90. Insc.
with measurements and names of rooms.
Pencil and water-colour
18⅝ × 14⅞ (47.3 × 37.8) D.1321–1896

A design for a chancel screen for the church of St. John the
Baptist at Little Yeldham is in the RIBA.

RIBA *Catalogue*, p.35

LLANBADARN FAWR, ABERYSTWYTH, Dyfed. Church of St. Padarn

Half cross section of roof. Scale *half inch*. c.1868. Insc. *darn Fawr* (the first part has been cut off), *Details of nave & chancel* and with measurements.
Pen and ink, and water-colour on tracing paper. Torn
16⅛ × 11 (40.7 × 27.8) D.1504–1896

This large and important church had been built in the early 13th century and by the mid 19th century was in urgent need of restoration. The *Ecclesiologist* noted in 1848 that a subscription had been started for the repair and shortly afterwards Butterfield was called in to do the work, but resigned after a dispute. Seddon was then approached and accepted the task. He wrote in his survey report: 'The church has fallen into a sad state of dilapidation from neglect and injudicious repairs. The nave roof, and the spire, in particular, are in an imminently dangerous condition from the decay of their principal timbers, and the side walls are tottering, from their outward thrust; in some parts they overhang the base 15 in., and in others they are rent from top to bottom'.

Part of the reason for this was not only that William Morris had written to the vicar advising against employing an architect for the restoration, but also the opposition of interested but over zealous antiquaries who wanted every stone of the fabric preserved. Certainly this faction, headed by J. L. Petit and the Archdeacon of York, objected quickly to Seddon's restoration proposals. However, after Seddon explained the seriousness of the problem, they 'conceded the necessity of the proposed works, and as the committee entrusted the execution of them to a builder of great experience in such matters (Mr Thomas Williams), in whom the architect reposed great confidence, all parties, though regretting the need, felt satisfied that it would be carried out in the proper spirit of conservation'. Accordingly, as much of the old walling of the nave as it was practicable to retain was kept, and the remainder was rebuilt in conformity with the original design. The spire was replaced, as was the porch. Seddon also added new roofs, a marble raredos, glass by Belhams (his design for the east window was altered by F. J. Shields) and new tiled floors.

The church was further restored by G. G. Pace in the 1960s.

Seddon showed a design for the Church 'about to be restored' at the Architectural Exhibition 1868 (no. 164).

Ecc, VII, 1848, pp.250-1
BN, 26 August 1870, p.148
Ecclesiastical Art Review, March 1878
Howell and Beazley, pp.58-9

LLANDAFF, Glamorgan. Cathedral

Plans, elevations, section and details (on 15 sheets) of doors, organ, marble panels for sedilia and a stained glass window. 1860-1. 1887.
D.1539, 1632-4, 1645, 1684, 1711 insc. *Llandaff Cathedral* or similar. D.1635, 1711 s. *J. P. Seddon*. D.1633-5, 1684 insc. *Prichard and Seddon* etc. D.1539, 1541 insc. *Seddon and Carter, Archts. Westminster & Cardiff*. D.1633, 1645, 1646, 1684 insc. with notes.
D.1539, 1541, 1646 pen and ink, and water-colour. D.1540, 1640 pencil, pen and ink, and water-colour. D.1632, 1635 pen and ink. D.1633, 1644, 1684 pencil and water-colour. D.1638 pencil, and pen and ink. D.1642, 1645 pencil. D.1539–1541, 1633–1635, 1638 on tracing paper.
D.1539–1541, 1632–1635, 1638, 1640, 1642, 1644–1646, 1684, 1711–1896.

Plan of organ. Scale ½ *in*
10¼ × 12⅞ (26 × 32.7) D.1632–1896

Organ. *Front* and *side* elevations. Scale ½ *inch*. d. *May 1860*
19 × 14½ (48.3 × 37) D.1635–1896

Organ. *Elevation. Side*. Details. Scale ½ *in*
12⅜ × 18¾ (31.5 × 47.6) D.1645–1896

Llandaff. Cathedral organ D.1635–1896

Organ. *Front elevation. Side. Section*. Details. Scale ½ *in*. Insc. *Pipes omitted* and with notes. d. *17 May [?] 1861*
12⅝ × 17 (32 × 43) D.1633–1896

Design for organ. Front and side elevations. Scale ½ *inch*. d. *18 March 1861*
14½ × 12 (36.8 × 30.6) D.1634–1896

Exhib. *Plans and Prospects*, no. 82

Organ. Front and side elevations
13½ × 11¾ (34.1 × 27.3) D.1638–1896

Organ. Front elevation and sketch side elevations. Wm. *1860*
17½ × 12 (44.5 × 30.5) D.1642–1896

Organ. Front elevation. Wm. *1860*
19 × 12¾ (48 × 32.3) D.1640–1896

Organ. Side elevation. Probably for Llandaff. Wm. *1860*
19 × 12⅝ (48.4 × 32) D.1644–1896

Design for pipes and organ. Insc. with notes about colours
16¾ × 10¾ (43 × 27.4) D.1646–1896

Ventilation openings in doors. North Norman door. South Norman door. South east door. Scale *inch*. d. *Feb 1887*
15 × 18 (38 × 46) D.1539–1896

Ventilation openings in doors. West door. Small south door. Small north door. Scale *inch*. d. *Feb 1887*
14½ × 20¼ (37 × 51.6) D.1541–1896

Priest's door in presbytery. Front elevation. Back. Detail. Scale *inch* and *full size*
13½ × 20⅛ (34.2 × 51.1) D.1540–1896

Sketch for window for Sir J. Harding. d. *Dec. 61*
10⅝ × 6¾ (27.1 × 17) D.1711–1896

Marble panels for sedilia. Scale ½ *full size*
14½ × 18⅞ (36.7 × 47.9) D.1684–1896

Design for Tombstone for Sir John Harding. Side elevation. End elevation. Top. Scale *1 inch to a foot*. Stamped *Prichard & Seddon* etc.
Pen and ink, and water-colour
17 × 11⅜ (43.2 × 29) D.1932–1896

Llandaff Cathedral was begun by Bishop Urban c.1120 and the main fabric completed by 1280. Minor alterations and additions

Llandaff. Probate Registry D.1064–1896

were made in the 14th and 15th centuries, and in 1485 Jasper Tudor, uncle of Henry VII, rebuilt the north west Tower. Little then happened until after the Reformation when the fabric began to deteriorate. By 1691 the decay was bad enough to cause the abandonment of choral services, and in 1720 storms damaged the north west tower. Worse was to come, however, because in 1723 the south west tower fell and at about this time the roofs also collapsed.

John Wood the Elder of Bath began a reconstruction scheme, partly in a classical style, in 1734, but it was not for another century that the first moves to restore the entire building were made. In 1840 T. H. Wyatt was called in and three years later he was appointed Honorary Cathedral Architect. In 1857 Wyatt resigned his post and it was filled by John Prichard who had, in fact, been made Diocesan Architect in 1847, and who, as a son of one of the priest-vicars, had restored the east window of the Lady Chapel in about 1843 and the rest of the Chapel c.1846-8. Seddon, consequently, was involved from the inception of his partnership with Prichard. It was through Seddon's friendship with the Pre-Raphaelites that Rossetti, Morris, Burne Jones and others did work in the Cathedral. (see Preface) The magnificent south west tower with its tall spire appears to have been the work of Prichard alone.

This restoration was largely complete by 1869. In 1886 Prichard died and Seddon was appointed Cathedral Architect (without salary). He continued to work on the interior completing, for example, the remaining stalls. When, however, he was faced with the prospect of saving the north west tower which was giving way at the foundations his advice was rejected in favour of that of J. L. Pearson who suggested getting in 'a practical builder' and the work was complete by 1890. Seddon felt he had lost prestige but he was, nevertheless, always held in the highest regard by the Church authorities.

In 1941 the Cathedral was hit by a land mine which gutted the nave. Restoration was begun under George Pace, of York, eight years later and finally completed in 1960. Unfortunately, it was carried out in a particularly unsympathetic manner not just from the point of view of the mediaeval fabric but also from that of

those 19th century fittings—among the best in the country of their time—which had survived the bombing. Thus, only fragments remain of the Sedilia carved by Edward Clarke and pieces of the choir stalls have been incorporated in an idiosyncratic way into the new organ console. Fortunately Prichard's magnificent Bishop's Throne in the production of which H. H. Armstead helped has survived, as has Seddon's ironwork for the doors. The organ which had been installed in the Cathedral in 1861 at a cost of £1,200 survives intact at Usk where it was taken in 1899.

There is a design for the font in the RIBA.

Howell and Beazley, pp.244-7
BN, 4 December 1857, p.1283; 6 September 1861, p.234
CEAJ, 1 December 1860, p.380; 1 September 1861, p.251, pl.26
BA, 10 February 1882, p.64
Ecc, XVII, 1856, p.314
RIBA *Catalogue*, p.35
Plans and Prospects, p.89

Probate Registry

Llandaff Probate Registry. South elevation. Scale ⅛th inch to a foot.
Insc. *Prichard and Seddon* etc.
Pen and ink, and wash on tracing paper
12½ × 18¾ (31.7 × 46.5) D.1064–1896

Contemporary accounts refer to the Probate Registry, which survives in Llandaff High Street, as being by Prichard alone, and this is perhaps supported by the absence of anything more than this single tracing in the Seddon collection. Eastlake certainly refers to it as being by Prichard, and Prichard did show a photograph of it at the Paris exhibition in 1867 (Group 1, class 4, no. 70). Howell notices that 'it is one of his best buildings, and shows his masterly use of materials in the contrast of smooth ashlar with finely-split rough stone'.

BN, 4 January 1867, p.9 (illus)
Eastlake, p.194 (108)
Howell and Beazley, p.24

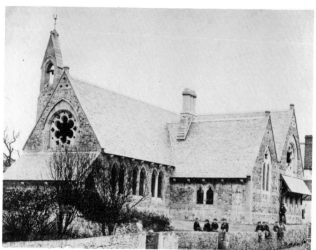

Llandaff. School D.950–1896

School

Photograph of front
$11\frac{1}{8} \times 14\frac{1}{2}$ (28.3 × 37) D.950–1896

The *Building News* referred to the school, which has now been demolished, as being by Prichard alone, and there seems no reason to doubt this. It was built by Thomas Williams for £900 of Bath stone and green sandstone from Bridgend, with bands of Pennant stone, and was completed by July 1867. The design relates in some respects to the partnership's earlier one for Llandough school, and also to that for the Llandaff Probate Registry.

BN, 26 July 1867, p.513

LLANDDEWI FELFRE (LLANDDEWI VELFREY), Pembroke. Church of St. David

Llanddewr Velfrey Church. Plans, elevations and thumbnail sketches of pews. Scale *inch.* Insc. *Prichard & Seddon.* Wm. *1860*
On the back is a design for a tankard
Pencil, pen and ink, and water-colour
$17\frac{1}{8} \times 11\frac{3}{4}$ (43.6 × 30) D.1624–1896

The *Ecclesiologist* reported in 1860: 'Messrs Prichard and Seddon have in hand the restoration of this small church. It contains chancel and north aisle nave with a north aisle to its eastern half, and a south porch. The work is generally well done, though the west door is surely unnecessary. The belfry cote is however extremely unsuccessful'.

The church should not be confused with St. Peters at Llampeter Velfrey in the same county which Prichard and Seddon designed in the same year.

Ecc, XXI, 1860, p.53
CB, 1863, p.77

LLANDEILO, Dyfed. Cottage

Design for cottage on estate. J. Charles Morris Esq., Pen y Bank, Carmarthen. Ground plan. First floor plan. *South elevation. East elevation. West elevation.* Section. Scale $\frac{1}{8}$th inch. s. *John P. Seddon.* Insc. with measurements and names of rooms
Pencil and water-colour
$13 \times 18\frac{7}{8}$ (32.9 × 48) D.1453–1896

House

J. Charles Morris Esq. Pen y Bank, Carmarthen. Elevations and details of *Door between dining room & drawg rm & between dining room & passage. Door between drawing room & hall & to hall & study.* Scale *inch* and $\frac{1}{2}$ *full size.* Insc. *Prichard and Seddon* etc. d. *1858*
Pencil, pen and ink, and water-colour
$13 \times 18\frac{3}{4}$ (33 × 47.8) D.1553–1896

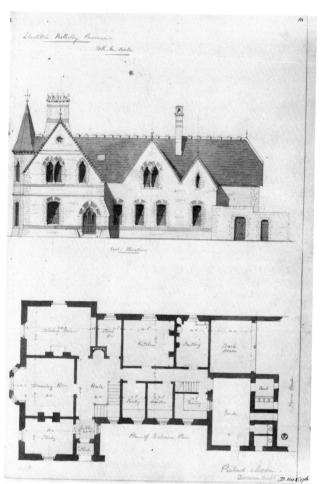

Llandeilo Bertholau. Parsonage D.1148–1896

LLANDEILO BERTHOLAU, Gwent. Parsonage

Llantillio Pertholly Parsonage. Plan of entrance floor and *east elevation.* Scale $\frac{1}{8}$th in. Insc. *Prichard and Seddon* and with measurements and names of rooms. d. *1858*
Pencil and water-colour
$18\frac{3}{4} \times 12\frac{3}{8}$ (47.5 × 31.5) D.1148–1896

LLANDENNY, Gwent.
Church of St. John. Possibly

Part *plan. South elevation. Section shewing alterations of windows* of roof raised one foot. Insc. with notes including *NB. this roof to be raised bodily one foot,* and *Llan* the rest is not legible. On the back is an elevation of a gate for Captn. Rivers
Pencil, part cut off
$14\frac{1}{2} \times 8$ (36.8 × 20.5) D.1575–1896

Prichard and Seddon restored the church for £700 in 1860-65

Ecc, XXI, 1860, p.53

LLANDOUGH, Glamorgan. School

Photograph, plans, elevations, sections and details (on 5 sheets).
D.953, 954, 996, 1356 are plates from *Examples of Building Construction,* published by J. R. Jobbins, 3 Warwick Ct. Holborn, July 1860. D.954, 996 engraving, pencil and water-colour. D.954 engraving. D.1356 engraving, pen and ink, and water-colour
D.952–954, 996, 1356–1896

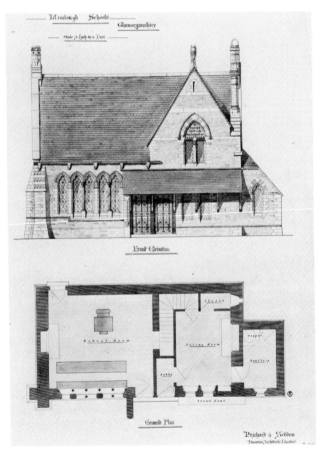

Llandough. School D.1356–1896

Photograph of completed building
$11\frac{1}{8} \times 14\frac{1}{2}$ (28.3 × 36.8) D.952–1896

Front elevation. Ground plan. Scale ¼ *inch to a foot*
$20\frac{5}{8} \times 14\frac{3}{4}$ (52.5 × 37.4) D.1356–1896
Exhib. 'Marble Halls', No. 71

Elevations and ground plan. Ground plan. Principal elevation. End elevation. Transverse Section. Scale ¼ *inch to a foot.* Numbered
Pl.65. d. *July 1860*
$19\frac{5}{8} \times 23\frac{1}{4}$ (49.8 × 59) D.953–1896
Exhib. Plans and prospects, No. 55

Longitudinal section and details. Longitudinal section. Scale ¼ *inch to a foot. Section and part of front elevation shewing doors and verandah.* Scale ½ *inch to a foot. Section and elevation of three light window in end. Side, plan, and elevation of Hipknob to roof including a sculpted figure of an angel and child.* Scale ⅛ *full size*
$18\frac{1}{4} \times 22\frac{1}{2}$ (46.3 × 57.3) D.996–1896

Details of chimneys, mouldings, etc. including plans, elevations and sections. Scale *1 inch to a foot. Details* ¼ *full size.* Numbered *Pl.70.* d. *Septr 1860*
$25\frac{1}{2} \times 19\frac{1}{2}$ (64.6 × 49.4) D.954–1896

The school which was converted from a barn at a cost of £350 was apparently completed by 1859 when the *Ecclesiologist* remarked: 'the style is First Pointed almost too decided and elaborate for the size and destination of the building'. The *Building News* remarked of the drawing which Seddon exhibited at the RA in 1861 (no. 683), that it had 'the good qualities which are incorporated in all their [Prichard and Seddon's] designs. The dressings are of white freestone, with occasional black blocks, the whole design as it is, is worked out in a vigorous manner'. The school, which survives as a village hall, should not be confused with that which Prichard built at Llandaff in 1867. (see LLANDAFF)

Ecc, XXI, 1859, p.210
B.N, 21 May 1861, p.427; 17 May 1867, pp.340, 343 (illus)
'*Marble Halls*', no. 71, pp.116-17
Plans and Prospects, p.65

LLANDYSOE, Gwent. Parsonage

Plans, elevations, sections and details (on 4 sheets).
D.1130, 1131, 1133 insc. *Lansoy.* D.1131 stamped and D.1132 lettered *Prichard and Seddon* etc. D.1131-3 insc. with measurements
D.1130 pen and ink. D.1131-3 pencil, pen and ink, and watercolour
D.1130–1133–1896

Ground and first floor plans. Scale ⅛*th.* Insc. with names of rooms. Alterations suggested in pencil. On the back sketch of bracket and gutter
$11\frac{3}{4} \times 17\frac{1}{4}$ (29.7 × 43.9) D.1131–1896

Elevation and transverse section. Scale ⅛*th.* Wm. *1862*
$12\frac{1}{2} \times 18\frac{1}{4}$ (31.6 × 46.3) D.1130–1896

Plans, elevations, sections and details of *chamber floor windows* and *kitchen windows.* Scale details *half full size.* Numbered in red *33*
$11\frac{5}{8} \times 17\frac{1}{4}$ (29.6 × 43.8) D.1132–1896

Details of ground floor windows. Scale *inch.* ½ *full size.* ¼ *full size.* Numbered in red *34*
$17\frac{1}{4} \times 11\frac{7}{8}$ (43.8 × 30.2) D.1133–1896

Prichard and Seddon prepared designs for the refitting and restoration of the church in 1857 which were apparently not carried out (*Ecc,* XVIII, 1857, p.397). The *Builder* noted in 1855 that tenders for the parsonage had been lodged and that Mr Brown's for £630, less £50.5s for old materials, had been accepted.

Br, 12 May 1855, p.224

LLANELEN, Gwent. School

Plans, elevations, sections and details (on 7 sheets). D.964-7, 969 insc. *Llanellen schools.* D.964-9 insc. or stamped *Prichard & Seddon* etc.
Pencil, pen and ink, and water-colour. D.965–970 on tracing paper
D.964–1896

Ground plan. Front elevation. Scale *eight feet to one inch. Drawing No 1.* Insc. with measurements and names of rooms
$17 \times 11\frac{7}{8}$ (43 × 30) D.969–1896

Chamber plan. East elevation. West elevation. Longitudinal Section. Scale ⅛ *inch. Drawing No. 2*
$16\frac{3}{4} \times 12$ (42.6 × 30.5) D.970–1896

Details of bell turret including plan, elevations, section and details. Scale ½ *inch* and *full size*
$22\frac{3}{4} \times 16\frac{1}{8}$ (57.9 × 41) D.964–1896

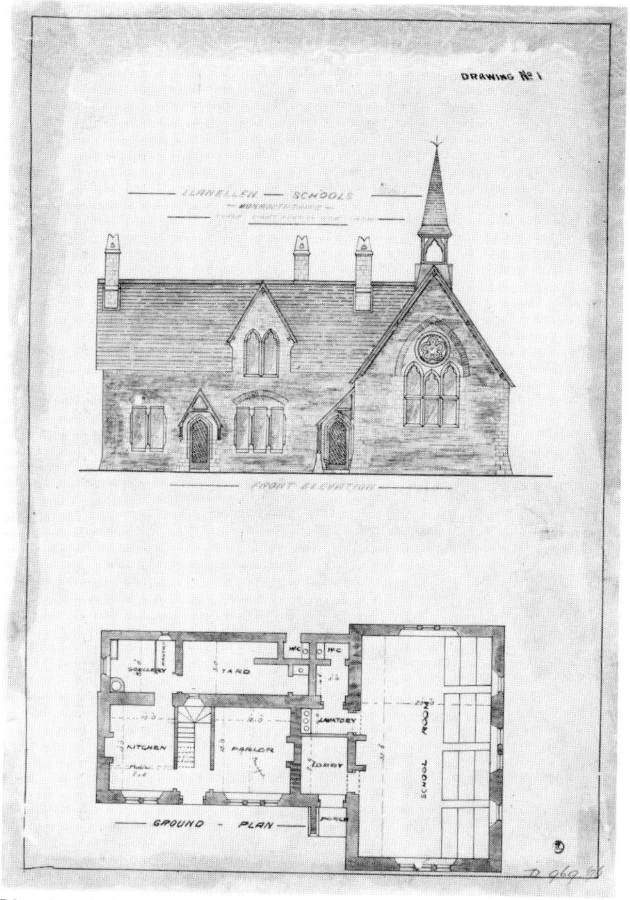
Llanelen. School D.969–1896

Details of circular window including plan, elevations, and section. Scale *half an inch to a foot*, *¼ full size* and *½ full size*
14⅛ × 19½ (35.8 × 49.5) D.965–1896

South window of school room. Plan, elevations, section and a detail. Scale *½ inch to a foot* and *¼ full size*
19⅜ × 14½ (49.2 × 36.8) D.966–1896

Details of windows including plans, elevations and sections. Scale *½ inch* and *¼ size*
17½ × 14¼ (44.5 × 36.5) D.967–1896

Plans, elevations and sections of entrance door and porch, *school room fireplace* and a *chimney*. Scale *½ inch to one foot*
16⅜ × 14 (41.6 × 36) D.968–1896

The school still survives. It was built as depicted in these drawings though the belfry and the door to the left of the schoolroom were omitted. The schoolroom window has since been altered and additions have been made to the building.

LLANFRECHFA, Gwent. Parsonage

Elevations and sections (on 2 sheets). 1856.
Insc. *Llanvrechva parsonage.*
D.1122 pen and ink and water-colour on tracing paper. D.1123 pencil, pen and ink and water-colour on tracing paper.
D.1122, 1123–1896

Front elevation. End elevation. Entrance elevation. End elevation. Scale *⅛th inch*. Also a rough sketch plan and details. Numbered in red *30*. Insc. with notes
12 × 18 (30.4 × 45.8) D.1123–1896

Section on line AB. Section on line CD. Scale *⅛th inch*. Numbered in red *29*
5¼ × 11⅞ (13.4 × 30.3) D.1122–1896

Howell and Beazley describe the parsonage, which still survives, as 'a splendidly colourful and elaborate affair of 1856'.

Howell and Beazley, p.212

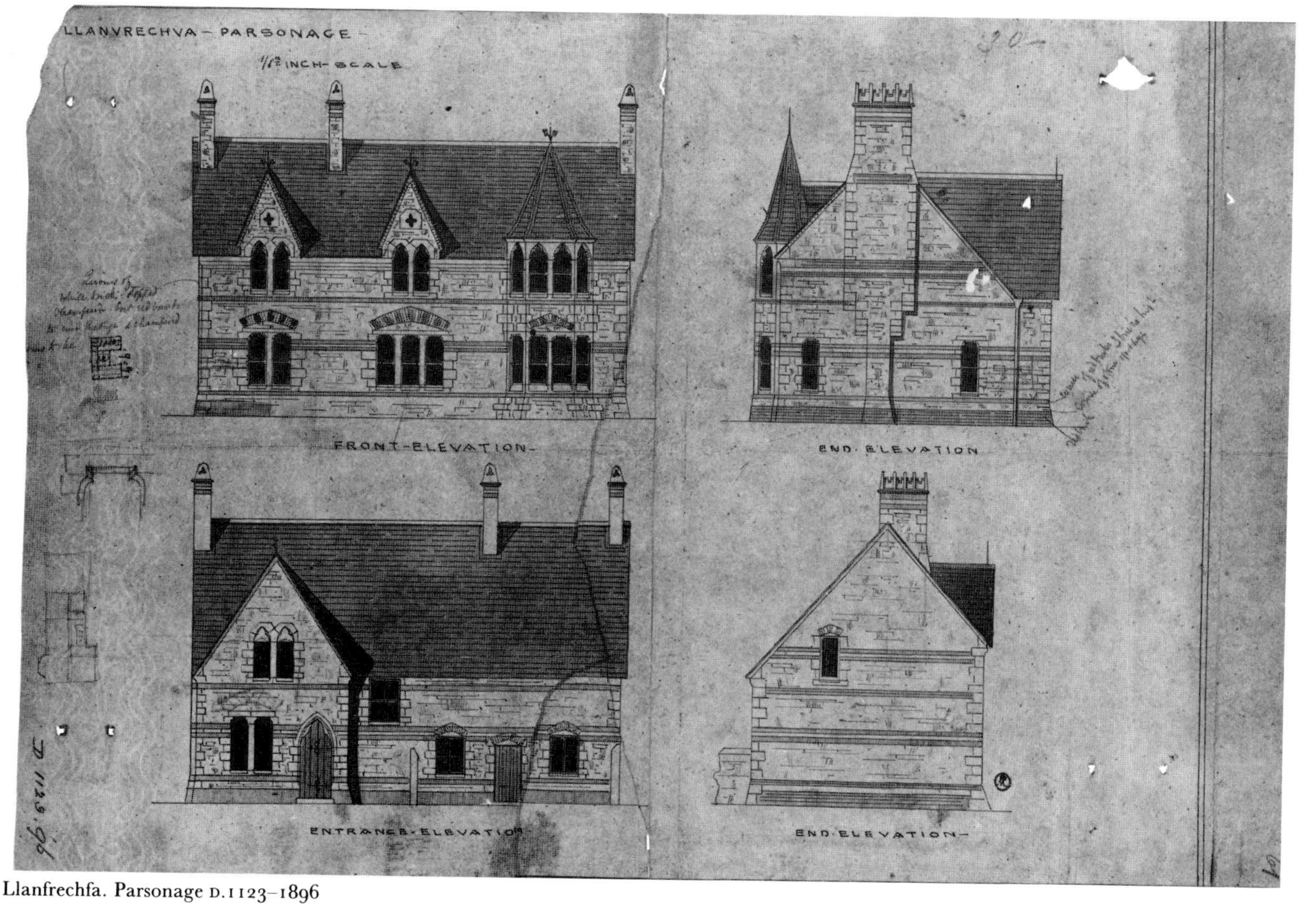

Llanfrechfa. Parsonage D.1123–1896

LLANGWM UCHAF, Gwent.
Church of SS Jeremy and John

Llangwin church. Plan of *tile pavement for chancel.* Scale ½ inch.
Insc. *John P. Seddon Archt. 12, Park Street, Westminster* and with
measurements.
Pen and ink, and water-colour
10¾ × 13½ (27.2 × 34.4) D.2045–1896

The *Ecclesiologist* reported in 1858 that the church was about to
be rearranged by Prichard and Seddon, and that the nave was to
be rebuilt from the foundations: 'the original Third Pointed
details will be preserved in this process and even the roof timbers
will be repaired and replaced'. This plan, however, dates from a
further restoration which Seddon carried out 1871-8. Seddon
was particularly proud of his restoration of the chancel screen
writing about it in the *Church Builder* in 1876 and showing his
drawings both at the Royal Academy (1878, no. 1061) and at
the Architectural Association (1878, no. 647).
　There is a design for a lectern at the RIBA.
　The church should not be confused with that of St. John at
Llangwm Isaf five hundred yards down the valley which
Prichard and Seddon restored in 1858 too. (*Ecc,* XIX, 1858, p.203,
BN, 29 April 1859, p.398).

Ecc, XIX, 1858, p.203
Br, 12 June 1858, p.416 (Tenders)
BN, 1 September 1871, p.1507
CB, 1876, pp.30–35
Howell and Beazley, p.187
RIBA *Catalogue,* p.35

Schools

*Llangwm schools Monmouthshire. Ground plan. First floor plan. Plan
of roof shewing position of chimney. Front elevation. End elevation of
house. End elevation of school. Section through school room. Half
section of school roof.* Scale ⅛ and ½ inch. s. *John P. Seddon.* d. *Feb
70.* Insc. with measurements and names of rooms.
Pen and ink, and water-colour on tracing paper
14⅞ × 21⅞ (37.8 × 55.6) D.1012–1896

Llangwn schools. Detail of desks including plan, front elevation
and *end elevation.* Scale inch. s. *J. P. Seddon Archt.* d. *Nov 21 1870*
Pencil
19 × 13 (48.1 × 33) D.1887–1896

LLANMARTIN, Gwent (Monmouth). Parsonage

Plan and entrance elevation. Insc. in pencil *Llanmartin P. Mon.*
Pencil, pen and ink, and wash on tracing paper
18 × 12¼ (45.7 × 31.1) D.1149–1896

Prichard and Seddon designed the church of St. Martin at
Llanmartin in 1858.

LLANTRISANT (or possibly LLANTRISANT FAWR), Gwent or LLANTRISANT, Glamorganshire. Church

*Llantrissent Church, Monmouthshire. Design for nave & chancel
pavement* and *section of floor shewing steps.* Scale *half inch.* Insc.
with notes including an *index to colour of tiles.*
Pen and ink and water-colour
16⅛ × 21 (41 × 53.4) D.2129–1896

It is not clear which Llantrisant this is. The parish records of
Llantrisant, Glamorganshire in the Glamorgan Record Office
include notes of restorations in 1866 and 1868, and Howell and
Beazley note that John Prichard worked there in 1873 (p.265).

LONDON, Kensington.
115–117 Lansdowne Villas, Brompton Road, S.W.3

Elevation of a fireplace wall showing two designs for
cupboards. Insc. *Richard White 115-7 Lansdowne Villas,
Brompton Road. The side of the Printers Arms corner* and *C. Seddon
& Co. South Molton St. London.*
Pencil, pen and ink, and water-colour
12⅞ × 19½ (32.7 × 49.6) D.1617–1896

LONDON, Kentish Town. Houses

Plans and elevations (on 3 sheets) for semi detached houses in
Middleton and Hungerford Roads, Camden Road, for Mr
Batson. Insc. with measurements and D.1061, 1062 with
names of rooms. D.1061, 1063 insc. *Houses to be built in
Middleton Road.*
Pen and ink and water-colour on tracing paper
D.1061–1063–1896

Basement Plan. Ground Plan. Alterations suggested in pencil.
Insc. *Semi-detached villas to be built on the Freehold Estate of—
Batson Esqre in Middleton & Hungerford Roads, Camden Road*
18¼ × 25⅝ (46.2 × 65) D.1062–1896

One pair story, two pair story plans
15¾ × 24 (40.1 × 61.1) D.1063–1896

*Front elevation of houses and fence wall and gates. Side elevation of
houses*
18⅜ × 24⅞ (46.8 × 63.2) D.1061–1896

School

Ground plans (on 2 sheets) showing different schemes. 1870.
s. *John P. Seddon* and insc. with names of rooms
Pencil and water-colour on tracing paper
D.1352, 1353–1896

Plan. Scale ⅛th. Insc. *Proposed new schools for Kentish Town.*
d. *1 March 1870*
22½ × 20 (57 × 51) D.1352–1896

Plan. Scale ⅛th. Insc. *Design for school buildings at Kentish Town.
Alternative design all on one floor. Both schoolrooms & both class
rooms also can be thrown into one at pleasure.* Initialled *J.P.S.*
d. *March 1870*
23¾ × 20¼ (60.4 × 51.3) D.1353–1896

Seddon submitted a design for laying out ground belonging to
the Governesses Institution at Kentish Town at the Architectural
Exhibition in 1852 (nos. 79, 178).
　The houses in Middleton Road still survive.

LONDON, Kingsbury. St. Andrew's Church (formerly in Wells Street, W.1)

Design (copies on 4 separate sheets) for an altar frontal for the
anniversary of the Festival of Saints and Martyrs. Scale *1½″ to
the foot.* Insc. *St. Andrews' Church, Wells Street. Festival altar cloth* or
similar. D.1901 insc. *Miss Leslie* and D.1903 *Approved* and
numbered *1.* D.1902 s. *J. P. Seddon Architect* and d. *September
1874.*
D.1901–1903 pencil. D.1900 pencil and water-colour. D.1903
on tracing paper
The largest 12⅝ × 18⅜ (32 × 46.7) D.1900–1903–1896

Design for Altar Frontal.
s. *John P. Seddon Architect, 1 Queen Anne's Gate Westmr.* d.
October 1874 and insc. in ink *For St. Andrews Ch. Well's St.—In
Lent. Approved design.* Numbered *2*
Pencil on tracing paper
14½ × 10⅝ (37 × 27) D.1904–1896

Incomplete drawing as above
16½ × 12¼ (42 × 31) D.1907–1896

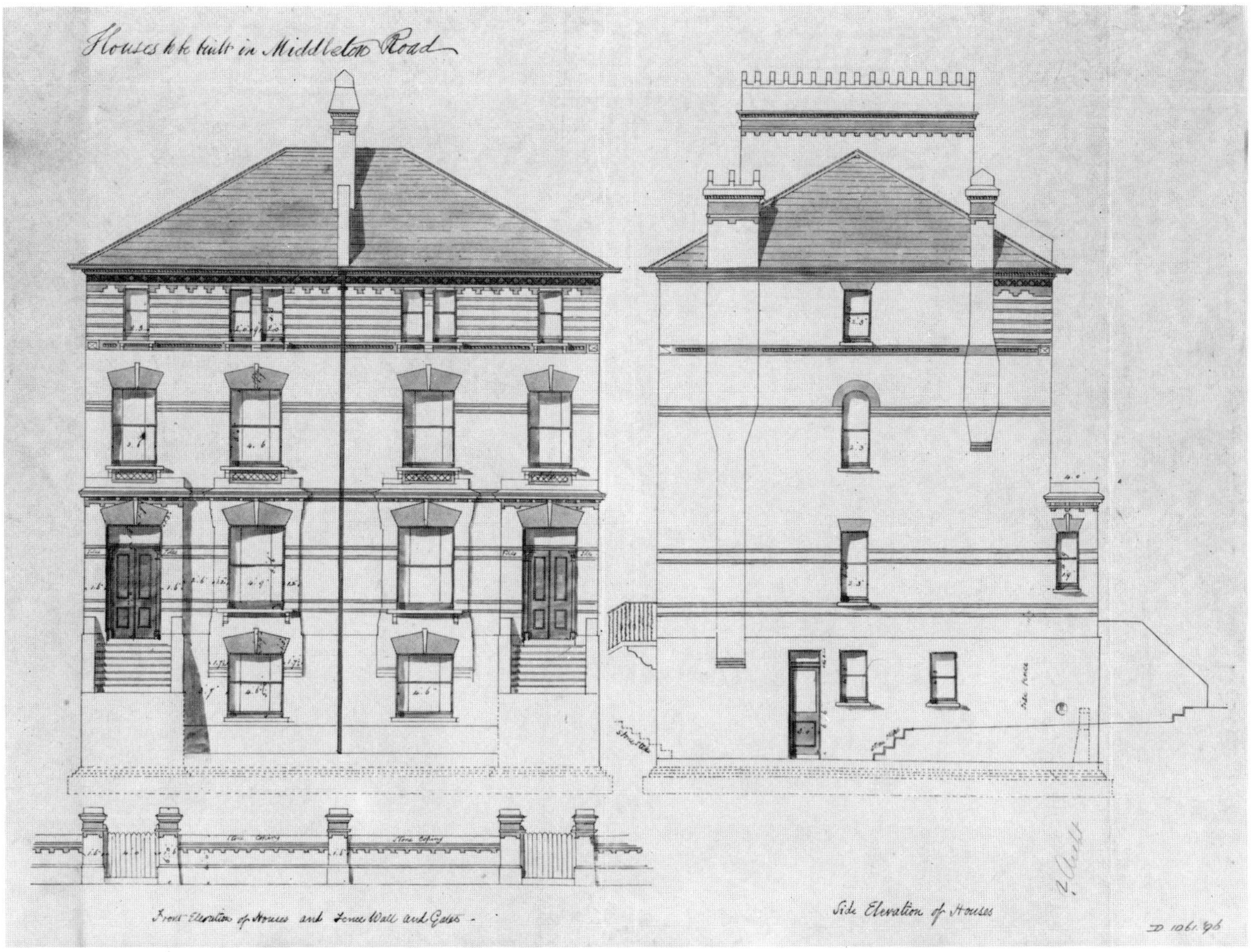

London, Kentish Town, Houses D.1061–1896

Sketch for Penitential Altar Frontal. S. Andrews Wells Street. Scale *1½″*. s. *John P. Seddon Architect.* d. *September 15–74*
Pencil on tracing paper
16 × 8⅞ (40.6 × 22.6) D.1905–1896

LONDON, Lambeth Palace Chapel

Details of tile flooring and design for altar frontal (on 3 sheets). 1878.
Insc. *Lambeth P. Chapel* or similar. D.1897 s. *J. P. Seddon* and D.2066 insc. *John P. Seddon Esqre 1 Queen Anne's Gate SW.* D.1896 pencil. D.1897 pencil and water-colour on tracing paper. D.2066 pen and ink with colour wood engravings pasted on.
D.1896, 1897, 2066–1896

Plan of part of the tile flooring. Scale ¾″. Numbered *689.* d. *May 1878*
13⅜ × 16½ (34 × 42) D.2066–1896

Design for an embroidered altar frontal
10 × 17⅜ (25.5 × 44.1) D.1896–1896

Details of *altar cloth.* Scale *full size.* d. *1878*
25½ × 25½ (64.8 × 64.8) D.1897–1896

Seddon's scheme was never executed; Clayton and Bell carrying out a modified design by William Burges instead. The chapel was bombed during the Second World War and no trace of any 19th century decoration survives. There are designs by Seddon for the decoration and for the altar, of 1877, one a perspective sketch by H. Gaye, in the RIBA.

Seddon showed his design for the restoration of the chapel at the RA in 1877 (1166).

Br, 11 May 1878, pp.481–482
RIBA *Catalogue*, pp.35–36

LONDON, Tulse Hill. Church

Perspective, plan, elevations and sections (on 7 sheets). Insc. *Tulse Hill Church.* D.713–716, 718, 719 lettered *Prichard and Seddon* etc. D.719 addressed *Llandaff & 7 Percy St. Bedford Sq.* D.714–716 pen and ink. D.713, 717–719 pen and ink and water-colour
D.713–719–1896

Perspective view of interior. Numbered *9*
20⅞ × 16 (53 × 40.7) D.719–1896

Plan of ground floor. Plan of Gallery. Scale linear. Insc. with details of the accommodation including *Total 1004*
15 × 21⅜ (38.2 × 54.3) D.713–1896

West elevation. Scale linear. Numbered *4*
22⅜ × 16¼ (56.8 × 41.3) D.714–1896

North elevation. Scale linear
22½ × 15¾ (57.1 × 40) D.716–1896

East elevation. Scale linear
22½ × 15¾ (57.1 × 40) D.716–1896

Transverse section. Section through gallery. Elevation of do (gallery). *Plan of soffit.* Scale linear. Insc. with notes
15¾ × 22½ (40 × 57.4) D.717–1896

Longitudinal section. Scale linear. Numbered *8*
15¾ × 22½ (40 × 57.4) D.718–1896

The *Ecclesiologist* noted that Prichard and Seddon's design, which was apparently submitted in competition for the church and not accepted, was 'florid . . . with gabled aisles'.

Ecc, XVII, 1856, p.310

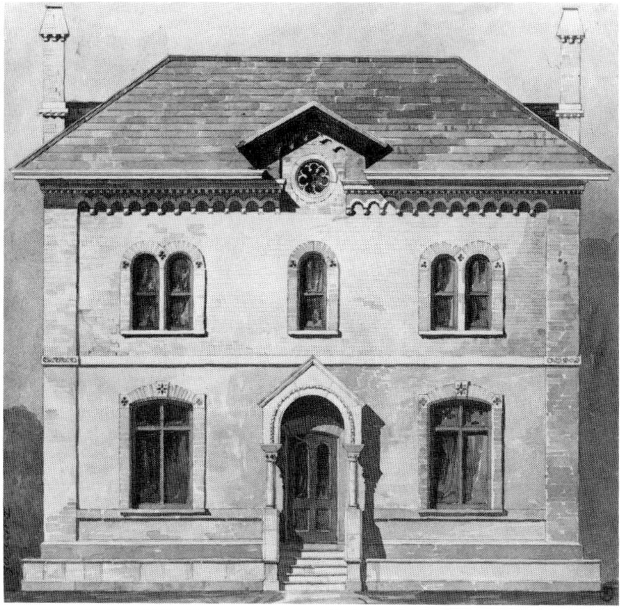

London, Tulse Hill, Houses D.1137–1896

Houses

Plans and elevation (on 2 sheets) of two houses for John Hales. 1851.
D.1137 pencil and water-colour. D.1136 pencil, pen and ink, and water-colour
D.1136, 1137–1896

Design for two houses to be erected on Tulse Hill, John Hales Esq. Plan of basement. Plan of attics. Scale linear. Insc. with notes, measurements, etc. and on the back *John Hales Esq., Contract drawings for houses on Tulse Hill.* s. *John P. Seddon Archt.* and *T. F. Allcock* and d. *Sep. 1851.* Numbered *2*
18 × 11½ (45.6 × 29.2) D.1136–1896

Front elevation
10 × 11¾ (25.5 × 27.5) D.1137–1896

This may be the drawing which Seddon exhibited at the Architectural Exhibition in 1852 (no. 284) 'Design for two houses now in course of erection upon Lower Tulse Hill, Surrey faced with Suffolk brick and stone dressing'.

The area was badly bombed during the war and these houses do not appear to have survived.

Parsonage

Plans, elevations and sections (on 2 sheets).
D.1171 pen and ink, and water-colour. D.1170 pen and ink, and wash.
D.1170, 1171–1896

Basement plan. Ground plan. Chamber plan. Attic plan. Scale linear. Lettered *Prichard & Seddon* etc. and insc. with names of rooms and measurements
15 × 21⅝ (38 × 55) D.1171–1896

Front elevation. Side elevation. Longitudinal section. Transverse Section. Scale linear. Insc. in pencil *Tulse Hill parsonage*
15 × 21⅝ (38 × 55) D.1170–1896

It is not clear whether this was ever carried out.

LONDON, Wandsworth. Villa

Plans, elevations, sections and details (on 17 sheets) for Captain Rivers. 1863-64.
D.1097–110 insc. *Design for villa Wandsworth* and D.1096, 1101-3, 1575. *Captain* or *Captn Rivers.* D.1097–1102, 1108 s. *John* or *J. P. Seddon.*
D.1097–1100 addressed *6, Whitehall, London* and D.1101, 1102 *12 Park St., Westminster.* D.1097–1101 initialled *R.C.J.*
D.1097-9, 1100 insc. with names of rooms. D.1097–1100, 1109 insc with measurements. D.1097–1100 include pencil alterations or additions.
D.1096 pencil. D.1102, 1106–1108, 1575 pencil and water-colour. Rest pencil, pen and ink, and water-colour.
D.1096–1111, 1575–1896

Basement plan. Ground plan. Front elevation. Side elevation. Section CD. Section AB. Scale *⅛th.* d. *Octr 30th 63*
19 × 12⅝ (48.2 × 32.1) D.1097–1896

Chamber plan. Attic plan. Back elevation. Side elevation. Scale *⅛th* d. *Oct 30th 63*
18⅛ × 12¼ (46.2 × 31.2) D.1100–1896

Basement plan. Ground plan. Chamber plan. Attic plan. Front elevation. Section AB. Scale *⅛th.* d. *Decr 12th 1863*
19 × 12⅝ (48.2 × 32.1) D.1098–1896

Side elevation. Side elevation. Back elevation. Section CD. Scale *⅛th* d. *12 Decr 1863*
18½ × 12⅝ (47 × 32.1) D.1099–1896

Ground plan and front elevation
18⅝ × 12⅝ (47.3 × 32.1) D.1096–1896

Detail of staircase window. Plan. Elevation. Section. Scale *half inch.* d. *May 31st 1864*
18½ × 12⅝ (47 × 32) D.1101–1896

Detail of cornice and gutter. Scale *½ inch*
18⅞ × 12¼ (48 × 31.2) D.1102–1896

Detail of chamber floor windows. Plan. Half outside, half inside elevation. Section. Scale *inch*
17¼ × 12⅜ (43.8 × 31.5) D.1103–1896

Drawing room window. ½ *exterior* and ½ *interior* elevations. *Section.* Details
12⅜ × 17¾ (31.5 × 45) D.1104–1896

Porch. Plan, elevations, section and detail
12½ × 17⅝ (31.6 × 44.8) D.1105–1896

Glazed doors. Plans, elevations and sections. (These do not appear in the elevations.)
12¾ × 19 (32.4 × 48.1) D.1106–1896

Details of windows
18⅞ × 12¾ (48 × 32.3) D.1107–1896

Doors. Plans, elevations and details. Scale *inch*
12¾ × 19⅛ (32.4 × 48.5) D.1108–1896

Breakfast room, drawing rm, back bed rm, dressing rm and *WC* windows. Plans, elevations, sections and details. Scale *½ inch* and *½ full size*
12⅞ × 19 (32.7 × 48.2) D.1109–1896

Staircase. Plans, elevation and details. Scale details *full size*
12⅞ × 19 (32.7 × 48.2) D.1110–1896

Staircase. Plan, elevation and details showing a different treatment of the bannister. Scale details *full size*
17¾ × 12⅞ (45.1 × 32.7) D.1111–1896

Elevation of a gate. On the back sketches for alterations to Llandenny church
8⅛ × 14½ (20.6 × 36.7) D.1575–1896

The house still survives in Viewfield Road, SW18 but has now been converted into flats.

Ecc, XXV, 1864, p.52

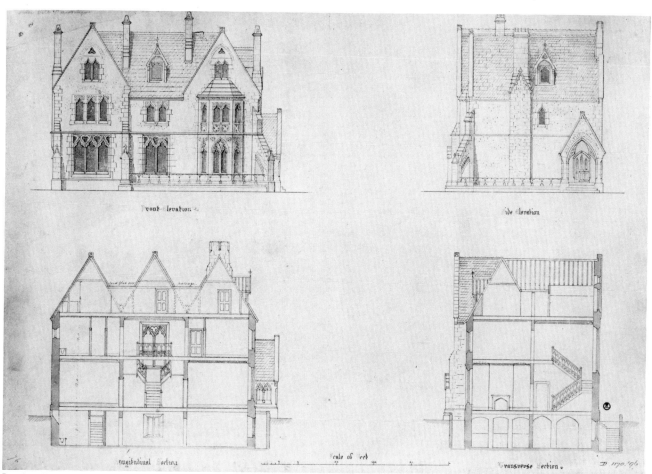

London, Tulse Hill, Parsonage D.1170–1896

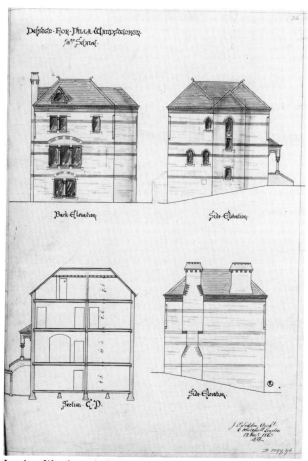

London, Wandsworth, Villa D.1099–1896

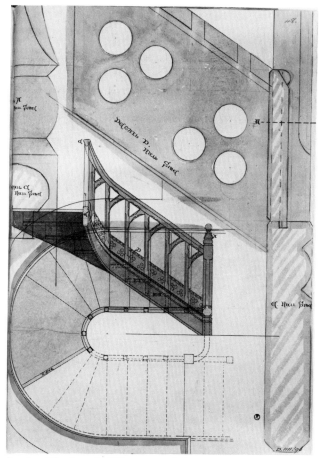

London, Wandsworth, Villa D.1111–1896

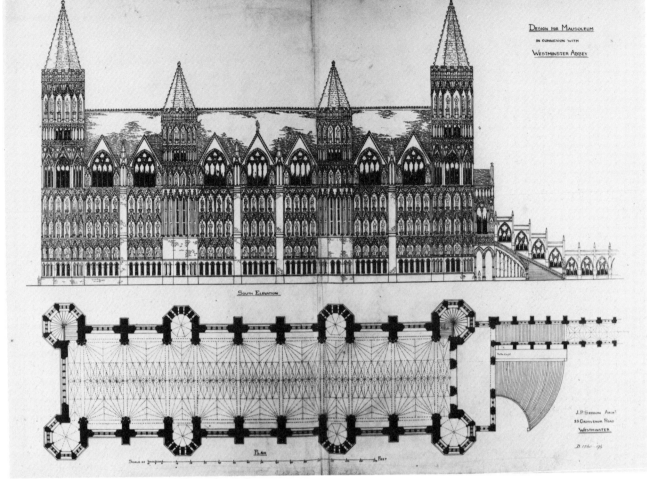

London. Westminster. Monumental Halls D.1260–1896

LONDON, Westminster. Church of St. Margaret

Plan, elevations and sections (on 3 sheets).
D.1261 pen and ink, and pencil. D.1262, 1764 pencil and water-colour.
D.1261, 1262, 1764–1896

St. Margaret's Westminster. Porch. Elevation. Plan. Scale ½ inch.
On the back plans of University College of Wales as about to be restored. d. *1882*
26⅝ × 19⅜ (67.5 × 49.3) D.1262–1896

Porch. *South elevation. Longitudinal section.* On the back designs for stained glass windows at St. Mary on the Hill, Chester
13⅜ × 21⅝ (34 × 55) D.1261–1896

Mosaic border round front. Scale 2″. Lettered *John P. Seddon Architect, Westminster*
13¾ × 8⅞ (35 × 22.6) D.1764–1896

There is a design for the font at the RIBA.

Founded in the 12th century but most of the present building is 16th century. The tower was rebuilt in 1735-7. Much restoration was carried out in the 19th century by G. G. Scott (1877) and J. L. Pearson amongst others. Pevsner notices that it was Pearson who designed the porches. The mosaic border does not appear to have been carried out.

N. Pevsner and B. Cherry, *London 1*, 1973, pp.493-95
RIBA *Catalogue*, p.35

Monumental Halls

Design for Mausoleum in connexion with Westminster Abbey. Plan. South elevation. Scale linear. Wm. *1888.* Insc. *J. P. Seddon Archt., 23 Grosvenor Road, Westminster*
Pen and ink
21½ × 29½ (54.6 × 75) D.1260–1896

Until the beginning of the 18th century the monuments in Westminster Abbey were confined to the eastern chapels with few exceptions. Guelfi's memorial to Secretary Craggs, quickly followed by those to Newton and Stanhope by Rysbrack, soon began, however, an invasion of white marble effigies into the transepts and nave. By the middle of the 19th century, consequently, almost all available space was filled, and concern began to be expressed. There were those who advocated the removal of everything while others were of the opinion that, as the Abbey could be considered to be a national mausoleum, something more positive should be done to provide accommodation for both the bodies and memorials of such future persons whom it was desired to commemorate there.

In 1854 Sir Gilbert Scott presented a report to Lord John Thynne, the Sub-Dean, suggesting that a 'wide and lofty cloister of great length' should be erected behind the old houses (now demolished) in Abingdon Street to house many of the marbles, and a few years later he produced another scheme, but nothing came of either of them.

By 1890, however, public disquiet was such that a Royal Commission was appointed to enquire into the lack of space in the Abbey. They inspected plans depicting various proposals for solving the problem submitted by J. L. Pearson, Somers Clarke, E. J. Tarver, L. Harvey and J. P. Seddon, but nothing came of these schemes either.

Harvey and Seddon's plans were divided into four parts. They proposed a cluster of six chapels radiating round the Chapter House; the restoration of the Norman ambulatory and

Another version of Seddon's design for the Monumental Halls, Westminster. c.1890. Water-colour in the collection of the Royal Institute of British Architects: Drawings Collection.

opening in to the cloisters and the new chapels; the building of a new ambulatory eastwards, and finally the construction of a huge Campo Santo along Abingdon Street, on the site suggested by Scott, of which they said 'the cost would, no doubt, be very great'. Indeed, this last proved correct for the estimate worked out at £480,000 of which £200,000 was for the Campo Santo, and a further £100,000 was estimated for the purchase of the buildings in Abingdon Street.

Drawings for a later, more elaborate, version of the scheme, prepared by Seddon in partnership with Edward Beckitt Lamb, the son of Edward Buckton Lamb, are in the RIBA.

'Marble Halls', no. 15, pp.51–52
RIBA *Catalogue*, p.37

MARSHFIELD, Glamorgan. School

Perspective from the front. c.1860. Insc. on the back *19th 11 o'clock commenced. 20th traced on stone, finished at 1 oc.*
Water-colour and preliminary pencil
$10\frac{1}{2} \times 14\frac{3}{4}$ (26.7 × 37.5) D.951–1896

Exhib. *Plans and Prospects*, no. 57

The school survives in the village of Castleton nearly $\frac{3}{4}$ mile down the road from Marshfield.

MEXBOROUGH, Yorkshire (West Riding). Church

Plans and details (on 2 sheets). 1891.
Insc. with notes, measurements, etc. D.1300 s. *John P. Seddon.*
D.1300 pen and ink. D.1301 pencil
D.1300, 1301–1896

Marshfield, School D:951–1896

Plan of proposed new church at Mexborough. Ground plan. *Plan of vestries at west end. Plan of heating chamber at West end.* Scale $\frac{1}{8}th$ inch to a foot. d. *1891.* Insc. with details of the *accommodation* including *total 644*
$19\frac{1}{4} \times 13\frac{3}{8}$ (48.7 × 34) D.1300–1896

Mexborough Church. Details of woodwork. Scale *inch* and *full size* (on the back plans of University College, Wales as about to be restored, d. *1886*).
27 × 20 (68.6 × 50.7) D.1301–1896

Apparently not built. Possibly an alternative design for All Saints of 1899 by Hodgson Fowler and H. L. Smethurst.

N. Pevsner, *Yorkshire The West Riding*, 1959, p.366

MONMOUTH, Gwent. Boy's school

Plans and elevations (on 4 sheets). 1870.
D.1008, 1360 insc. *Monmouth new boy's school* and s. *J. P. Seddon Archt. 12 Park St. Westminster.*
D.1358, 1359 pencil. D.1008, 1360 pencil and water-colour on tracing paper
D.1008, 1358–1360–1896

Block plan. d. *24 Decr 1870.* Scale linear. Numbered *23*
13 × 16⅛ (33 × 41) D.1360–1896

Plan. d. *22 Decr 1870.* Numbered *21.* Insc. *Desk accommodation for 114 children. Space for 190 children* and with measurements and names of rooms
7¼ × 14⅛ (18.5 × 35.8) D.1008–1896

Sketch ground plan, side and end elevations, and transverse and longitudinal sections
22 × 16⅜ (55.7 × 41.5) D.1358–1896

Sketch ground plan, side elevation and sections
21⅜ × 17¼ (54.4 × 44) D.1359–1896

School

Plans and elevations (on 2 sheets) for alterations and additions. 1870. Insc. *Design for alterations and additions to Monmouthshire schools,* with names of rooms and *J. P. Seddon Archt. 12 Park St. Westminster*
Pencil, pen and ink, and water-colour on tracing paper
D.1350, 1351–1896

Block plan. Scale *1/16th* and linear. d. *Dec 2* (the rest torn off)
10⅝ × 16¾ (27 × 42.5) D.1350–1896

First floor plan. Front elevation. End elevation. Elevation at EF. Section on AB. Scale ⅛*th.* d. *Dec 16 1870.* Numbered *17*
26⅛ × 18 (66.2 × 45.7) D.1351–1896

Hospital

Design for hospital, enclosure, pump, etc. at Monmouth. Plan of enclosure. Elevation of pump. Plan of pump. Plan of gate. Front elevation of gate. Plan of angle pier. Elevation of angle pier. Section of of angle pier. Scale ⅛*th* and details ½ *inch.* s. *John P. Seddon Architect.* d. *1868*
Pencil and water-colour on tracing paper
23½ × 15⅜ (59.8 × 39.1) D.1985–1896

Another drawing by Seddon for this scheme is in Monmouth Museum. If it was built then it has now been demolished.

MONMOUTH, OVERMONNOW, Gwent. National School

Design for alterations and additions to Over Monnow National Schools. Block plan. Scale *1/16th* and linear. Insc. *J. P. Seddon, Architect, 12, Park St. Westminster.* d. *Dec 20th 1870*
Pen and ink, and water-colour on tracing paper
12 × 17½ (30.6 × 44.5) D.1355–1896

Prichard and Seddon restored the Romanesque church at Overmonnow three years later.

The Schools at Monmouth and Overmonnow are discussed in K. Kissack *op. cit.*

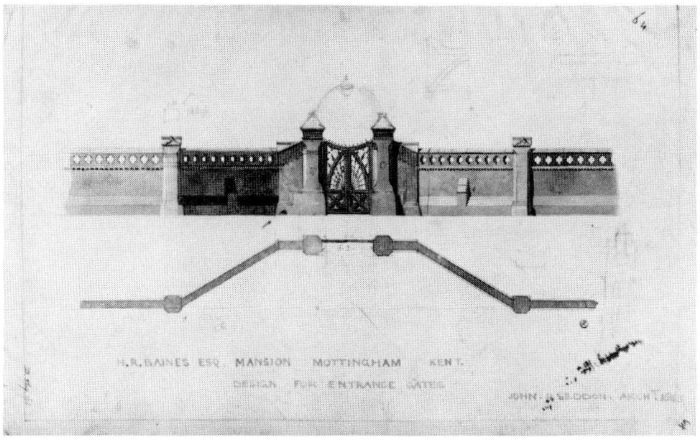

Mottingham House. Design for entrance gates D.869–1896

MOTTINGHAM, Kent. Mottingham House

Plans, elevations, sections and details (on 6 sheets) for additions to a house for H. R. Baines. 1852-53.
Insc. *Mottingham House, nr. Blackheath. H. Baines esq.* D.867, 869, 872 insc. *John P. Seddon* and D.868, 870, 871 *Prichard and Seddon.*
D.867 pen and ink, and water-colour. D.872 pencil and water-colour. D.868–871 pencil, pen and ink, and water-colour.
D.867–872–1896

Plan of entrance floor. Scale linear. d. *14 May 1852.* Numbered *1*
9⅛ × 14⅛ (23.2 × 36) D.867–1896

Porch. Plan, elevations and details. Scale *one inch to a foot* and *full size.* d. *Aug. 1852*
24.5 × 18¾ (62.3 × 47.6) D.872–1896

Design for verandah. Elevations and plan of roof. d. *June* 1853
14¼ × 21¾ (36.2 × 55.2) D.871–1896

Detail of verandah. Scale *inch.* Insc. with measurements and d. *June 1853*
18½ × 12¾ (47 × 32.1) D.870–1896

Design for entrance gates. Plan and elevation. d. *1853*
12⅝ × 20¼ (32.2 × 51.5) D.869–1896

Design for entrance gates. Part elevation, section and detail. Insc. *to be in English oak.* Scale *2 inch*
15¼ × 21⅞ (38.7 × 55.4) D.868–1896

Mottingham House was demolished in the early 1960s and a block of flats, Colview Court, built on the site. Some outbuildings and parts of the boundary wall—the latter as depicted in D.869—survive, but the gates have regrettably disappeared. These are in Mottingham Lane, London, SE9. The existing wall was designed to provide gateways for several houses besides Mottingham House on both sides of Mottingham Lane, but with one exception these houses have all been demolished and replaced with more modern ones. The exception is a much smaller house than appears in any of the designs listed below.

MOTTINGHAM, Kent (probably). Villas

Plans and elevations (on 8 sheets) for eight villas. 1858.
Insc. *H. R. Baines Esq. Design for villa,* or similar, with measurements and names of rooms and *Prichard & Seddon* etc.
D.1013, 1018, 1023, 1027, 1030, 1031 pencil and water-colour.
D.1028, 1029 pencil, pen and ink, and water-colour
D.1013, 1018, 1023, 1027–1031–1896

Plan of entrance floor. Front elevation. Scale ⅛*th.* d. *May 1858.* Numbered *1*
18⅞ × 12⅜ (47.9 × 31.4) D.1013–1896

Plan of entrance floor. Entrance elevation. Scale ⅛*th in.* d. *1858.* Numbered *2*
18⅞ × 12½ (47.9 × 32) D.1018–1896

Ground plan. Front elevation. Sketch perspective view. Scale ⅛ *inch.* Numbered *3.* Alterations suggested in pencil
18⅞ × 12½ (48 × 32) D.1029–1896

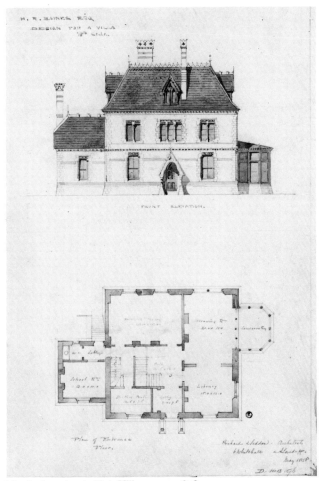

Mottingham (probably). Villa D.1013–1896

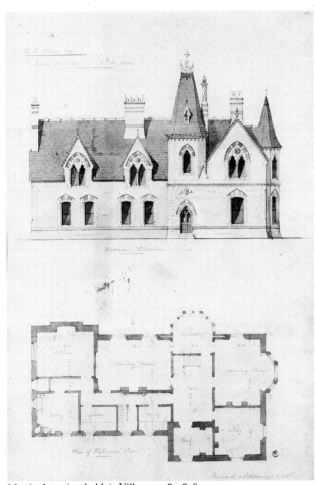

Mottingham (probably). Villa D.1018–1896

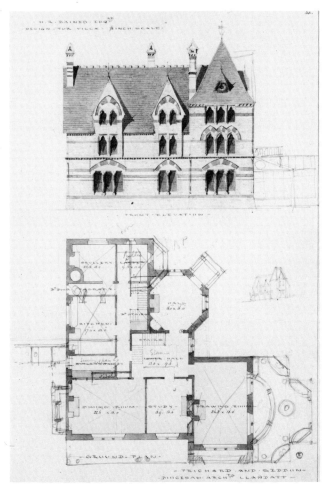

Mottingham (probably). Villa D.1029–1896

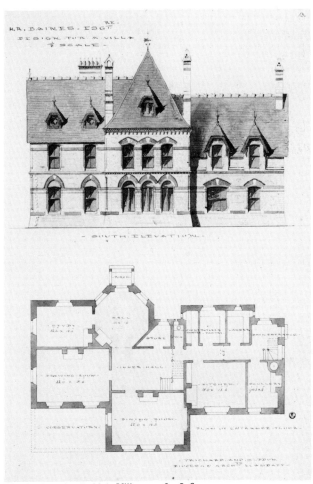

Mottingham (probably). Villa D.1028–1896

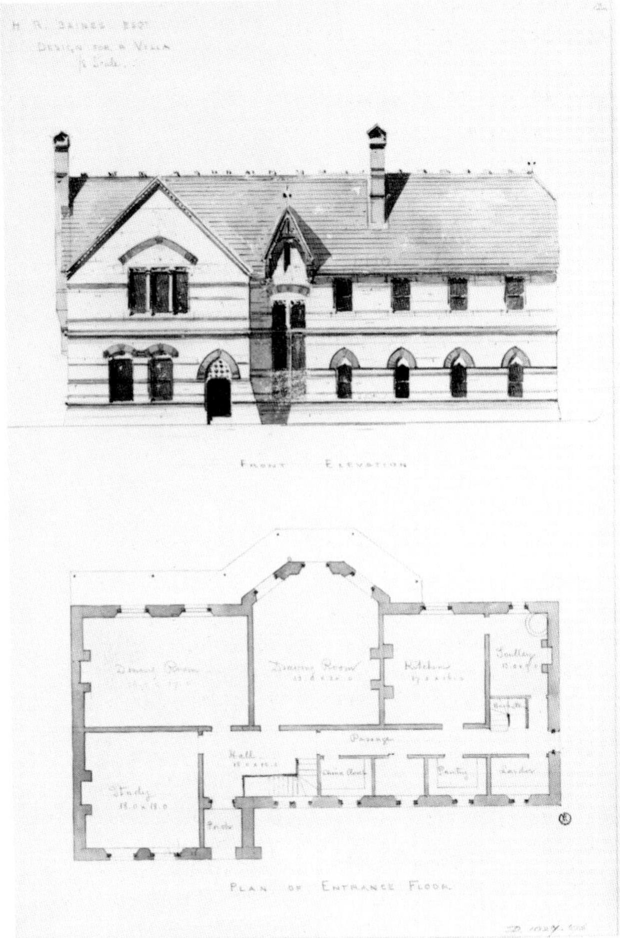

Mottingham (probably). Villa D.1027–1896

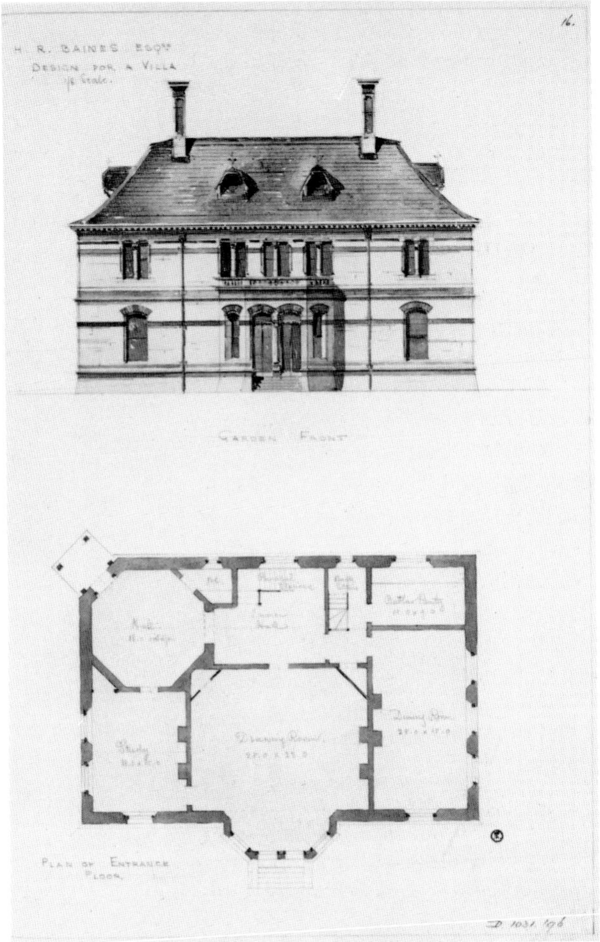

Mottingham (probably). Villa D.1031–1896

Plan. *Front elevation.* Scale $\frac{1}{8}$ *inch.* Numbered *4*. Wm. *1857*
$18\frac{7}{8} \times 12\frac{1}{4}$ (48 × 31.1) D.1030–1896

Plan of entrance floor. South elevation. Scale $\frac{1}{8}$. Numbered *5*
$18\frac{7}{8} \times 12\frac{5}{8}$ (48 × 32) D.1028–1896

Ground plan. Entrance elevation. Scale $\frac{1}{8}$ *inch.* Numbered *6*
$18\frac{3}{4} \times 12\frac{7}{8}$ (47.7 × 30.7) D.1023–1896

Plan of entrance floor. Front elevation. Scale $\frac{1}{8}$
$18\frac{7}{8} \times 12\frac{3}{4}$ (48 × 32.3) D.1027–1896

Plan of entrance floor. Garden front. Scale $\frac{1}{8}$
$18\frac{7}{8} \times 12\frac{5}{8}$ (48 × 32.2) D.1031–1896
(another version of D.1030)

Probably designed for the grounds of Mottingham House. See above.

MOUNTAIN ASH, Glamorgan. Church of St. Margaret

Plans, elevations, sections and details (on 10 sheets). 1860-61. D.691–695, 698–700, 1563 insc. *Mountain Ash Church* or similar. D.691, 692, 700, 1563 stamped or insc. *Prichard and Seddon* etc. D.691–695 s. *A. Llandaff.* D.691–695, 700 bear a seal insc. *Incorporated Society for Promoting the enlargement building and repairing of Churches and Chapels* and a printed notice warning about alteration to plans and forfeiture of their grant. D.693, 697 pen and ink, and water-colour. Rest pencil, pen and ink, and water-colour.
D.691–695, 698–700, 1563, 1574–1896

Ground plan. Scale $\frac{1}{8}$*th inch.* d. by the seal *16 July 1860* and *21st Jan. 1861*. Numbered *1*. Insc. with details of the *Accommodation* including *Total 501*
$12\frac{3}{4} \times 19\frac{1}{8}$ (32.5 × 48.5) D.691–1896

West elevation. East elevation. Scale *8 feet to one inch.* d. by the seal *16 July 1860* and *21st Jan 1861*. Numbered *3*
$12\frac{3}{4} \times 19\frac{1}{8}$ (32.5 × 48.5) D.693–1896

South elevation. Scale $\frac{1}{8}$*th inch.* d. by the seal *16 July 1860* and *21st Janr 1861*. Numbered *2*
$12\frac{3}{4} \times 19\frac{1}{8}$ (32.5 × 48.5) D.692–1896

Longitudinal section. Scale $\frac{1}{8}$*th inch.* d. by the seal *16 July 1860* and *21st Janr 1861*. Numbered *4*
$12\frac{3}{4} \times 18\frac{1}{8}$ (32.5 × 45.9) D.694–1896

Half section AB. Half section CD. Details of seats including *Plan* and *front elevation.* Scale *8 feet to one inch* and *7 feet to one inch.* d. *16 July 1860* and *21st Janr 1861*. Numbered *5*
$18\frac{5}{8} \times 12\frac{3}{4}$ (47.2 × 32.5) D.695–1896

Half external elevation and internal section. Scale *2 feet to one inch.* Numbered *7*
$15\frac{3}{4} \times 21\frac{7}{8}$ (40 × 55.5) D.698–1896

Part transverse section and part *longitudinal section.* Scale $\frac{1}{2}$ *inch to a foot.* Numbered *16*
$22\frac{3}{8} \times 15\frac{1}{2}$ (56.8 × 39.5) D.699–1896

Detail of Nave roof. Transverse section and part *longitudinal section.* Scale $\frac{1}{2}$ *inch.* Numbered *6*. d. by the seal *16 July 1860*
$16 \times 22\frac{1}{2}$ (41 × 57) D.700–1896

Sketch plan and elevation of gateway
$7\frac{7}{8} \times 9\frac{1}{4}$ (20 × 23.5) D.1574–1896

Details of entrance gates. Plans, elevations, sections and details. Scale $\frac{1}{2}$ *inch to a foot.* $\frac{1}{2}$ *full size* and $\frac{1}{4}$ *full size.* An alternative design for one of the lanterns is sketched on
$14 \times 20\frac{1}{2}$ (35.4 × 52.1) D.1563–1896

There are two designs for altar and altar rails in the RIBA.

The church was built to cope with the expanding population—1853 300, 1863 6,000 inhabitants—of a district comprising parts of the parishes of Aberdare and Llanwonno. Construction was carried out by Thomas Williams and the church consecrated on 14 August 1862. It was enlarged by Prichard in 1883 and a new chancel and tower were added by E. Bruce Vaughan in 1898.

Br, 30 August 1862, p.624
Ecc, 1860, p.323
CB, 1863, p.180
RIBA *Catalogue*, p.36

NEWCHURCH, Gwent. Church

Sections (2) of roofs. Insc. *New Church, Monmouthshire* and with measurements
Pencil and water-colour
D.1552, 1523–1896

Section of *chancel roof*. Insc. with width of span *13′6″*
17⅛ × 26¾ (43.5 × 68) D.1522–1896

Section of *nave roof*. Insc. with width of span *15′8″*
17⅜ × 25½ (44.2 × 64.8) D.1523–1896

The church was rebuilt by Seddon in 1864.

Howell and Beazley, p.187

NEWPORT, Gwent
Cathedral Church of St. Woolos

Plans and elevations (on 10 sheets) for alterations and additions. D.1293-5, 1315 insc. *S. Woolos Church Newport* and D.1287 *Proposed south aisle St. Woolos Ch. Newport.* D.1293-5 insc. *Prichard and Seddon* etc. and D.1287, 1288 *John P. Seddon Architect Westminster* and in pencil *& J. C. Carter, Cardiff.* D.1295, 1315 insc. *Those parts teinted red are intended to be new* and D.1293, 1294 *Those parts teinted with the lighter colour are proposed to be new.*
D.1287-9, 1292 pen and ink. D.1290, 1291 pencil. Rest pen and ink, and water-colour
D.1287–1295, 1315–1896

Ground plan. Scale ⅛*th.* Alterations suggested in mauve crayon. Insc. with details of the *Accommodation.* Numbered *1*
18⅜ × 25 (46.5 × 63.6) D.1295–1896

Ground plan showing new alterations
20⅛ × 27 (51.2 × 68.6) D.1292–1896

Elevation of east end. Scale ⅛*th inch*
13⅛ × 19 (33.4 × 48.3) D.1293–1896

South elevation. Scale ⅛*th inch*
18⅛ × 24⅝ (46.1 × 62.5) D.1294–1896

Transverse section thro' nave. Longitudinal section thro' nave & chancel
18¾ × 13¼ (47.5 × 33.5) D.1315–1896

Side elevation. Scale ⅛″
11 × 16½ (28 × 41.8) D.1287–1896

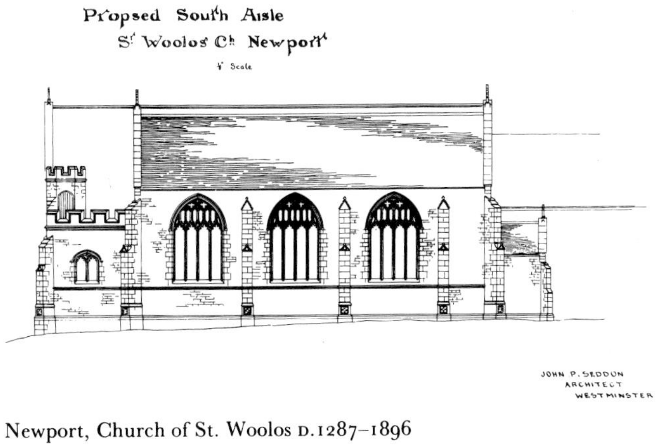

Newport, Church of St. Woolos D.1287–1896

Part end elevation
12¾ × 18⅝ (32.3 × 47.2) D.1289–1896

Sketch and elevation and part section
19¾ × 13⅜ (50 × 33.9) D.1291–1896

Transverse section. Longl section. Scale ⅛″
19¼ × 13 (49 × 33.1) D.1288–1896

Transverse and longitudinal sections. Insc. with notes
16½ × 12⅞ (42 × 32.6) D.1290–1896

St. Woolos Church, of Norman foundation, became a Cathedral in 1921 when the new diocese of Monmouth was created out of the diocese of Llandaff. Besides Seddon's work, most of which appears to have been carried out, W. G. and E. Habershon and Sir Harold Brakspear restored the building in 1853-4 and 1913 respectively and W. D. Caröe added the large new chancel in 1960-4.

Howell and Beazley, pp.205-6.

NEWPORT, CHRISTCHURCH, Gwent.
Church

Doorhandle of porch to church at Christchurch near Newport Monmouthshire. Front elevation. Side elevation. Shape of piece of metal formed into dog's head. Scale *about real size.* On the back pencil sketch of a church window. c.1864. Insc. *from sketch by J. P. Seddon*
Pen and ink, and pencil
12¾ × 13¼ (29.8 × 33.8) D.1954–1896

The church, one and a half miles north-east of St. John's church at Maindee, was rebuilt by Seddon in 1864. It was burnt out in 1949, but opened again in 1952 after restoration by G. G. Pace.

Howell and Beazley, p.208

NEWPORT, MAINDEE, Gwent.
Church of St. John the Evangelist

Section and part elevations of the roof. Insc. *Maindee Church. Newport. Monmouthshire* and with width of span *23′9″*
Pencil, pen and ink, and water-colour
30¾ × 29¾ (80.5 × 75.5) D.1524–1896

Prichard and Seddon had apparently completed their designs for the new church by April 1859 when the *Builder* noticed that various tenders for the erection had been received, but that they averaged £5,000, and the architects were being asked to modify the design so as to bring the cost down to £2,000. The *Ecclesiologist* remarked: 'the plan comprises a chancel with a vestry at its north-western end, a nave and south aisle, with an engaged tower at the west end of the latter, and a south chancel aisle for children. The style is developed Pointed, and some polychrome is introduced. The tower is slender, in excess; but the octagonal broach spire is good, though the spire-lights set on the cardinal sides seem treated with rather too early a feeling. There is a western porch'. One interesting point about the design which they omitted to mention was that it did not include a chancel. This is substantially how the church was built and it would appear that financial savings were made by not including the spire and the statue of St. John on the west end. Eastlake notes that the cost without the spire was £3,000. The tower top, described by Goodhart Rendel as 'a weak pseudo Welsh thing', was not, in fact, added until 1911. The north aisle was perhaps added at this time too, it does not appear in early illustrations of the church.

Seddon showed a design for the church at the RA in 1861 (no. 704). A design by Seddon for the font is at the RIBA.

Br, 16 April 1859, p.267
Ecc, XX, 1859, p.208. XXI, 1860, p.258 (illus)
BN, 6 October 1865, p.206 (window depicting Ascension)
Magazine of Art, 1897, pp.49 & 52 (mentions glass by Seddon)
Eastlake, Appendix, p.103
Howell and Beazley, p.208

NEW TREDEGAR, Glamorgan. Church

Plans, elevations, sections and details (on 8 sheets).
Insc. Proposed new church, New Tredegar
Pen and ink on tracing paper
D.1279–1286–1896

Plan. Insc. *Accommodation. Nave 258. Aisle 76. Chancel 26. Total 362*
$11 \times 19\frac{1}{8}$ (28×48.7) D.1279–1896

South elevation
$10\frac{1}{2} \times 15\frac{1}{2}$ (26.7×39.5) D.1280–1896

West elevation. East elevation. Scale $\frac{1}{8}''$
$10\frac{3}{4} \times 18\frac{1}{8}$ (27.5×46.2) D.1282–1896

North elevation
$10\frac{1}{4} \times 17\frac{1}{8}$ (26×43.4) D.1283–1896

Longitudinal section. Section thro' nave. Section thro' chancel. Scale $\frac{1}{8}''$
$14\frac{1}{8} \times 17$ (35.9×43.2) D.1281–1896

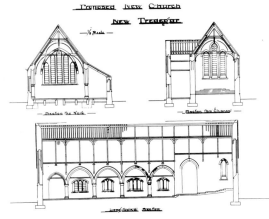

New Tredegar, Church D.1281–1896

Details at east end. Plan. Elevation. Section. Scale $\frac{1}{2}'' = 1$ *foot*
$25\frac{3}{8} \times 20$ (64.5×50.7) D.1284–1896

Details west end. Plan. Elevation. Section. Scale $\frac{1}{2}'' = 1'$
$25\frac{1}{4} \times 19\frac{7}{8}$ (64×50.3) D.1285–1896

Details of windows. Scale $\frac{1}{2}''$ and *full size*
$25\frac{3}{8} \times 19\frac{7}{8}$ (64.3×50.3) D.1286–1896

NORTHAMPTON. Church of St. James

Design for altar frontal. St James' Northampton. Scale *inch & half to a foot.*
Insc. *J. P. Seddon Archt. 1 Queen Anne's Gate, Westminster.*
d. *March 1878*
Pencil and water-colour
$12\frac{3}{4} \times 18\frac{3}{4}$ (32.5×47.5) D.1899–1896

NORWOOD, Surrey. The Rylands

Plans, elevations and sections (on 2 sheets) for an addition for Charles F. Leaf. 1859. Insc. *Prichard and Seddon* etc. and *Chas. F. Leaf Esqre. The Rylands, Norwood. Additions* added on D.881.
Pen and ink, and water-colour on tracing paper. D.880 with added pencil
D.880, 881–1896

Plan. Elevation. Section. Scale $\frac{1}{4}$ *of an inch to a foot.* d. *29 June 1859*
$21\frac{3}{8} \times 15\frac{1}{8}$ (55×38.5) D.880–1896

Half plan below. Framed for revolving shutters. Half plan below. Framed for ordinary shutters. Half plan above. Half exterior and *half interior* elevations and *section*
$16\frac{3}{8} \times 21\frac{1}{4}$ (41.6×54) D.881–1896

Gothic addition comprising three bay window and steps to garden, to late 18th century house.

OLDCASTLE, Gwent. Church of St. John

Oldcastle Church, Monmouthshire. Section and part elevation of roof. Insc. with width of span *18'6"*
Pencil and water-colour
$18 \times 28\frac{3}{8}$ (45.7×72) D.1519–1896

Oldcastle Ch. Mon. Design for west window. Scale *2 inch.* Insc. *John P. Seddon Archt. 12, Park St. Westminster.* d. *23 Feby 1864.*
Initialled *R.M.* (?)
Pencil, ink and water-colour
$22\frac{3}{8} \times 17\frac{1}{4}$ (56.7×43.6) D.1748–1896

The church was rebuilt by Seddon on the existing foundations and he used the original Romanesque windows. The *Ecclesiologist* criticised the ritualistic arrangements. The church leaflet indicates that the west window depicting angels with musical instruments is by Chance. There is a design for seating in the RIBA.

Ecc, xxv, 1864, p.53
Howell and Beazley, p.165

ORCOP, Herefordshire. School

Orcop Schools Herefordshire. Perspective view and ground plan.
c.1853
Pencil and water-colour
$22\frac{1}{4} \times 15\frac{3}{4}$ (56.7×40.2) D.995–1896

Abuts the churchyard and is now a private house. The schoolroom has been converted to a garage, a porch has been added to the door to the master's house, and the left chimney has gone. The bell gable over the schoolroom window is dated 1853.

Seddon also restored the church.

Orcop, School D.995–1896

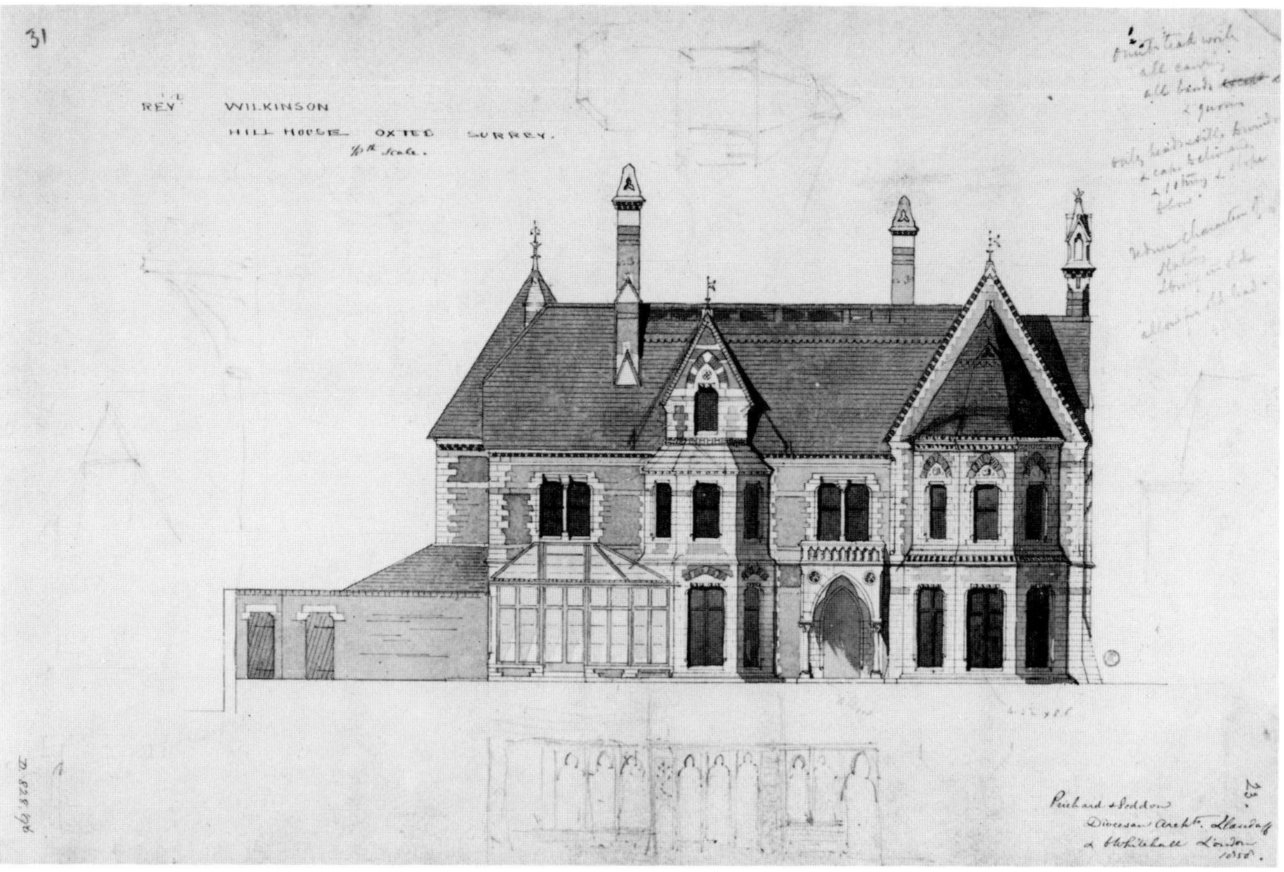

Oxted, East Mill House D.828–1896

OXTED, Surrey. East Hill House

Plans, elevations, sections and details (on 20 (19) sheets) for rebuilding for Rev. Thomas Wilkinson. 1858-60.
D.827–829, 839, 841-4, 849 insc. *Design for re-building Hill House Oxted, Surrey for the Rev'd Wilkinson* or similar. D.846, 848, 852, 853 insc. *Hill House, Oxted*; D.850, *East Hill House, Oxted* and D.1615 *East Hill Oxted.* D.840–844 s. *James Howard.* D.827, 828, 840, 841, 843, 844, 846, 848, 852-4, 1615 insc. *Prichard and Seddon* etc. and D.850 *send tracing to Mrs Wilkinson, Christchurch Road, Roupell Park, Brixton.* D.829, 839-41, 850 insc. with names of rooms and D.826, 829, 839, 840, 844, 845, 850, 854 with measurements.
D.846-9, 853, 1615 pencil and water-colour. D.852 pen and ink, and water-colour on tracing paper. Rest pencil, pen and ink, and water-colour.
D.826–829, 839–850, 852–854, 1615–1896

Plan of bedroom floor. Elevation next road. Scale $\frac{1}{8}$*th*
$21\frac{3}{8} \times 14\frac{3}{4}$ (54.4×37.5) D.829–1896

Elevation of garden front. Sketches of details. Scale $\frac{1}{8}$*th.* d. *1858* and insc. *Omit teakwork all carving* etc.
$12\frac{3}{8} \times 18\frac{1}{2}$ (31.4×47.2) D.828–1896

East elevation. West elevation. Scale $\frac{1}{8}$*th.* d. *1858*
$19\frac{1}{8} \times 12\frac{3}{4}$ (48.5×32.6) D.827–1896

Transverse and longitudinal sections, and details of skirtings, gallery rail, doors and ceiling
$20\frac{1}{2} \times 14\frac{1}{4}$ (52.2×36.3) D.826–1896

Ground plan. Cellar plan. Sketch elevation of entrance gateway. Scale $\frac{1}{4}$ (one sheet cut into two)
$24\frac{1}{4} \times 37\frac{3}{8}$ (61.7×95) D.839, 840–1896

First floor plan. Sketch elevation of upper part of stable. Scale $\frac{1}{4}$ *in.* d. *1859*
$21\frac{1}{4} \times 29\frac{7}{8}$ (53.8×75.9) D.841–1896

Entrance elevation. Scale $\frac{1}{4}$ *in.* Insc. with notes about the colour of the bricks, etc.
$16\frac{1}{4} \times 22$ (41.2×56.1) D.842–1896

Back elevation. Scale $\frac{1}{4}$
$15 \times 20\frac{3}{4}$ (38×52.5) D.843–1896

Transverse section showing arrangement of flues. Scale $\frac{1}{4}$
$15\frac{3}{8} \times 21$ (39.1×53.4) D.844–1896

Plan of *library.* Part elevation and section of entrance porch. Scale $\frac{1}{2}$ *in.* d. *May 1859*
$13\frac{1}{4} \times 19\frac{3}{8}$ (33.5×49.2) D.852–1896

Designs for chimney pieces. Scale *inch.* d. *May 1860*
$12\frac{7}{8} \times 19\frac{1}{8}$ (32.7×48.5) D.1615–1896

Bedroom windows, garden front. Scale *inch* and *full size.* d. *3 June 59*
$13 \times 11\frac{3}{4}$ (29.8×30) D.848–1896

Plan, elevations and sections of conservatory. d. *8 June 59*
$22\frac{5}{8} \times 16\frac{1}{8}$ (57.5×41) D.845–1896

Elevations and a plan of chimney stacks. d. *30 June 59*
$12\frac{1}{2} \times 17\frac{1}{4}$ (31.7×44) D.847–1896

Detail of window in gable and of dormers including sketches of metal finials. Scale $\frac{1}{2}$ *inch* and *full size.* d. *July 59*
$12 \times 15\frac{3}{4}$ (30.6×39.9) D.846–1896

Front door. Scale *inch* and *full size*
$13\frac{1}{8} \times 19\frac{1}{4}$ (33.2×49) D.853–1896

Details of porch. Scale *full size.* d. *1859*
$24\frac{5}{8} \times 18\frac{1}{4}$ (62.6×46.3) D.849–1896

Entrance gates and wall. *Plan,* elevations and detail of *part of gate* and *part of iron hinges to door.* Scale $\frac{1}{2}$ *inch,* $\frac{1}{2}$ *full size* and *full size.* d. *Aug 1859*
$12\frac{1}{4} \times 18\frac{1}{4}$ (31.2×46.5) D.854–1896

Entrance lodge, stables, etc. Plan; *elevation of Lodge etc.* Elevation of *end of stables & side of lodge. Elevation of stables etc. Section AB. Section of lodge.* Scale $\frac{1}{8}$*th inch.* Wm. *1859.* Alterations suggested in pencil
$18\frac{1}{2} \times 12\frac{1}{2}$ (47.2×31.8) D.850–1896

Cottage Fence

Sketch elevation of a *Cottage Fence*. Scale *$1\frac{1}{2}$ inches*. Insc. in ink *Oxted*
Pencil and wash
$11 \times 17\frac{1}{4}$ (27.7×44) D.1579–1896

PENARTH, Glamorgan. Church

Plan, elevations and sections (on 8 sheets). c.1865-66.
D.1263-70 insc. *New Church, Penarth*
Pen and ink, and water-colour on tracing paper
D.1263–1270–1896

Plan of site. Scale linear
$13\frac{1}{8} \times 19\frac{5}{8}$ (33.5×49.8) D.1263–1896

Plan. Plan of heating chamber. Scale linear.
Insc. *Accommodation 780*
$13\frac{1}{2} \times 19\frac{3}{8}$ (34.3×49.2) D.1264–1896

West elevation. Scale linear
$19\frac{1}{2} \times 13\frac{3}{8}$ (49.6×34) D.1265–1896

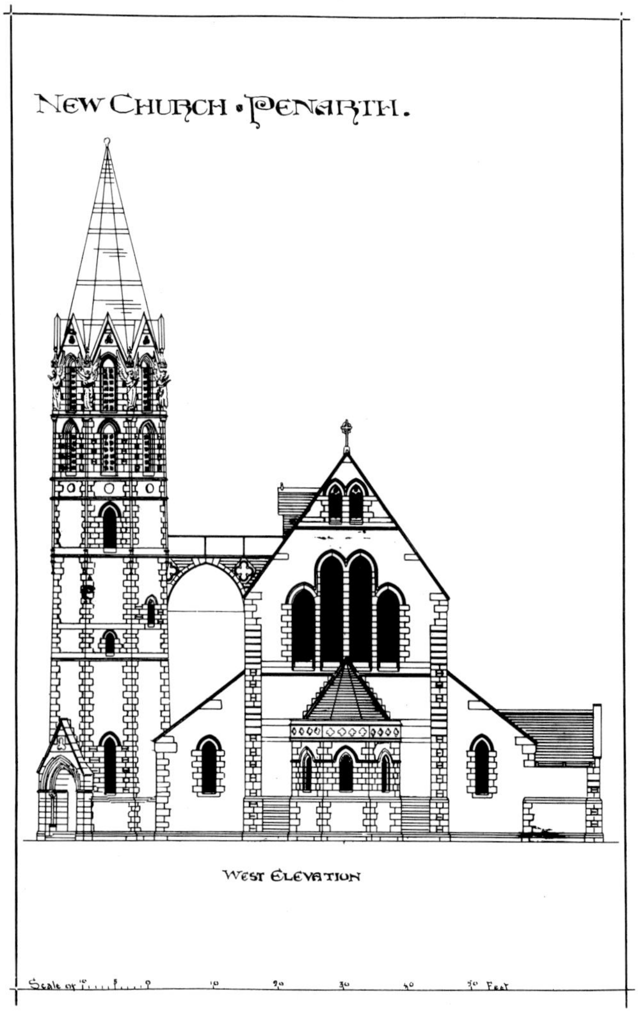

Penarth, Church D.1265–1896

South elevation
$13\frac{1}{4} \times 19\frac{5}{8}$ (33.7×49.8) D.1266–1896

East elevation. Scale linear
$13\frac{1}{4} \times 19\frac{3}{4}$ (33.8×50.2) D.1269–1896

Cross section through transepts. Scale linear
$13\frac{1}{8} \times 19\frac{5}{8}$ (33.4×49.7) D.1267–1896

Longitudinal section. Scale linear
$13\frac{1}{4} \times 19\frac{5}{8}$ (33.8×49.7) D.1268–1896

Cross section including tower
$13\frac{1}{4} \times 19\frac{5}{8}$ (33.8×49.8) D.1270–1896

These designs were never carried out. They appear to be of c.1865-6 and may have been an alternative scheme for St. Augustines designed and built by Butterfield at that time. They do not appear to be an early scheme for Seddon and Carter's All Saints, Penarth which was put up in 1891. (On All Saints see, *Br*, 4 October 1890, p.274. *BN*, 26 June 1891, p.874 and 891 (illus). *Academy Architecture*, 1892, p.16. *Howell and Beazley*, p.272. The church was burnt in 1926 and rebuilt).

Billiard Room

Plan. *S. Elevn. Cross Section. Longl section. Billiard rm for Penarth*
Pen and ink on linen
$9\frac{1}{2} \times 12\frac{1}{2}$ (24×32) D.1435–1896

Possibly an addition to the Conservative Club which Seddon and Carter designed in 1885 (*Br*, 16 May 1885, p.705).

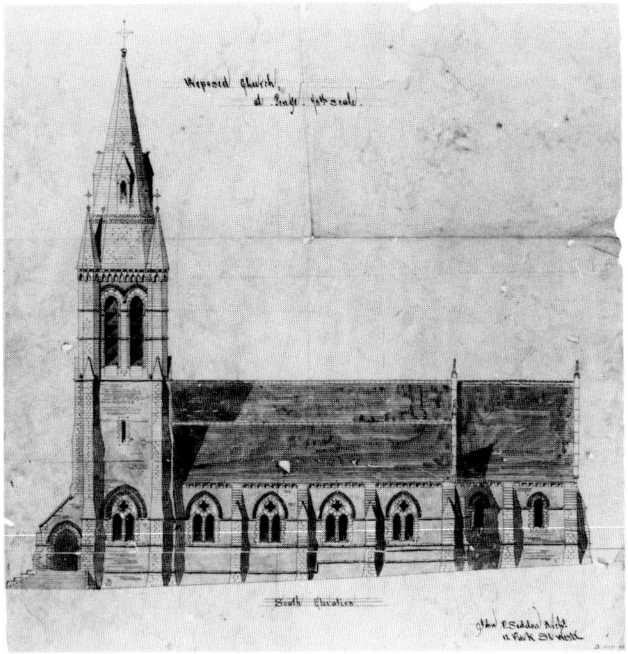

Penge, Church D.1297–1896

PENGE, Kent. Church

Plans and elevation (on 3 sheets) for new church.
D.1296 insc. *Proposed church at Penge* and D.730 *Design for church at Penge.* D.730, 1297, s. *John P. Seddon Archt.* D.1297 addressed *12 Park St. Westr.*
D.730 pencil and water-colour. D.1296 pen and ink, and water-colour on tracing paper. D.1297 pen and ink, pencil, and water-colour.
D.730, 1296, 1297–1896

Ground plan. Scale *16 feet to the inch* and linear. Insc. *The church might be finished nearer this boundary & further from this road. Accommodation 1000.* Initialled *J.P.S.*
$8\frac{7}{8} \times 15\frac{3}{4}$ (22.4×40) D.730–1896

Ground plan. Scale *$\frac{1}{8}$th.* Insc. with details of the *accommodation* including *Total 1058 adults.* Small alteration suggested in pencil
$17\frac{1}{2} \times 25$ (44.3×63.7) D.1296–1896

South elevation. Scale *$\frac{1}{8}$th*
$24\frac{5}{8} \times 24\frac{3}{8}$ (62.5×61.8) D.1297–1896

The church was not built apparently. These drawings could relate to Holy Trinity (consecrated 1870); St. Paul (1866, by Bassett Keeling, now demolished) St. John the Divine (mid 19th century) or Christchurch (1886).

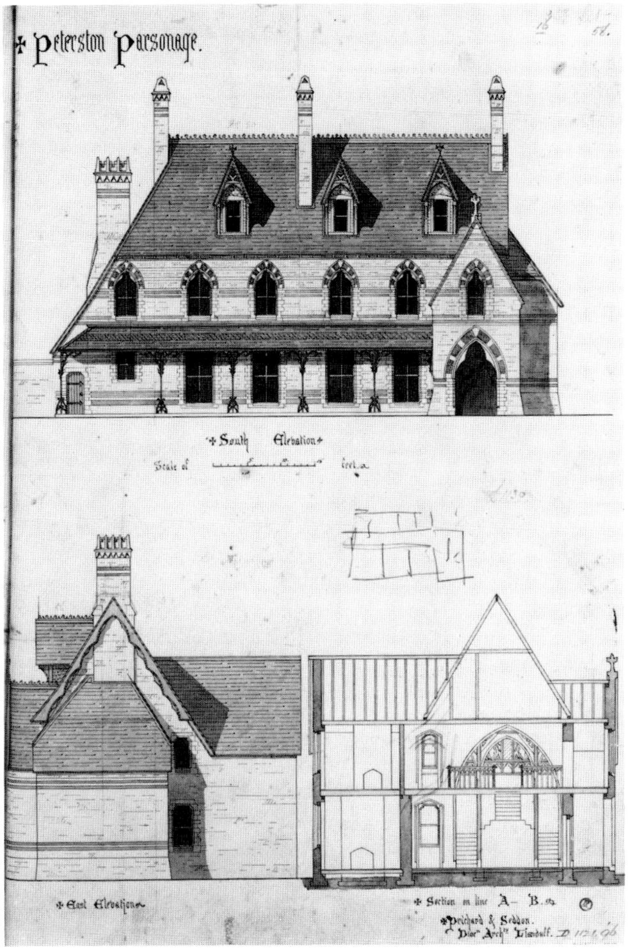

Peterston Super Ely, Parsonage D.1121–1896

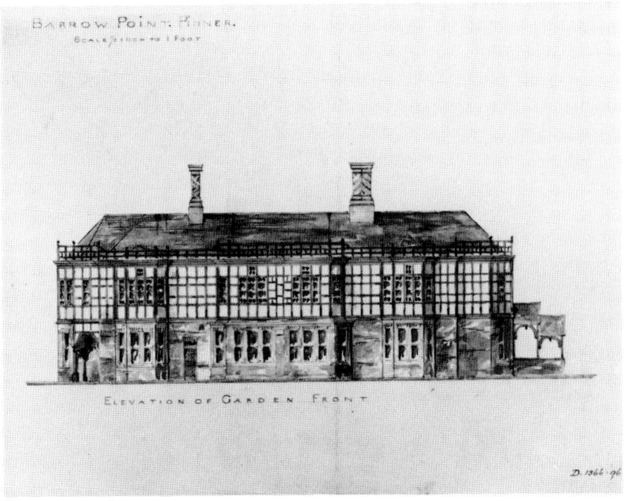

Pinner, Barrow (Barra) Point D.1366–1896

PETERSTON SUPER ELY, Glamorgan (possibly). Parsonage

Plans, elevations and sections (on 4 sheets) showing two schemes. c.1857
D.1158, 1159 insc. *Peterston parsonage.* D.1158, 1159, 1121A lettered *For the Revd C. Lewis.* All lettered *Prichard and Seddon.* D.1122, 1159 insc. with names of rooms.
Pencil, pen and ink, and water-colour
D.1121, 1121A, 1158, 1159–1896

Ground plan. One pair plan. Scale $\frac{1}{8}$. Insc. *3rd set.* Numbered in red *17*
$17\frac{1}{4} \times 11\frac{3}{4}$ (44×29.8) D.1121A–1896

South elevation. East elevation. Section on line AB. Rough sketch plan. Scale linear. Insc. *£1130* and *3rd set.* Numbered in red *16*
$17\frac{1}{4} \times 11\frac{3}{4}$ (44×29.8) D.1121–1896

Ground plan. One pair plan. Scale $\frac{1}{8}$*th*
$18\frac{1}{8} \times 12\frac{5}{8}$ (45.8×32) D.1159–1896

South elevation. East elevation. Section through study. Scale $\frac{1}{8}$*th*
$18\frac{1}{8} \times 12\frac{5}{8}$ (45.8×32) D.1158–1896

The *Ecclesiologist* noted in 1857: 'Peterston parsonage by Messrs Prichard and Seddon, seems, in its plan, to waste space in the somewhat ambitious staircase and to be far too small in the 'study'. The style is pointed; with the ornamental detail in parts a good deal exaggerated, and a verandah with iron posts and tracery made a part of the original design. The expense will be £1,100.

Ecc, XVIII, 1857, p.258
(Plans and specification for the church at Peterston super Ely dated 1860 by David Vaughan are in the Records Office at Cardiff.)

School

Peterstone schools. Plan. *Entrance elevation. Side elevation. End elevation. Longitudinal section. Transverse section.* Scale $\frac{1}{8}$ *inch. Prichard and Seddon* etc. Insc. in pencil *not executed*
Pencil, pen and ink, and water-colour
$19 \times 12\frac{1}{4}$ (48.4×31.1) D.955–1896

PINNER, Middlesex. Barrow (Barra) Point

Plans, elevations and sections (on 7 sheets).
Insc. *Barrow* or *Barra Point Pinner* or similar, and D.1371, 1365 with names of rooms.
D.1370 pencil. D.1372 pencil, pen and ink. Rest pencil and water-colour.
D.1365, 1366, 1368, 1370–1372, 1376–1896

Ground plan. Scale $\frac{1}{8}$
$13\frac{1}{2} \times 18$ (34.3×45.5) D.1371–1896

Sketch ground plan. Scale $\frac{1}{8}$
$13\frac{5}{8} \times 13\frac{5}{8}$ (34.7×34.7) D.1368–1896

First floor plan. Scale $\frac{1}{8}$
$13\frac{3}{8} \times 15\frac{3}{4}$ (34×40) D.1365–1896

Elevation of garden front. Scale $\frac{1}{8}$ *inch to 1 foot*
$12\frac{1}{8} \times 16\frac{1}{8}$ (30.9×40.9) D.1366–1896

Elevation of entrance front. Scale $\frac{1}{8}$ *inch to 1 foot*
On the back Raffles Davison Rambling sketches, no. 49, Birchington
$13\frac{3}{8} \times 18\frac{5}{8}$ (34×47.4) D.1376–1896

Detail of bay window. Scale $\frac{1}{2}$ *inch* and linear
On the back an engraving of the Ecclesiastical Art Exhibition, Victoria Embankment, London
$18\frac{3}{4} \times 12\frac{5}{8}$ (47.6×32.1) D.1372–1896

Plan, elevation and section of porch. d. *July 25 1874.*
On the back a drawing for Woodhall (see below)
$18\frac{1}{4} \times 12\frac{3}{8}$ (46.3×31.2) D.1370–1896

Woodhall

Plans, elevations, sections and details for *Proposed alterations and additions* (the last torn off) for *W. Bar*[ber] (part torn off). Scale *8 feet to 1 inch* and ½ *inch to 1 foot*. Insc. with notes and measurements.
Pencil and water-colour on tracing paper
16¼ × 12⅛ (41.2 × 30.7) D.1367–1896

Tracing from the drawing on the back of D.1370–1896 (see above). Insc. *W. Barber Esq Pinner.*
Pencil.
Seddon did other work for Barber, see next sheet.

Cottage

Plans, elevations and sections (on 2 sheets). 1855.
Insc. *Proposed cottage at Pinner for W. Barber Esq.* s. *John P. Seddon Architect*
Pencil, pen and ink, and water-colour
D.1471, 1472–1896

Garden front. Elevation to road. Entrance front. End elevation. Scale *8 feet to 1 inch* and linear. d. *1855* but one gable d. *1885* and initialled *J.B.* Stamped *Hendon Union Rural Sanitary* (the next word is illegible) *approved subject to compliance with the Bye Laws.* s. *Thomas Brigwater.* Alterations suggested in pencil
20 × 14½ (50.7 × 36.8) D.1471–1896

Ground floor plan. Bedroom plan. Roof plan. Section CD. Section EF. Section AB. Longitudinal section. Scale *8 feet to 1 inch.* d. *1855.* Insc. with measurements and names of rooms. Alterations suggested in pencil
19½ × 14⅝ (49.5 × 37.2) D.1472–1896

See previous entry. It is not clear whether this cottage is Woodhall or not.

PONTNEWYDD, Gwent.
Church of the Holy Trinity

Perspective, elevations and detail (on 4 sheets). 1857-59.
D.696, 697, 1979, lettered *Prichard and Seddon* etc. D.690, 1979 insc. *Cwm Bran Church.*
D.690, 697, 1979 pencil and water-colour. D.696 pencil, pen and ink and water-colour. D.1979 on tracing paper.
D.690, 696, 697, 1979–1896

Study for Cwm Bran Ch. Perspective from the south west
22¼ × 16¼ (56.7 × 41.3) D.690–1896

Elevations of tower. Scale ⅛ *of an inch to a foot*
12¼ × 19 (31.3 × 48.1) D.696–1896

South elevation. Scale ⅛*th inch* s. *A. Llandaff.* The sheet bears the seal of the *Incorporated Church Building Society.* d. *22 Decr 1857*
13¾ × 19⅝ (35 × 49.9) D.697–1896

Iron Hinges to door leading out of (a word here is not legible) *chancel.* Insc. *of hammer wrought iron* and d. *Oct. 59*
14⅞ × 24⅝ (37.8 × 62.5) D.1979–1896

A drawing for the font is at the RIBA.

The *Ecclesiologist* noted: 'This new church, by Messrs Prichard and Seddon, comprises nave and south aisle—not extending to the west end, dwarf south-west porch, chancel, and north-west vestry. The ritual arrangements are good—the pulpit projecting from the chancel into the nave on the north side. The style is Middle-Pointed—with some eccentricities. The aisle is divided from the nave by two broad arches rising from a low pier, and there is a much narrower arch eastward, opening into the eastern end of the aisle, where is placed the organ, and above which rises a thin square tower, with a very tall transomed belfry stage, surmounted by a four-gabled roof, from the intersection of which springs a pinnacle. There is some constructional colour in bands of red stone, and in the voussoirs of arches and windows. We should counsel greater simplicity and austerity of design'.

The church has been altered internally. There is a new font and screen, and the chancel was 'modernised' c.1900. None of the original glass survives and much of the original decoration has been painted over.

Ecc, VIII, 1857, p.394
RIBA *Catalogue*, p.36

Parsonage

Plans, elevations, sections and details (on 6 sheets) depicting three different schemes. 1857-59.
Insc. *Cwm Bran Parsonage* and lettered *Prichard and Seddon* etc. D.1124, 1125, 1172–1174 insc. with measurements, names of rooms, etc.
Pencil, pen and ink, and water-colour
D.1124, 1125, 1172–1175–1896

Cellar plan. Ground plan. Bedroom plan. South elevation. Transverse section. Scale ⅛. Some alterations suggested in pencil
15⅛ × 21½ (38.5 × 54.5) D.1174–1896

North elevation. East elevation. West elevation. Longitudinal section. Scale ⅛*th*
15⅛ × 21½ (38.5 × 54.5) D.1173–1896

Ground plan. Bedroom floor plan. *Front elevation. Back elevation.* Scale ⅛*th in.* d. *1857.* Slight alterations are suggested in pencil
14 × 18¾ (29.7 × 44) D.1172–1896

East elevation. West elevation. Transverse *section.* First floor *window in west elevation.* Ground floor window in west elevation *half exterior* and *interior.* Details of another window. Scale ⅛*th* and ½ *inch.* Numbered *12*
11¾ × 17¼ (29.7 × 44) D.1175–1896

Plan of cellars. Ground floor plan. Elevation of south front. Alterations to study suggested in pencil. Numbered in red *10.* Scale ⅛*th.* d. *Oct 1859*
17⅜ × 11¾ (44 × 29.8) D.1124–1896

First floor plan. West elevation. Elevation of *entrance front. Section on the line CD. Section on the line AB.* Numbered in red *11* Scale ⅛*th.* d. *Oct 1859*
17⅜ × 11¾ (44 × 29.8) D.1125–1896

The *Ecclesiologist* noted in 1860 that the parsonage was a small house to cost £500 and that the style was: 'pointed, with coloured bands: and much more character is given than we should have thought possible for the sum named'. The cheaper scheme as depicted in D.1124, 1125 was built though the plan and elevations were simplified still further in execution. The present porch is of 'rustic' timber.

Ecc, XXI, 1860, p.51

School

Plans, elevations, sections and details (on 6 sheets) for alterations and additions. 1859.
D.957, 959–962 insc. *Prichard and Seddon* etc. D.959–963 insc. *Cwm Bran Schools.* D.957, 958, 960, 963 insc. with measurements
Pencil, pen and ink, and water-colour. D.957, 958 on tracing paper
D.958–963–1896

Ground plan and *Plan of new bedroom over scullery. Front elevation. East elevation. Section thro class rooms. Section thro girls school & class rooms. Section thro scullery and bedroom over.* Scale ⅛*th inch*
21¾ × 17¼ (55.2 × 44) D.958–1896

Plan of site. Scale linear in *chains. West elevation. East elevation. Longitudinal section.* Scale ⅛ *inch*
22¾ × 16½ (57.7 × 42) D.959–1896

Ground plan. South elevation. Section on line AB. Section on line CD. Scale ⅛*th inch* and linear. Insc. with names of rooms
22⅞ × 16¾ (58 × 42.6) D.962–1896

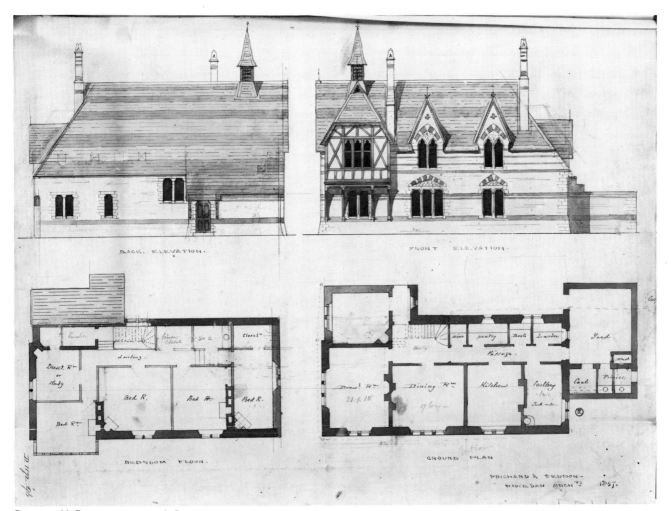

Pontnewydd, Parsonage D.1172–1896

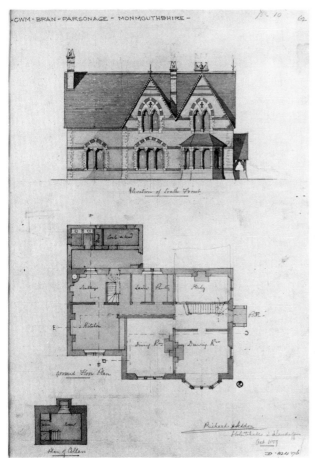

Pontnewydd, Parsonage D.1124–1896

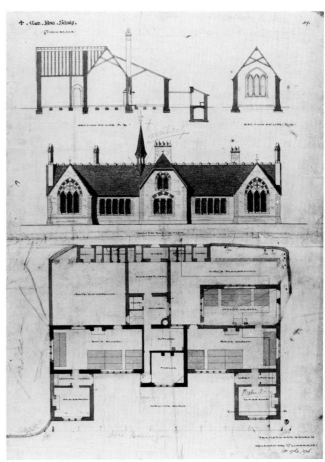

Pontnewydd, School D.962–1896

Turret. Plans, elevations, sections and details. Scale $\frac{1}{2}$ *in* and *full size*. d. *Dec. 59*
$12\frac{7}{8} \times 18\frac{3}{4}$ (32.6 × 47.7) D.960–1896

Plans, elevations and sections of a door and window. Scale $\frac{1}{2}$ *inch*
$12\frac{3}{4} \times 16\frac{3}{4}$ (32.3 × 42.5) D.961–1896

Plans, elevations and details of chimneys, a window, and a brick cornice. Scale $\frac{1}{2}$ *inch* and *full size*
$22\frac{7}{8} \times 16\frac{1}{2}$ (58 × 41.8) D.963–1896

School (possibly for)

Detail of Desks. Plan. Front elevation. End elevation. Scale *inch*. d. *Dec 1859*
$18\frac{3}{8} \times 9\frac{1}{2}$ (46.7 × 24.1) D.957–1896

D.958–963 show the school largely as built. The tower shown in D.958 was not built. The school was enlarged still further later in the century, possibly by Seddon.

REDRUTH, Cornwall. Church

Redruth Ch. Principle door. Plan, half elevations and details. Scale *1 in.* s. *John P. Seddon* and d. *June 1884.* On the back is a sketch of a pulpit
Pencil and water-colour
$12\frac{1}{2} \times 20\frac{1}{8}$ (31.9 × 51) D.1552–1896

ROCKFIELD, Gwent.
Church of St. Cenedlon (Kenelm)

Design for lych gate. Rockfield Ch. Plan. Elevation. Longitudinal section. Cross section. Details. Scale $\frac{1}{2}$ *inch* and $\frac{1}{4}$ *full size*. Insc. *John P. Seddon Archt.* d. *Augst 4th 1877*
Pencil and water-colour
$13 \times 18\frac{3}{4}$ (32.8 × 47.6) D.1594–1896

Seddon restored the church in 1859-60. The lych gate was built as in this drawing.

Ecc, xx, 1859, p.76
Howell and Beazley, p.174

ROSSDOHAN, near Sneem, Co. Kerry, Ireland. House

Plans, elevations, sections and details (on 14 sheets) for Dr Samuel Thomas Heard. 1875-81.
D.1378, 1379, 1381, 1383-6, 1388, 1683, 1560 insc. *House for Dr Heard at Rosdohan, Ireland*, or similar. D.1378, 1382-5, 1387, 1560 s. *J* or *John P. Seddon Archt.* and D.1378, 1384, 1385 addressed *1 Queen Anne's Gate, Westminster*. D.1378, 1388, 1560 insc. with measurements. Most insc. with notes, etc.
D.1378, 1381, 1385, 1387, 1560 pencil and water-colour.
D.1379, 1380, 1382-4, 1386 pencil. D.1388 pencil, pen and ink, and water-colour. D.1381A Lithograph.
D.1378–1381, 1381A, 1382–1388, 1560, 1683–1896

Ground plan. Front facing the sea. Scale $\frac{1}{8}$th. and linear. d. *Feb 1876*
$23\frac{1}{2} \times 16\frac{1}{8}$ (59.6 × 41) D.1378–1896

Section on line AB. Section on line CD. Section on line EF. Section on line GH. Section on line KL. s. *S. Heard* and with other signatures which are illegible. d. *23 Nov 75*. Scale $\frac{1}{8}$th and linear
$23\frac{1}{4} \times 15\frac{5}{8}$ (59.1 × 39.8) D.1388–1896

Perspective view of drawing room showing ceiling and one wall
$15\frac{1}{8} \times 14\frac{3}{4}$ (38.5 × 37.5) D.1380–1896

Plan looking up of drawing room ceiling. Scale linear. d. *May 1876*
$13\frac{1}{2} \times 21\frac{5}{8}$ (34.3 × 55) D.1382–1896

Side of drawing room. Scale *inch*
20×14 (51 × 35.5) D.1379–1896

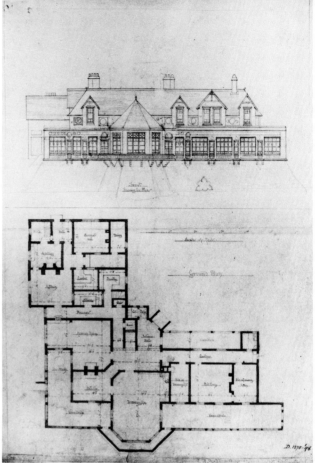
Rossdohan, House D.1378–1896

Side of drawing room. Scale linear. d. *Febr 1881*. Plate from *The Architect* 26 March 1881
$13\frac{3}{8} \times 18\frac{1}{2}$ (34 × 47) D.1381A–1896

Details of drawing room including elevation of a part of one wall. Scale *inch*. d. *April 1878*
$21\frac{1}{8} \times 24\frac{1}{4}$ (53.5 × 61.5) D.1384–1896

Plan, elevation and section of part of the *Drawing room*. Scale *one inch to one foot*. d. *Septr. 1877*
$21\frac{1}{8} \times 28\frac{5}{8}$ (54.2 × 72.8) D.1385–1896

Drawing room roof, details. Scale *inch* and *half inch*
22×29 (56 × 73.5) D.1386–1896

Detail of cornice to drawing room. Scale *full size*. d. *June 1878*
$22 \times 14\frac{3}{8}$ (56 × 36.6) D.1387–1896

Details of ornament. Scale *full size*. d. *April 79*
$21\frac{3}{4} \times 14\frac{1}{4}$ (55.2 × 36.6) D.1383–1896

Elevations of staircase and landing. Scale $\frac{1}{2}$ *inch*
$14\frac{1}{8} \times 21\frac{1}{8}$ (35.8 × 53.7) D.1381–1896

Detail of best doors. Scale *inch* and *full size*. d. *October 75*
$18\frac{1}{8} \times 28\frac{3}{4}$ (46 × 73) D.1560–1896

Part elevation of a coloured capital
$18\frac{1}{4} \times 14\frac{1}{2}$ (46.4 × 36.8) D.1683–1896

The house was burnt in 1922 and what remained was demolished by a South African, Fitzgerald who bought the ruin probably in the early 1930s and built himself a Dutch colonial house to the designs of various architects, including Michael Scott, on the northern part of Seddon's foundations. This was burnt c.1955 and that all that now survives is a shell. Seddon's cliffside arches can, however, still be seen.

A, 26 March 1881, p.219
Information kindly supplied by J. D. Williams, J. Leslie and T. E. Stoakley.

Rossdohan, House D.1380–1896

ST. LYTHANS, Glamorgan. Church

St. Lythans church. Details of roof. Longitudinal section. Transverse section. Details. Scale ½ inch to a foot and larger. Insc. sketched and measured by J. P. Seddon and with measurements 12⅝ × 18¾ (32 × 47.7) D.1500–1896

A simple late mediaeval building which Seddon restored.

Howell and Beazley, p.274

SHOTLEY HALL

Furniture as proposed for Shotley Hall. Design for cabinet. Design for hall bracket. Design for flower stand. Design for hall table. Design for wall seats. Design for wall seat. s. with a monogram of the letters *J.P.S.* Insc. *Seddon & Co London* and with notes about cost. Numbered *1*
Pencil and water-colour
19⅝ × 13⅜ (49.8 × 34.1) D.1824–1896

Tracing of flower stand, hall table and wall seats as above
9¼ × 13⅛ (23.5 × 33.4) D.1823–1896

Tracing of cabinet and wall bracket as above. Insc. *Shee No. 1*
9½ × 13⅛ (24.2 × 33.5) D.1819–1896

It is not clear which Shotley Hall this is.

Southerndown Hotel D.873–1896

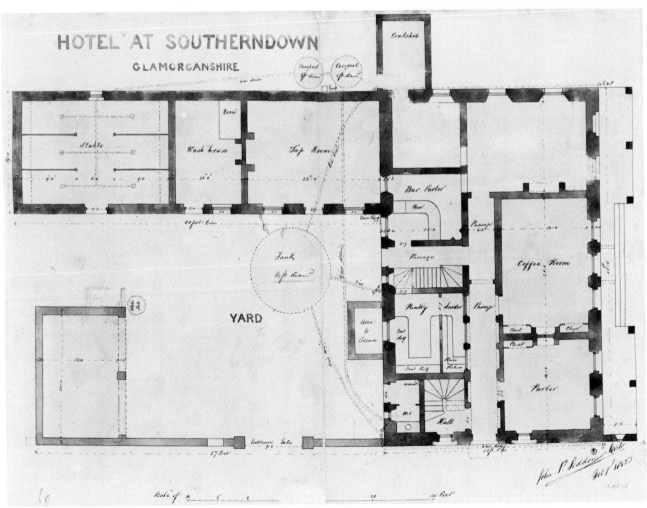

Southerndown, Hotel D.877–1896

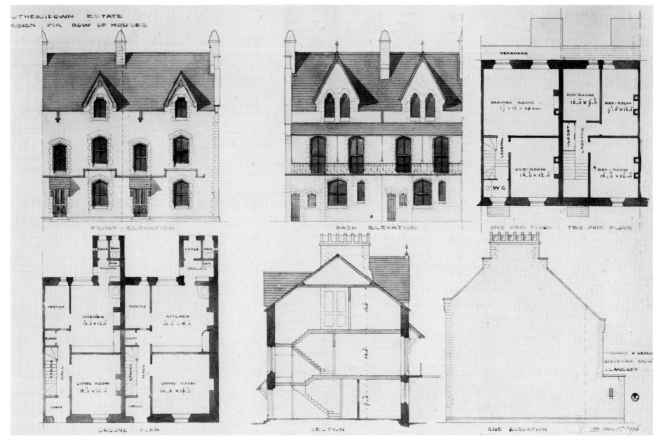

Southerndown, Houses D.1045–1896

SOUTHERNDOWN, Glamorgan.
Dunraven Arms Hotel, later the Southerndown Hotel and now the Welsh Sunshine Home for Blind Babies

Perspective, plans, elevations, sections and details (on 7 sheets). 1852-53.
D.876, 877, 879 s. *John P. Seddon.* D.876, 877 insc. with names of rooms and D.876, 877, 879 with measurements.
D.879 pen and ink, and water-colour. D.875 pencil and wash on tracing paper. Rest pencil, pen and ink, and water-colour.
D.873–879–1896

Perspective view
16¼ × 21⅞ (41.2 × 55.4) D.873–1896
Exhib. Marble Halls, no. 125. Illus. *Br*, 15 January 1853, p.37.

Plan of entrance floor. Scale linear. d. *Feby 1852*
15 × 10⅜ (38.1 × 26.3) D.877–1896

Hotel at Southerndown Glamorganshire. Plan of ground floor. Scale linear. d. *Feby 1852*
19¾ × 26¼ (51 × 66.5) D.876–1896

Southerndown Hotel. Side elevation
19¾ × 26¼ (51 × 66.5) D.878–1896·

Southerndown hotel. Front and side elevations, and a transverse section. Scale ⅛. d. *1852*
12⅜ × 15¾ (31.4 × 40.3) D.879–1896

Detail of verandah rackets
12 × 9⅜ (36 × 23.7) D.875–1896

Details of verandah. Scale ½ *inch*
9⅜ × 13 (23.8 × 32.9) D.874–1896

The story of Seddon's meeting with Prichard while working at Southerndown has been told in the Preface. Five tenders were received for the new hotel in the summer of 1852 and that of

J. Brown of Stoke's Croft, Bristol, for £1,339, accepted. By January 1853 the *Builder* reported that the work was nearly completed noticing that the hotel was built: 'to supply the want of proper accommodation which has long been felt by visitors who during the summer months have been in the habit of frequenting this watering place of South Wales'. They further noticed that: 'the projecting wall at the further end of the raised terrace is for the purpose of protecting the front somewhat from the wind which is violent at some seasons . . . the hotel is arranged so that the portion to be let privately is separate from that wherein its ordinary business if carried on'. Construction was of local limestone, and some Bath stone. The name Dunraven Arms, which was soon dropped, was inspired by Dunraven Castle, the home of the Dowager Countess of Dunraven, on the opposite side of the valley. Several additions have been made to the hotel in the 20th century.

Br, 15 January 1853, p.37
Public Library Journal (Cardiff), March 1903, IV, Part 2, p.29
Howell and Beazley, p.279

Houses

Plans, elevations, sections and details (on 7 sheets). 1856-58.
D.1045, 1047–1051 insc. *Prichard and Seddon* etc. and with measurements and names of rooms.
D.1045–1048, 1051 pencil, pen and ink, and water-colour.
D.1049, 1050 pencil and water-colour.
D.1045–1051–1896

[*So*]*utherndown estate.* [*D*]*esign for row of houses. Ground plan. One pair floor* plan. *Two pair floor* plan. *Front elevation. Back elevation. End elevation. Section.* Wm. *1853*
13½ × 20¼ (34.2 × 51.4) D.1045–1896

Houses to be erected at Southerndown. Plan of entrance floor. Plan of 1st floor. Front elevation. Section. Scale ⅛ *inch.* s. *George James.* d. *1856.* Alterations suggested in pencil
12¼ × 18⅜ (31.1 × 46.5) D.1047–1896

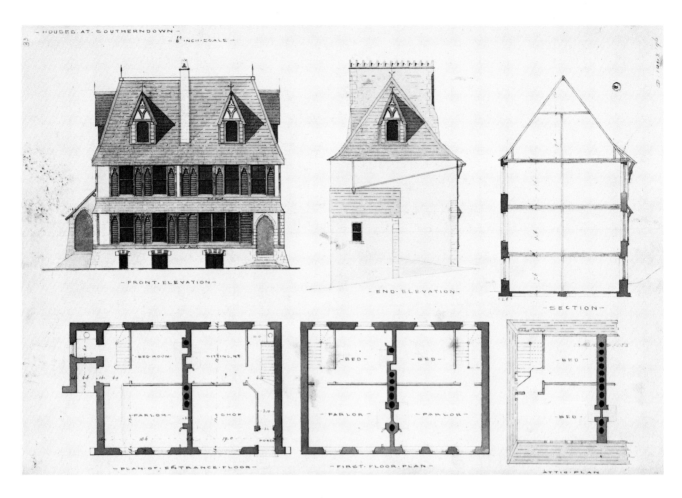

FRONT ELEVATION

END ELEVATION

SECTION

PLAN OF ENTRANCE FLOOR

FIRST FLOOR PLAN

ATTIC PLAN

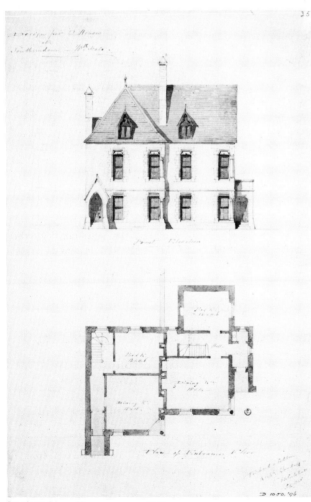

Southerndown, Houses D.1050–1896

Houses at Southerndown. Detail of basement window. Detail of chimney. Basement plan. Back elevation. Scale ⅛th inch and *inch* $12\frac{3}{8} \times 18\frac{3}{8}$ (31.5×46.5) D.1048–1896

Houses at Southerndown. Detail of basement window. Detail of Chimney. Basement plan. Back elevation. Scale ⅛th inch and *inch* $12\frac{3}{8} \times 18\frac{3}{8}$ (31.5×46.4) D.1051–1896

Plan of entrance floor. Front elevation. Scale ⅛th d. *Sep. 1858* $17\frac{1}{8} \times 11\frac{5}{8}$ (43.5×29.5) D.1050–1896

Design for 2 houses at Southerndown. Plan of first floor. Side elevation. Scale ⅛. d. *Sep 58* $17\frac{1}{8} \times 11\frac{5}{8}$ (43.5×29.5) D.1049–1896

Possibly for

Plan, elevation and section of a house. Alterations suggested in pencil $17\frac{3}{8} \times 12\frac{1}{4}$ (44.1×31.2) D.1046–1896

D.1048, 1051 and D.1049, 1050 are pairs.

These houses were presumably designed for the land left to Seddon by his maternal grandfather Mr Charles Magnus Thomas on which the Southerndown Hotel was also built.

STROUD, Gloucestershire. School of art

Plans and sections (on 3 sheets). 1890.
D.1348, 1349 insc. *School of Art, Stroud.* and lettered *John P. Seddon & W. H. C. Fisher architects. C. F. Kell Photo-litho, 8 Furnival St., Holborn, E.C.* D.1510 insc. *School of Art etc. Stroud* and *Seddon and Fisher Archts.* Each insc. with measurements. D.348, 1349 lithographs with added pencil. D.1510 pencil and water-colour on tracing paper.
D.1348, 1349, 1510–1896

Basement plan. Ground floor plan. Scale ⅛". Numbered *1* $20\frac{7}{8} \times 14$ (53×35.6) D.1349–1896

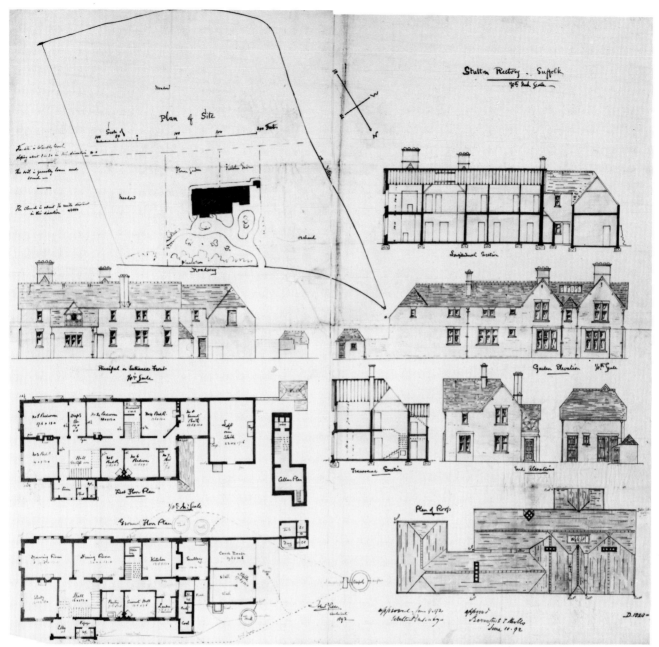

Stutton, Rectory D.1320–1896

First floor plan. Heating chamber plan. Plan at A. Section thro lavys. Scale ⅛″. Numbered 2
20⅞ × 14 (53 × 35.6) D.1348–1896

Roof. Section over front part. Part sectn over large window at back. Part sectn eaves at back. Scale ½ inch to a foot. d. 17.12.90
13¾ × 19¼ (34.9 × 48.9) D.1510–1896

The School, an elaborate Ruskinian Gothic building in Lansdown, was complete by 1899.

D. Verey, Gloucestershire: the Cotswolds, p.431.

STUTTON, Suffolk. Rectory

Plans, elevations, sections and details (on 2 sheets). 1892. D.1320 pen and ink, and water-colour on linen. D.1547 pencil
D.1320, 1547–1896

Stutton Rectory, Suffolk. Plan of site. Cellar plan. Ground floor plan. First floor plan. Plan of roofs. Principal or entrance front. Garden elevation. End elevation. Transverse section. Longitudinal section. Scale ⅛th inch and linear. s. & d. John P. Seddon Architect 1892 and Walter Ponsonby approved Jan 9.92. Insc. Barrington and Mills [?] approved June 10.92. and with notes about the site,

measurements and names of rooms
30 × 32 (76 × 81) D.1320–1896

Stutton Parge, details of doors. Scale inch. Insc. with notes. On the back printed plans of Aberystwyth as about to be restored
18 × 24⅛ (45.8 × 61.2) D.1547–1896

SWINDON (GORSE HILL), Wiltshire. Church of St. Barnabas

Plans, elevations and details (on 2 sheets) of doors. c.1885. Stamped Dutton and Powers, Art Craftsmen in Metals, etc., Manchester. Insc. Gorse Hill Church and D.1565 Swindon Pencil, pen and ink, and wash on tracing paper.
D.1564, 1565–1896

Door between vestry and chancel. Plans, elevations and details. Scale inch
11 × 17⅝ (28 × 44.7) D.1564–1896

West doors. Plan. Inside and outside elevations. Scale inch. Insc. Two pairs doors as this
14½ × 19⅛ (36.7 × 48.6) D.1565–1896

The church survives in Cricklade Road.

TEMPLETON, Dyfed. Church of St. John

Plan and elevation (on 2 sheets) showing alterations to existing
building. 1858.
Pencil and water-colour
D.701, 702–1896

Ground plan. Insc. *Templeton*, with details of the *Accommodation*
including *Total 250 adults & children promiscuously*, and *The
aisle shd be on the other side. Prichard & Seddon* etc. d. *Dec 1858*.
9⅝ × 12⅜ (24.4 × 31.3) D.702–1896

South elevation. Insc. *wd not slate roof with copings be more
suitable? How about money for it?* Initialled *J.P.*
9⅝ × 12⅜ (24.4 × 31.3) D.701–1896

The *Ecclesiologist* noticed Prichard and Seddon's design in 1860:
'It is very simple . . . with merely nave and chancel, a small
vestry north of the chancel, and a western bell gable. The style is
Early-pointed. The church was consecrated on 25 June 1862 and
cost about £750.

Ecc, XXI, 1860, p.50
CB, 1862, p.170

TRURO, Cornwall. Church

Sketch plans and sections (on 3 sheets) depicting different
schemes. 1880.
D.1302, 1306 insc. *Design for a church near Truro.* D.1302.
D.1303 pencil. D.1306 pen and ink on linen.
D.1302, 1303, 1306–1896

Sketch ground plan and transverse section. Scale *1″ = 16 feet.*
Insc. *Accomdn 600 in nave.* Numbered *1*
13¾ × 12¾ (34.8 × 32.3) D.1302–1896

Sketch ground plan and transverse section. Insc. with
measurements. Numbered *2*
15 × 12⅝ (37.9 × 32.1) D.1303–1896

Ground plan. Scale linear. s. *John P. Seddon* and insc. with
details of the *Accommodation* including *850 adults & 100
children*, and *estimate nave and school £7,500.* d. *Dec. 1880*
8½ × 13⅛ (21.7 × 33.4) D.1306–1896

Apparently not built. Pevsner lists no church by Seddon near
Truro.

TYNANT, Glamorgan. Church

Perspective view, plan, elevations and sections (on 6 sheets) for
Thomas Booker. 1854. Not executed.
Lettered *Prichard and Seddon* etc. D.685-9 insc. *Tynant Church.*
Pen and ink, and water-colour. D.685–689 mounted on linen.
D.684–689–1896

Perspective from the south east. Insc. *not executed. For Thos
Booker* Esq.
19½ × 12⅝ (49.6 × 32.1) D.684–1896

Ground plan. Scale linear. Insc. with details of *Accommodation*
including *Total 456 sittings.* d. *Oct. 1854*
16½ × 22½ (42 × 57.1) D.685–1896

West elevation. Scale linear
22½ × 16½ (57.1 × 42) D.686–1896

Probably exhib. at the Architectural Exhibition, 1854-5, no. 309.
'W. Elevation. Church about to be erected by Thomas Booker
MP at Tyn-y-nant in parish of Radyr nr Cardiff'.

East elevation. Scale linear
22½ × 16½ (57.1 × 42) D.687–1896
Probably exhib. at the Architectural Exhibition, 1854-5,
no. 311 (see above).

Tynant, Church D.684–1896

Longitudinal section looking north. Scale linear
22½ × 16½ (57.1 × 42) D.688–1896

Transverse section looking east. Scale linear
22½ × 16½ (57.1 × 42) D.689–1896

Seddon also showed a south elevation at the Architectural
Exhibition, 1854-5, no. 313 which is not included in this collection. The *Ecclesiologist* noticed Prichard and Seddon's design in
1856 remarking: 'The west spirelet, of stone, rises too much into
the proportions of a small spire'.

J. Hilling, *Plans and Prospects* suggests that this church may be
an early design for All Saints at Cwmavon, near Port Talbot,
Glamorgan.

Ecc, XVII, 1856, p.310

ULLENHALL, Warwickshire. Vicarage

Plans, elevations and sections (on 12 sheets) depicting three
different schemes for the Rev. J. George. 1873.
D.1336-42, 1344-47, 1465 insc. *Design for Ullenhall Vicarage* or
similar. D.1336-41, 1345-47 insc. *John P. Seddon Architect.*
D.1336, 1338, 1340, 1342, 1344, 1346 insc. with names of
rooms. D.1342, 1344, 1465 stamped *Approved Ecclesiastical
Commissioners for England*, insc. *conditionally see specification* and
s. *Clark and Smallwood.* D.1336, 1341, 1342, 1344-46 insc. with
measurements.
D.1336, 1338, 1340-42, 1344-46 pencil, pen and ink, and
water-colour. D.1337, 1339, 1347, 1465 pencil and water-
colour.
D.1336–1342, 1344–1347, 1465–1896

Plan of roof timbers. Roof plan. Section on AB. Section CD. Section on EF. Plan of fowl house. Side elevation of fowl house. End elevation of fowl house. Longitudinal section thro' stables. Cross section thro' stables. Scale ⅛th and linear. d. *July 1* (rest missing)
24⅛ × 16½ (61.3 × 41.9) D.1345–1896

Cellar plan. Ground plan. First floor plan. 2nd floor plan. Loft plan. Scale ⅛th. d. *June 14th 1873* and insc. *For the Rev'd J. George*
24⅜ × 16⅝ (61.9 × 42.2) D.1346–1896

North east elevation. South east elevation. North west elevation. South west elevation. Side elevation of stables. Scale ⅛th and linear. d. *July 1873*
24⅜ × 16½ (61.8 × 41.9) D.1347–1896

Ground plan. Cellar plan. Some lightly sketched elevations. Scale *8 ft to an inch* and linear. d. *September 26 1873.*
12½ × 18 (31.8 × 45.6) D.1336–1896

First floor plan. Attic plan. Scale *8 ft to an inch.* d. *September 26 1873*
12⅛ × 17¾ (30.9 × 44.9) D.1338–1896

Roof plan. Plan of roof timbers. North west elevation. Scale *8 ft to an inch.* d. *September 26 1873* and insc. *Amended plan*
18⅛ × 12 (46 × 30.7) D.1340–1896

South west elevation. Scale *8 ft to an inch* and linear. d. *September 26 1873*
12 × 17½ (30.5 × 44.3) D.1337–1896

North east elevation. Scale *8 ft to an inch* and linear. d. *September 26 1873* and insc. *Amended plan*
12¼ × 17½ (31 × 44.4) D.1339–1896

South east elevation. North west elevation. South west elevation (cut through)
19½ × 14⅝ (49.6 × 37.3) D.1465–1896

South east elevation. Section on line AB. Section on line CD. Section on line EF. Scale *8 feet to an inch* and linear. d. *September 26 1873*
18½ × 12⅜ (47 × 31.5) D.1341–1896

Cellar plan. Ground plan. *Front elevation.* Scale *8 feet to an inch* and linear. d. *December 3 187[3]* (on 2 sheets)
20⅛ × 15⅛ (51.2 × 38.3) D.1342–1896

Chamber plan. Roof plan. Attic plan. Plan of loft etc. over stables. Section on AB. Section on CD. Section on EF. Scale *8 feet to an inch.* d. with a stamp *12 Dec 1873*
21½ × 15⅛ (54.6 × 38.4) D.1344–1896

Seddon designed the church of St. Mary at Ullenhall in 1875. (The pulpit and reading desk were illustrated in the *BA*, 10 February 1882.)

UPAVON, Wiltshire. Church of St. Mary

Part section and part elevations of roof showing *rafters, ceiling* and *cradling.* Scale linear. Insc. (crossed out in blue crayon) *Upavon Church Wilts* and with measurements. c.1875.
Pen and ink on tracing paper
10¾ × 20 (27 × 50.7) D.1517–1896

Basically Norman, the chancel restored by T. H. Wyatt and the nave by Seddon.

Lit. Pevsner, *Wiltshire*, 1963, pp.482–3

WARE, Hertfordshire. Billiard room

Plan, elevations, sections and details (on 2 sheets) of billiard room. Both insc. *Gwyn Jeffrys Esq. Billiard room.* 1874
Pencil and water-colour
D.1533, 1538–1896

Plan. End elevation. ½ *side elevation. Cross section.* ½ *longitudinal section.* Details. Insc. *At Ware*
22 × 30 (56 × 76) D.1538–1896

Amended design. ½ *side elevation.* ½ *longitudinal section. Cross section.* Scale ½″ *to a foot.* d. *January 2 1874.* s. *John P. Seddon, Architect.* Insc. with measurements
15¾ × 28¼ (40 × 71.7) D.1533–1896

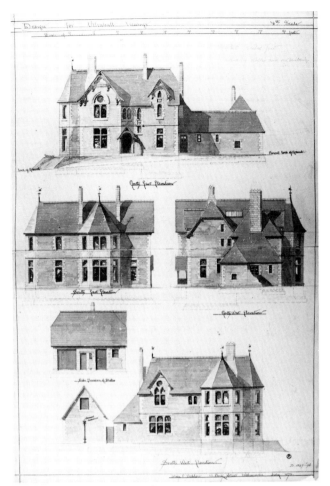

Ullenhall, Vicarage D.1347–1896

WESTON UNDER PENYARD, Herefordshire. School

Plans, elevations, sections and details (on 9 sheets) depicting three schemes. c.1860.
D.986–933 insc. *Weston-under-Penyard, Herefordshire. Design for Schools.* D.986–988, 990–993 stamped *Prichard and Seddon.* D.989, 990 insc. with measurements and D.986, 989, 990 with names of rooms.
D.986, 987, 990–992 pencil, pen and ink, and water-colour.
D.988, 989, 993 pen and ink, and water-colour. D.994 pencil and wash.
D.986–994–1896

Ground plan. First floor plan. Transverse section (of house). Thumbnail sketch elevation. Scale *8 feet to one inch.* Numbered *1.* Alterations indicated in pencil
18⅝ × 12⅞ (47.5 × 32.6) D.986–1896

North elevation. South elevation. Scale *8 feet to one inch.* Numbered *2*
18⅝ × 12⅞ (47.5 × 33.4) D.987–1896

West elevation. East elevation. Longitudinal section. Scale *8 feet to one inch.* Wm. *1860.* Numbered *3*
18⅞ × 13⅛ (47.5 × 33.4) D.988–1896

Ground plan. Front elevation. Scale *8th inch to a foot.* s. *J. P. Seddon*
19 × 13 (48.4 × 33) D.989–1896

Part of front elevation
20⅞ × 29¾ (52.7 × 75.5) D.994–1896

Ground plan. Chamber plan. Front elevation. Side elevation. Section on line AB. Scale *8 feet to one inch.* Numbered *1* and insc. *as executed*
19¼ × 15½ (49 × 39.4) D.990–1896

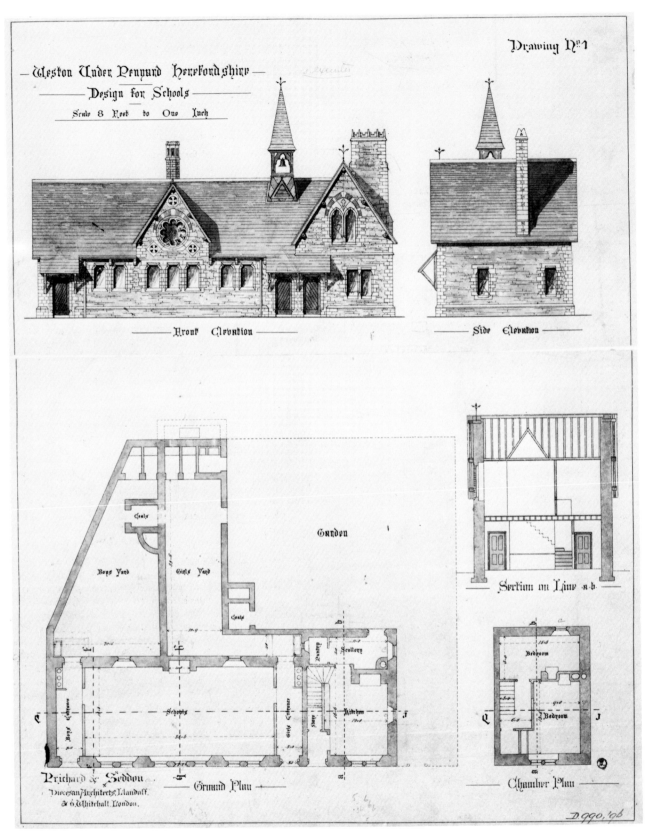

Drawing Nº 1

Weston Under Penyard Herefordshire
Design for Schools
Scale 8 Feet to One Inch

Front Elevation

Side Elevation

Section on Line a·b

Boys Yard

Girls Yard

Garden

Coals

Coals

Schools

Kitchen

Scullery

Pantry

Store

Boys Entrance

Girls Entrance

Bedroom

Bedroom

Prichard & Seddon
Diocesan Architects, Llandaff.
& 6, Whitehall, London.

Ground Plan

Chamber Plan

D.990, '96

Weston under Penyard D.990–1896

Back elevation. North elevation. Scale 8 feet to one inch. Numbered 2
$17\frac{1}{4} \times 12\frac{3}{4}$ (43.8×32.5) D.991–1896

Roof plan. Longitudinal section CD. Section on line CF. Section on line GH. Numbered 3
$17\frac{1}{4} \times 12\frac{1}{4}$ (43.8×31) D.992–1896

Plan, elevations and sections of chimneys. Scale $\frac{1}{2}$ *inch to a foot* and $\frac{1}{4}$ *full size.* Wm. *1859.* On the back is an elevation of part of a Gothic window
$19\frac{1}{2} \times 14$ (49.6×35.5) D.993–1896

D.986-8 depict the first scheme, D.989, 994 the second and D.990-3 the third. The third scheme was built with a few minor alterations to details. The amended design for the porches indicated by Seddon on D.990 was carried out. The bell turret and spire have now gone and several new class-rooms have been added at the back.

Seddon was also involved in alterations to the church at Weston-under-Penyard in 1865 (documents in Hereford Record Office).

WHITCHURCH, Herefordshire. Church

Plan of proposed tiling. Scale *1 inch.* Insc. *J. F. Campbell, Esq., Woodseat* and *General Nicholl, The Grange, Whitchurch, nr Ross.* d. *June 94*
Pencil, pen and ink, and water- and body-colour
$29\frac{3}{4} \times 19\frac{7}{8}$ (75.6 × 50.6) D.2127 1896

Seddon designed the School at Whitchurch in 1858 (*Ecc*, XIX, 1858, p.277).

WYESHAM, Gwent. Church of St. James

Plans, elevations, sections and details (on 6 sheets). 1872.
D.1298, 1299, 1511-13, 1571 insc. *Wyesham Church* or similar.
D.1298, 1512, 1513, 1571 s. or insc. *John* or *J. P. Seddon* and
D.1512 addressed *12 Park St., Westminster.*
D.1298, 1299 pencil. D.1512, 1513 pencil, pen and ink and water-colour on tracing paper. D.1511 pen and ink on tracing paper. D.1571 pencil and water-colour on tracing paper.
D.1298, 1299, 1511–1513, 1571–1896

Plan. South elevation. End elevation. Transverse section. Scale $\frac{1}{8}$*th.* d. *1872.* Insc. with details of the *accommodation* including *total adults & children 225.*
$18\frac{3}{4} \times 14$ (47.6 × 35.5) D.1298–1896

Alternative plan and section. Scale $\frac{1}{8}$*th.* Insc. *to hold 200* and with itemised *estimate without chancel*
$10\frac{1}{2} \times 16\frac{7}{8}$ (26.8 × 43) D.1299–1896

Part section and part elevation of roof. Scale linear. Insc. with measurements
12 × 16 (30.5 × 40.7) D.1511–1896

Details of roof including part section and part elevations. Scale $\frac{1}{2}$ *inch.* d. *June 27 1872.* Insc. with details of size of the *scantlings* and stamped *Incorporated Church Building Society. Plans approved.* The date *July 6 1872* has been added in manuscript
$16\frac{1}{2} \times 14\frac{3}{8}$ (42 × 36.6) D.1512–1896

Part section and details of roof. Scale *inch.* Insc. *this roof is exceedingly stiff* and with a note and measurement. Torn
$19\frac{5}{8} \times 22\frac{1}{4}$ (50 × 56.5) D.1513–1896

Details of *doorcase & screws of gunmetal.* Scale *full size.* Insc. with a note about the position of the screws. d. *June 5th 1873*
$10\frac{3}{8} \times 8\frac{5}{8}$ (26.5 × 22) D.1571–1896

The *British Architect* noticed the church in 1885 remarking that it was: 'studiously plain, but well suits the lovely pastoral site it occupies, and forms part of a pleasing group with the schools alongside, built by the same architect . . . The interior of this church is extremely pleasing; the cost was only some £1,700'. The church is unusual in Seddon's oeuvre in that it has a saddle-backed tower. The schools still survive though the church is now surrounded by modern housing estates. A board over the door of the church records that the Incorporated Church Building Society gave £70 towards its cost.

Br, 17 August 1885, pp.30-1 (illus)

AUSTRALIA, Melbourne. Bank

Elevations (on 2 sheets). 1880.
D.1361 pencil. D.1423 pen and ink on tracing paper.
D.1361, 1423–1896

Side elevation. Insc. *Melbourne bank*
$14\frac{1}{4} \times 19\frac{3}{4}$ (36.3 × 50.3) D.1361–1896

Front elevation
$20\frac{3}{8} \times 14$ (51.7 × 35.6) D.1423–1896

The bank was proposed for a prominent site in the City of Melbourne. The conditions were rather unusual as the *British Architect* explained: 'Stone being costly, it was necessary that its use should be economised to the utmost extent; terra cotta, or some such material, being substituted for the general framework, and intermediate surfaces being plated with mosaic or tilework, so as to produce an artistic effect at moderate expenditure.

Mr Seddon has, therefore, contemplated in his design the employment of Messrs. Rust's glass mosaic (in the same manner that he has used it upon the facade of Messrs. Rust's manufactory on the Albert Embankment), enclosed within a framework of rose-coloured terra cotta. The roof would be covered with green slates. The portion of the building represented in our illustration is the principal facade, with offices on ground floor and mezzanine, answering to the one storey, 30 feet high, of the bank behind them. Over these is, on the first floor, the suite of rooms for the manager, and above, two floors of bedrooms'.

The bank does not appear to have been built.

BA, 9 January 1880 (illus)

TURKEY, INSTANBUL. Crimean War Memorial Church

S-Constantinople. Exterior *Elevation of one bay of nave. Half section thro' nave looking east. Interior elevation of one bay of Nave.* Plans of each of preceding. Insc. *Prichard and Seddon* etc. A circular device pasted onto the sheet bears the motto *Magna est veritas et prevalebit*
$24\frac{1}{4} \times 29$ (61.5 × 73.5) D.735–1896

The decision to build a memorial church to the Crimean war in Constantinople was taken at a meeting on 28 April 1856 presided over by the Duke of Cambridge. An open competition for designs was favoured and the rules stated that the style of the proposed church should be a modification, to suit the climate, of the 'Pointed, or Gothic' and that 'the neglect on the part of any architect of this provision will absolutely exclude from competition'. The design was to be for a church big enough to accommodate 700 people and was to cost not more than £20,000. The judges were to be the Bishop of Ripon, Sir Charles Anderson, Bart, the Dean of Ely, Professor Willis, and A. J. Beresford Hope, and the first prize was £100. Some 41 designs were sent in early in 1857 and the committee's choice was 1st W. Burges, 2nd G. E. Street, 3rd G. Bodley. The design by W. Slater was recommended for an extra prize, and Mention was made of those by C. Gray, R. P. Pullan, G. Truefitt, Weightman, Hadfield and Goldie, William White, A. Bell Howell and Budd, and Prichard and Seddon. In fact, after work had begun on Burges's design it was abandoned because of high building costs, and G. E. Street's design was carried out instead. The building was completed by 1869.

Br, 28 Feb 1857, pp.115-16
Victorian Church Art, 1971, p.45

Designs for unidentified localities

Specific Clients

ABERGAVENNY, Lord

Sketch elevations of chimneypieces, and details of dining tables (on 3 sheets).
D.1610, 1611 pencil and water-colour. D.1891 pencil. D.1610 and 1611 are one sheet cut into two.
D.1610, 1611, 1891–1896

Designs for chimneypieces for Lord Abergavenny. Scale *inch to a foot*
$10\frac{1}{8} \times 15$ (26.2 × 38) D.1610–1896

Design for a chimneypiece. s. *John P. Seddon Archt.*
$9\frac{1}{2} \times 15$ (24.4 × 38) D.1611–1896

Details of *Lord Abergavenny's dining tables*. Scale $\frac{1}{8}$*th full size*.
Insc. with measurements and *Pitch pine*
$13\frac{7}{8} \times 21\frac{1}{4}$ (35.3 × 54) D.1891–1896

BROCK, Allan

Design for a screen for Allan Brock Esq. Plan. Elevation. Scale *inch.*
Insc. *Seddon delt.* d. *April 6th 64*
Pencil and water-colour
$18\frac{1}{8} \times 12\frac{3}{4}$ (46.1 × 32.3) D.1859–1896

BURRELL, Sir Percy

Design for inscription for granite tomb. Scale *inch & quarter to a foot* and linear. The tomb is inscribed *In reverend and beloved memory of Sir Percy Burrell Bart MP. Died 19 July 1876. Born 12 Feb 1812. Married 26 Aug 1865 Henrietta Katherine Daughter and co-heir of Sir Geo. Brooke Pechell Bart MP.* Insc. *J. P. Seddon Archt. 1 Queen Anne's Gate Westminster SW.* d. *Decr. 1877*
Pencil
$8\frac{5}{8} \times 12\frac{1}{8}$ (21.8 × 30.7) D.1924–1896

BURROUGHES, T. H.

Plans, elevations, sections and details (on 2 sheets) of cottages. Both insc. with measurements and names of rooms.
D.1437 pencil and water-colour.
D.1437, 1448–1896

Cottage for T. Burroughs Esq. Ground plan. Chamber plan. End elevation. Front elevation. Back elevation. Sketch section.
Insc. *Lingwood Lodge, Norwich*
$10\frac{3}{4} \times 15\frac{1}{4}$ (27.2 × 38.7) D.1437–1896

Design for double cottage for T. H. Burroughes Esq. Ground plan. Chamber plan. Front elevation. Back elevation. End elevation. Cross section. Longitudinal section. Plan of dormer. Details. Scale $\frac{1}{8}$ *of an inch to a foot*, $\frac{1}{2}$ *an inch to a foot* and linear. Insc. *John P. Seddon Archt. 12 Park St. Westminster*. d. *Jan 29 1870*
$19\frac{1}{8} \times 13\frac{1}{8}$ (48.4 × 33.4) D.1448–1896

BYASS, R. B.

Plans, elevations and sections (on 10 sheets) depicting two different schemes for a villa.
Insc. *Prichard & Seddon* etc. D.1057–1059 initialled *R.C.J.*
D.1052-57, 1059, 1060 insc. *Design for a villa for R. B. Byass Esq* and D.1052, 1053, 1056, 1060 with names of rooms.
D.1052, 1053, 1056 pen and ink on tracing paper. D.1054, 1055, 1057-59 pencil, pen and ink on tracing paper
D.1052–1054, 1054A, 1055–1060–1896

Basement plan. Ground plan. Scale $\frac{1}{8}$*th*
$18\frac{7}{8} \times 12\frac{3}{4}$ (48 × 32.2) D.1052–1896

First floor plan. Attic plan. Scale $\frac{1}{8}$*th*
$18\frac{7}{8} \times 12\frac{3}{4}$ (48 × 32.2) D.1053–1896

Front elevation. Back elevation. Scale $\frac{1}{8}$*th*
$18\frac{7}{8} \times 12\frac{3}{4}$ (48 × 32.2) D.1054–1896

End elevation. End elevation. Scale $\frac{1}{8}$*th*
$18\frac{7}{8} \times 12\frac{3}{4}$ (48 × 32.2) D.1054A–1896

Section AB. Section CD. Scale $\frac{1}{8}$*th*
$18\frac{7}{8} \times 12\frac{3}{4}$ (48 × 32.2) D.1055–1896

Ground plan. First floor plan. Scale *8 feet to one inch*
$16\frac{1}{8} \times 23\frac{1}{8}$ (41 × 58.8) D.1056–1896

Elevation of entrance front. Scale $\frac{1}{8}$*th*
$16\frac{1}{4} \times 21\frac{1}{4}$ (41.2 × 54) D.1059–1896

Cellar plan. Second floor plan. Section on line CD. Scale *8 feet to one inch*
$16\frac{1}{4} \times 23\frac{1}{4}$ (41.2 × 59) D.1060–1896

Garden front. Scale $\frac{1}{8}$*th*
$16\frac{1}{2} \times 22\frac{3}{4}$ (42 × 57.7) D.1057–1896

Front next yard. End elevation. Section AB. Elevation of *stable.*
Scale $\frac{1}{8}$*th*
$22\frac{5}{8} \times 16\frac{1}{2}$ (57.6 × 41.8) D.1058–1896

CHANCE, R. L.

Design for sideboard. Elevation. Plan. Scale *inch.* Insc. *R. L. Chance Esqr* and with notes. s. *J. P. Seddon.* d. *1863*
Pencil, pen and ink, and water-colour
$18\frac{1}{2} \times 12\frac{7}{8}$ (46.8 × 32.7) D.1800–1896

Copy of above. s. *J. P. Seddon Archt* and addressed *12 Park*
Pen and ink, and water-colour on tracing paper
$17\frac{5}{8} \times 12$ (44.8 × 30.5) D.1801–1896

Design for bookcase & commode. Walnut. Scale *inch.* Insc. *R. L. Chance Esq.* s. *John P. Seddon.* d. *1863.*
Pencil and water-colour
$12\frac{7}{8} \times 18\frac{5}{8}$ (32.7 × 47.3) D.1793–1896

Tracing of above
$9\frac{1}{4} \times 15$ (23.4 × 38) D.1816–1896

Design for pier table & glass on bracket. Design for commode of simple character. Insc. *R. L. Chance Esq.* s. *John P. Seddon Archt 12 Park St Westminster*
$12\frac{3}{4} \times 18\frac{1}{4}$ (32.5 × 46.5) D.1856–1896

Design for ch[imne]y glass for dining rm. Plan. Elevation. Scale *inch.*
Insc. *R. L. Chance Esq* and with notes. s. *John P. Seddon.* d. *1863*
Pencil and water-colour
$18\frac{5}{8} \times 12\frac{7}{8}$ (47.3 × 32.7) D.1858–1896

CORNISH, J. G.

Boundary walls. General view. Elevation of boundary wall and gates. Scale $\frac{1}{2}$ *inch* and $\frac{1}{8}$ *inch* (on 2 sheets, one is traced from the other). Insc. *Prichard & Seddon* etc. and with notes.
D.1588 pencil, pen and ink, and water-colour. D.1605 pencil, and pen and ink on tracing paper
$13 \times 19\frac{1}{8}$ (33 × 48.5) D.1588–1896
$8 \times 8\frac{7}{8}$ (20.3 × 22.5) D.1605–1896

FREEMAN, E. A.

Plans, elevations and a section (on 2 sheets) depicting alternative designs for a bay window. D.882 insc. *E. A. Freeman Esq. Design for bow window. Prichard & Seddon* etc. and *Rev'd Dr Millard, High St., Oxford.* Scale $\frac{1}{8}$*th inch*
D.882 pencil, pen and ink, and wash on tracing paper. D.884 pen and ink, and pencil.
$11 \times 8\frac{3}{8}$ (27.8 × 21.2) D.882–1896
$21\frac{1}{2} \times 15$ (55 × 38.3) D.884–1896

R. B. Byas. Villa D.1059–1896

JOB, W.

Design for hall table for W. Job Esq. Elevation. Section. Side. ½ *plan of top.* ½ *plan below.* Scale *inch.* Insc. *Seddon*
Pencil and water-colour
$12\frac{5}{8} \times 18\frac{5}{8}$ (32 × 47.3) D.1880–1896

LEAF, W.

Design for chandelier. W. Leaf Esq. s. *J. P. Seddon.* d. *1862*
Pencil
13 × 8¾ (33 × 22.2) D.1948–1896

Design for gas bracket for boudoir. W. Leaf Esq. s. *J. P. Seddon.*
d. *1862*
Pencil
$8\frac{7}{8} \times 13$ (22.4 × 33) D.1949–1896

MATTHEWS, Reverend

Two sketch elevations of a house. Insc. *Revd Matthews* and
s. *J. P. Seddon Architect.* d. *April 1872*
Pencil
$16\frac{1}{4} \times 11\frac{3}{8}$ (41.4 × 28.9) D.1440–1896

MEEKING, C.

*Sketch for organ for C. Meeking Esq. Plan at AA. Plan at BB.
Elevation. Section.* Scale *1 inch to a foot.* Insc. with notes abouts
materials and cost, and with measurements. s. *John P. Seddon.*
d. *1862*
Pencil, pen and ink and water-colour
22 × 15⅛ (56 × 38.7) D.1639–1896

Elevation of an organ showing two different treatments.
Possibly for C. Meeking.
Pencil, pen and ink, and water-colour
18 × 12½ (46 × 31.7) D.1641–1896

MOORE, W. F. N.

*W. F. N. Moore Esq. Design for hall table. Front. Side. Top of
table. Design for flower stand. Bracket in hall.* Scale *inch.* s. *J. P.
Seddon.* d. *June 1863*
Pencil and water-colour
$18\frac{5}{8} \times 12\frac{7}{8}$ (47.3 × 32.7) D.1883–1896

Tracings of above. s. *J. P. Seddon Archt. 12 Park Street,
Westminster*
$7\frac{1}{2} \times 12\frac{1}{4}$ (20 × 31.3) D.1864, 1865–1896

Design for wardrobe. s. in blue crayon *John P. Seddon.* Insc. in
blue crayon *Moore Esq.* and with notes
Pencil and water-colour
$13\frac{1}{4} \times 13\frac{1}{8}$ (33.6 × 33.2) D.1787–1896

POOLE, M. R.

*No. 2 Cottage for Mr Poole. Details of masonry. Plans, elevations
and a section of chimneys and windows.* Scale ½ *inch.* s. *J. P.
Seddon, Architect, 12 Park St. Westr.* d. *Nov 9 1871.* Insc. with
measurements
Pen and ink, pencil and water-colour
$13 \times 9\frac{3}{8}$ (33 × 23.9) D.1436–1896
(Possibly the Rev'd Poole for whom Seddon designed
Hoarwithy church, etc.?)

POWYS KECK, H. J. (?)

Perspective sketch. Ground plan. First floor plan. Front elevation. Side elevation. Section on line AB. Small house *for H. J. Powys Keck* [?] *Esq.* s. *J. P. Seddon, 1 Queen Anne's Gate.* Insc. with names of rooms and measurements. Wm. *1875*
Pencil, pen and ink, and water-colour
17⅞ × 11¾ (44.2 × 30) D.1443–1896

PRICHARD, J.

Mr Prichard's dining table. Inlaid work omitted. Part top view showing inlay of architect's drawing instruments. Insc. *This molding has been omitted in execution.* Scale *⅛th real size* and *full size*
Pen and ink, and wash on tracing paper
14¾ × 19⅝ (37.4 × 50) D.1875–1896

RANSOME

Design for tomb for — Ransome Esqre. Plan of top. Side view. Head. Front and details. Scale *⅛th real size* and *full size.* s. *John P. Seddon 12 Park St.* (part torn off)
Pen and ink, and water-colour
12¾ × 18½ (32.4 × 47.2) D.1933–1896

ROBINSON, G.

Design for a lodge for G. Robinson Esq. Ground plan and plan of garden. *First floor plan.* Two elevations. Scale *⅛th* (On the back is a part plan of a school). s. *John P. Seddon.* d. *Aug 1886.*
Insc. with measurements and names of rooms
Pencil and water-colour
14¼ × 10¾ (36.3 × 27.2) D.1456–1896

SPORUN, Lewis

Flat monumental slab to memory of Lewis Sporun Esq.
Design (3 copies) for a memorial slab insc. *Until the day break and the shadows flee away.* s. *John P. Seddon.* D.1767A insc. in pencil.
D.1766 pencil and water-colour. D.1767 pen and ink on tracing paper. D.1767A Lithograph
Largest 18 × 12⅛ (45.5 × 30.7) D.1766–1767A–1896

VERDON, Sir George

Plans, elevations sections and details (on 5 sheets) for additions to a cottage. Each insc. *Additions to cottage for Sir George Verdon. J. P. Seddon, 1 Queen Anne's Gate Westminster* and with notes, measurements and names of rooms
Pencil, ink and water-colour
D.1466–1470–1896

Ground plan no. 1. Principal front elevation no. 3. Scale linear
24 × 16¾ (61 × 42.4) D.1466–1896

First floor plan no. 2. Plan of floor in roof no. 4. Side elevation no. 4. Side elevation no. 4. Section AB no. 2. Section CD no. 2. Section EF no. 2. Section AB no. 4. Scale linear
17 × 24 (43 × 61) D.1467–1896

Roof plan. Roof plan no. 2. Part plans of drawing room. *Section of drawing room.* Scale linear
24½ × 16⅝ (62.1 × 42.3) D.1468–1896

Detail drawing no. 8. Plans, elevations, sections and details of dormer, gable, cornice, etc. Scale linear and *full size.* d. *Sept. 1879*
29⅜ × 21 (74.7 × 53.3) D.1470–1896

Detail drawing no. 9. Plans, elevations, sections and details of chimneys, a door and dining room fireplace and window. Scale linear and *full size.* d. *September 1879*
21 × 29⅜ (53.2 × 74.7) D.1469–1896

WARD, J. E.

Cottage for J. E. Ward Esq. Ground floor plan. First floor plan. Roof plan. Front elevation. Side elevation. Back elevation. Side elevation. Section. Plan of coal house & earth closet. End elevation. Scale linear.
Insc. with measurements and names of rooms
Pencil, pen and ink, and water-colour
12⅛ × 18½ (31 × 47) D.1464–1896

WESTHOPP, M. R. (?)

Mr Westhopps [?] *firedogs. Plan. Side view. End.* Details. Scale *1½*
Pencil and wash on tracing paper
4⅛ × 13⅜ (10.3 × 34) D.1981–1896

WILDE, S. C.

Design for eight cottages for S. C. Wilde Esq. Half plan of ground floor. Half plan of upper floor. Front elevation. Back elevation. End elevation. Section. Scale 8th. Insc. *J. P. Seddon Architect, 12 Park St. Westminster* and with names of rooms and measurements and *£914 for 8 cottages.* d. (?) *1869*
Pen and ink, and water-colour
17¼ × 24 (43.8 × 61) D.1491–1896

Cottages, Stables, a Toll House, etc.

Design for a triple cottage. Ground plan. Chamber plan. Front elevation. Scale linear and *⅛ of an inch to a foot.* Insc. *John P. Seddon Archt. 12 Park St. Westminster.* d. *Mar 1st 1871.* Insc. with measurements and names of rooms
Pencil, pen and ink, and water-colour
19 × 13¼ (48.4 × 33.7) D.1451–1896

Design for a row of six cottages. Half ground plan. Half plan of upper floor. Front elevation. Scale ⅛. Lettered *J. P. Seddon Archt. 12 Park St. Westminster.* Insc. with notes, measurements and names of rooms
Pencil, ink and water-colour
12⅞ × 18½ (32.6 × 47.1) D.1454–1896

Ground plan of a double cottage. Insc. with names of rooms, measurements, etc. and *belongs to Mr Seddon*
Pencil, pen and ink, and wash on tracing paper
12½ × 9 (31.8 × 22.7) D.1455–1896

Plans, elevations and details of a pair of cottages. Insc. with notes, measurements and details for *BN* and *plan and perspective for book*
Pen and ink, and pencil
13⅛ × 19⅛ (33.5 × 48.5) D.1458–1896

Plans, elevations, sections and details (on 2 sheets) of a pair of cottages. Lettered *J. P. Seddon, 12 Park St. Westmr* and insc. with names of rooms and measurements
D.1446 pen and ink, and water-colour on tracing paper.
D.1447 pencil and water-colour
D.1446, 1447–1896

Design for a pair of cottages. Ground plan. Plan of upper floor. Front elevation. Back elevation. Side elevation. Cross section. Thumbnail perspective sketch. Scale ⅛
12 × 17⅛ (30.5 × 43.5) D.1446–1896

Details of double cottage. Plan, elevations and sections of chimney, windows and door. Scale ½ *inch*
13 × 18⅝ (33 × 47.5) D.1447–1896

Design for a cottage. Ground plan. Plan of bedrooms etc. Front elevation. Back elevation. Side elevation. Side elevation. Elevations and sections of details. Scale *⅛th of an inch to a foot* and *½ an inch to a foot.* Insc. *John P. Seddon Archt. 12 Park St. Westminster,* and with names of rooms and measurements. d. *May 1871*
Pen and ink, and water-colour
19⅛ × 13¼ (48.4 × 33.8) D.1449–1896

Design for a row of cottages. Ground floor plan. First floor plan. Plan of attics. Front elevation. Section. Insc. *J. P. Seddon Archt. 12, Park St. Westminster* and with names of rooms, measurements and *three bedrooms each* and *to be returned*
Pencil, pen and ink, and water-colour
$18\frac{3}{4} \times 12\frac{3}{4}$ (47.5 × 32.5) D.1450–1896

Design for a cottage. Ground plan. Chamber plan. Front elevation. Side elevation. Back elevation. Section AB. Scale linear. On the back part of an elevation of the reredos at St. Peter's, Mancroft, Norwich
Pen and ink
$14 \times 21\frac{1}{2}$ (35.6 × 53.8) D.1476–1896

Sketch plans, elevations and sections (on 1 sheet in 2 pieces) for a stable with a central clock tower
Pencil
$15\frac{7}{8} \times 12\frac{1}{8}$ (40.3 × 30.7) D.1369–1896
$16\frac{3}{4} \times 13\frac{1}{4}$ (42.5 × 33.8) D.1452–1896

Design for a toll house. s. *John P. Seddon*
Pencil and water-colour
$10\frac{3}{8} \times 13\frac{3}{8}$ (26.4 × 36.5) D.1590–1896

Elevation of above showing gates on either side
Pen and ink, and brown wash
$12\frac{3}{8} \times 20$ (31.5 × 50.6) D.1591–1896

Gardener's cottage and entrance gates. No. 14. Elevation of entrance gate with part of the side elevation of lodge. Scale linear
Pencil, pen and ink, and water-colour
$11\frac{1}{4} \times 17\frac{1}{8}$ (28.6 × 43.6) D.1587–1896

Plans, elevations and sections (on 3 sheets) of a small building comprising a single room with pitched roof. On the back are printed plans of the University of Wales, Aberystwyth
Pencil
Each $13\frac{1}{2} \times 19\frac{7}{8}$ (34.4 × 50.3) D.1373–1896

See also *Ecclesiastical including Monuments* D.1587–1896

Ecclesiastical including Monuments

Sketch perspective of west entrance of a large church
Pen and ink on tracing paper
$9\frac{1}{2} \times 7\frac{1}{2}$ (24 × 19.3) D.1309–1896

Plan. East elevation. West elevation of a church. Insc. with details of the *accommodation* including *total 223*
Pencil, pen and ink, and water-colour
$17 \times 12\frac{1}{2}$ (43 × 31.8) D.1308–1896

Ground *plan* of a church. Insc. with details of the *accommodation* including *Totals 762 adults 16 children*
Pencil on tracing paper
$19\frac{1}{8} \times 29\frac{1}{8}$ (48.7 × 74) D.1311–1896

Elevations of ends of a church
Pen and ink on linen
$15\frac{1}{8} \times 12\frac{1}{8}$ (38.4 × 30.8) D.1307–1896

Sketch ground plan of a part of a church
Pencil
$5\frac{3}{8} \times 5\frac{3}{4}$ (13.7 × 14.5) D.734–1896

Sketch plan and elevation *of church to hold 300* people. On the back plan and elevation of a bay window. Scale *1 inch to a foot.*
Pencil
$13\frac{1}{2} \times 14\frac{3}{4}$ (34.5 × 37.4) D.1441–1896

Plan, elevations and sections of a church with seats for 48 people
Pen and ink, and pencil
$20\frac{1}{8} \times 16$ (51.2 × 40.8) D.1313–1896

Section of a church showing design for decoration of the nave and chancel
Pencil, pen and ink, and water-colour
$11\frac{3}{4} \times 19\frac{3}{8}$ (29.7 × 49.4) D.1688–1896

As above
Pencil, pen and ink, and water-colour
$11\frac{1}{2} \times 19\frac{7}{8}$ (29.2 × 50.5) D.1687–1896

Perspective sketch, plan and part sections of a timber roof probably for a church
Pencil
$11\frac{5}{8} \times 18\frac{1}{8}$ (29.5 × 46) D.1529–1896

Perspective, plan, and sections of a timber roof possibly for part of a church
Pencil
$19\frac{1}{8} \times 13\frac{1}{4}$ (48.5 × 33.7) D.1530–1896

Part elevation and sections of a timber roof probably for a church. Insc. *John P. Seddon, Architect, 12 Park Street Westminster SW* and with measurements, etc.
Pen and ink, and water-colour on tracing paper. Torn
$16\frac{1}{4} \times 10\frac{5}{8}$ (41.2 × 26.8) D.1537–1896

Detail of hinges on outside door west porch. s. *John P. Seddon Architect.* d. *July 14, 74*
Pencil
$36\frac{5}{8} \times 26\frac{3}{4}$ (93 × 68) D.1988–1896

Elevations, sections and details of woodwork (including a chancel screen?) for a church. Scale linear
Pencil, pen and ink
$22 \times 29\frac{5}{8}$ (56 × 79.2) D.1631–1896

Perspectives and ground plan (on 2 sheets) for a church
D.1316 pencil, pen and ink, and water-colour. D.1317 pencil and water-colour
D.1316, 1317–1896

Perspectives from the south east and south west
$24\frac{1}{2} \times 16\frac{1}{2}$ (62 × 41.8) D.1317–1896

Unidentified Church D.1317–1896

Ground plan. Insc. with details of the *accommodation* including *grand total 560* and with measurements
$16\frac{1}{2} \times 24\frac{1}{2}$ (41.8 × 62) D.1316–1896

Perspective from the north east of a church
Wash over preliminary pencil
$14\frac{1}{8} \times 17\frac{1}{4}$ (36.3 × 43.7) D.1318–1896

Plans and elevations of an organ loft. Insc. *this is the new arrangmt to suit organ gallery as executed*
Pencil
$29\frac{7}{8} \times 22\frac{1}{8}$ (75.8 × 56.3) D.1312–1896

Design for part of a ceiling apparently the chancel and apse of a church including the inscription *Holy Holy Lord God of Hosts Glory be to God*
Pencil
$16\frac{1}{2} \times 10\frac{3}{4}$ (41.8 × 27.3) D.1664–1896

St. Donats. Nave roof. Section, elevation of *one bay* and details. Scale $\frac{1}{2}$ *in* and *full size*. Insc. *The nave roof is in every respect an accurate restoration of the grand old roof now existing* and with notes and measurements
Pen and ink, and wash on tracing paper
$12\frac{1}{4} \times 18\frac{3}{8}$ (31.1 × 46.7) D.1509–1896

Design for a tile floor for a church. Scale *inch*. Insc. with notes
Pencil, pen and ink, and water-colour
$10\frac{1}{4} \times 14\frac{3}{8}$ (26 × 36.4) D.2038–1896

Design for tiling the floor of a chancel. Insc. with measurements
Pencil and water-colour
$20\frac{5}{8} \times 11\frac{5}{8}$ (52.5 × 29.6) D.2074–1896

As above
$21\frac{1}{4} \times 13\frac{1}{4}$ (54 × 33.7) D.2075–1896

Design for *Pavinging* [*sic*] *at East end of nave*. Scale *2" to a foot*
Pencil and water-colour
$11\frac{5}{8} \times 13\frac{3}{4}$ (29.5 × 34.8) D.2041–1896

Design for tiling part of the floor of a church. Insc. with measurements and notes
Pencil and water-colour
$11\frac{1}{2} \times 13\frac{3}{4}$ (29.2 × 34.7) D.2051–1896

Design for tiling part of the chancel of a church. Scale $\frac{1}{2}$
Pencil and water-colour
$6\frac{5}{8} \times 5\frac{1}{2}$ (16.8 × 14) D.2085–1896

Design for tiling chancel and aisle of a church. Insc. in ink with notes
Water-colour on graph paper
$4\frac{3}{8} \times 3\frac{5}{8}$ (11.2 × 9.4) D.2095–1896

Design for tiling part of a floor probably for a church. Some of the tiles are insc. with the names of saints, etc.
Pencil and water-colour on tracing paper
$6\frac{1}{2} \times 9\frac{1}{2}$ (16.5 × 24) D.2099–1896

Sketch perspective for a free-standing monument.
Insc. *J. P. Seddon*
Pencil
11 × 8 (28 × 20.3) D.1922–1896

Designs (on 6 sheets) for twenty two coffin-like or slab monuments including plans, elevations and details. Scale *half inch*, $\frac{1}{4}$ *full size* and linear. s. in mauve crayon *J. P. Seddon* and insc. with numbers etc. up to *39*
Pen and ink
$13 \times 10\frac{1}{2}$ (32.8 × 26.6) D.1925, 1927–1931–1896

Design for two tombstones and a coffin-like monument.
s. *J. P. Seddon*
Pencil and water-colour
$12\frac{1}{2} \times 10$ (32 × 25.4) D.1926–1896

Unidentified Church D.1318–1896

Design for a monument D.1938–1896

Perspective view of a large monument with fountains and a canopy to contain three groups of statuary
Pencil, and pen and ink
$26\frac{7}{8} \times 20\frac{1}{8}$ (68.2 × 51.1) D.1938–1896

Is this perhaps the 'Design for a fountain proposed to be executed in Ransome's Patent Stone, for Australia', which Seddon showed at the Architectural Exhibition, 1866 (167)?

Design for a tomb. Plans, elevations and details. Scale $\frac{1}{8}$*th* and *full size*. The slab inscribed *In memory of Thomas Jenkins aged 60 Born Jan 1 1800 Died Dec 31 1860*. Insc. in roundel *Prichard & Seddon* etc. and d. *Oct 1860*
Pen and ink, and water-colour on tracing paper
$13\frac{3}{8} \times 19$ (34 × 48) D.1939–1896

Design for a reredos
Pen and ink, and water colour
$21\frac{1}{2} \times 27$ (54.7 × 68.4) D.1769–1896

Design for the base of a lectern (?)
Pencil, pen and ink
$14 \times 13\frac{1}{2}$ (35.5 × 34.2) D.1622–1896

Unidentified House D.1362–1896

Elevation and details of a roof. Insc. *urch. Herefordshire* and
L of roof (the rest torn off). Scale ½ *inch*, ¼ *full size, full size.*
Insc. *[J] P. Seddon Archt. Park St. Westminster SW.* d. *July 15th
1865.* Initialled *RCJ.*
Pencil and water-colour on tracing paper
12⅝ × 18¾ (32 × 45.4) D.1506–1896

Section and part elevation of a roof probably for a church
Pencil
11⅞ × 18⅛ (30.1 × 46) D.1527–1896

Perspective sketch, section and details of a timber roof for a
church
Pencil
13¼ × 19 (33.8 × 48.3) D.1531–1896

Houses and Villas

Plans, elevations and sections (on 10 sheets) for a house
Pen and ink, and water-colour on tracing paper
D.1014–1017, 1019–1022, 1025, 1026–1896

Basement plan
7⅛ × 7½ (18 × 19.2) D.1015–1896

Ground plan. Insc. with names of rooms in pencil
6⅞ × 9½ (17.3 × 24.1) D.1026–1896

First floor plan
5⅛ × 8⅛ (13 × 20.7) D.1019–1896

Second floor plan
6¼ × 7⅞ (15.9 × 20) D.1017–1896

Front elevation
6¼ × 9 (16 × 23) D.1025–1896

Back elevation
5⅝ × 8⅝ (14.3 × 22) D.1014–1896

End elevation
6⅝ × 6⅝ (16.7 × 16.7) D.1021–1896

End elevation
6⅝ × 6 (16.7 × 15.2) D.1022–1896

Longitudinal section. Insc. with measurements
6¾ × 8¾ (17 × 22.1) D.1020–1896

Transverse section
7 × 5⅝ (17.8 × 14.3) D.1016–1896

Perspective view of a half-timbered house
Water-colour over preliminary pencil
12 × 17⅛ (30.6 × 43.5) D.1362–1896
Tracing of above
12½ × 19¼ (31.7 × 49) D.1363–1896

Ground plan. Back elevation. Side elevation. (The front elevation
has been cut off) of a house. Insc. with measurements and
names of rooms. On the back sketch elevations and plans for a
house at Birchington. d. *Oct 78* and s. *John P. Seddon*
Pencil and water-colour
13⅜ × 16 (34 × 40.5) D.1442–1896

Front. Back. Side. Side. Elevations of a house. Scale *4 feet to 1
inch*
Pencil on tracing paper
20⅛ × 25½ (51 × 64.6) D.1421–1896

Plans, elevations and a section (on 9 sheets) of a house. D.1483,
1485, 1488, 1490. insc. with names of rooms and D.1485, 1490
with measurements.
D.1482, 1484, 1486, 1489 pen and ink on tracing paper.
D.1485, 1490 pencil, pen and ink on tracing paper. Rest pen
and ink and wash on tracing paper.
D.1482–1490–1896

Cellar plan
2¾ × 2½ (6.9 × 6.4) D.1488–1896

Ground plan
5¼ × 11½ (13.4 × 29.2) D.1490–1896

First floor plan. Alterations suggested in pencil
$5\frac{3}{8} \times 11\frac{1}{2}$ (13.7 × 29.3) D.1485–1896

Second floor plan
$5\frac{3}{8} \times 4\frac{3}{8}$ (13 × 11.2) D.1483–1896

Front elevation
$5\frac{1}{4} \times 11\frac{1}{2}$ (13.5 × 29.3) D.1489–1896

End elevation
$5\frac{3}{8} \times 5\frac{1}{2}$ (13.5 × 14.1) D.1486–1896

End elevation
$5\frac{3}{4} \times 5\frac{1}{2}$ (14.6 × 14.1) D.1482–1896

Back elevation
$5\frac{5}{8} \times 11\frac{3}{8}$ (14.3 × 29) D.1484–1896

Transverse section
$6 \times 5\frac{3}{4}$ (15.2 × 14.5) D.1487–1896

Sketch *first floor* plan of a house
Pencil
$12\frac{3}{8} \times 17\frac{1}{8}$ (31.5 × 43.6) D.1438–1896

Sketch plan of a house. Insc. with measurements and
lower 1 foot
Pen and ink, and pencil
$7\frac{1}{2} \times 11\frac{5}{8}$ (19.1 × 29.6) D.1439–1896

Sketch plans and elevations of a detached half-timbered house.
Insc. with the names of some rooms
Pencil
$13\frac{1}{4} \times 20$ (33.7 × 51) D.1474–1896

Sketch plans, elevation and section of a house. Insc. with
names of rooms
Pencil
$18\frac{7}{8} \times 12\frac{1}{2}$ (48 × 31.6) D.1044–1896

Plan, and front and side elevations of a house. Insc. with
names of rooms
Pencil and wash
$19 \times 12\frac{3}{8}$ (48 × 31.5) D.1043–1896

Plan and *elevation* of a house. Scale $\frac{1}{8}$ *inch*. Insc. *Prichard and
Seddon* etc.
Pencil, pen and ink, and water-colour
16×13 (40.7 × 33) D.1036–1896

Plans, elevations and sections (on 4 sheets) of a villa. Insc.
*Design for villa residence. John P. Seddon Archt. 12 Park Street
Westminster S.W.* Initialled *R.C.J.* D.1039–41 insc. with names
of rooms
Pen and ink and water-colour
D.1039–1042–1896

Ground plan. Front entrance elevation. Scale $\frac{1}{8}$*th.* Insc. with notes
and measurements in pencil
$18\frac{3}{4} \times 12\frac{1}{2}$ (47.5 × 31.5) D.1039–1896

Chamber floor plan. Back elevation. Scale $\frac{1}{8}$*th*
$18\frac{3}{4} \times 12\frac{1}{2}$ (47.5 × 31.5) D.1040–1896

Basement plan. Attic plan. End elevation. End elevation. Scale $\frac{1}{8}$*th*
$18\frac{3}{4} \times 12\frac{1}{2}$ (47.5 × 31.5) D.1041–1896

Transverse section. Longitudinal section. Section thro kitchen, etc.
Scale $\frac{1}{8}$*th*
$18\frac{3}{4} \times 12\frac{1}{2}$ (47.4 × 31.5) D.1042–1896

Plans, elevations and sections (on 2 sheets) of a villa. Insc.
Design for villa and *John P. Seddon Archt. 12 Park St., Westminster
SW.* Initialled *RCJ*
Pen and ink, and water-colour. D.1037 with added pencil
D.1037, 1038–1896

*Basement plan. Ground floor plan. Chamber floor plan. Attic floor plan.
Entrance front. Section AA.* Scale $\frac{1}{8}$*th.* Alterations suggested in
pencil
$18\frac{3}{4} \times 12\frac{1}{2}$ (47.5 × 31.5) D.1037–1896

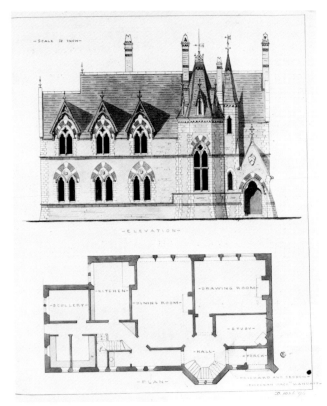

Unidentified House D.1036–1896

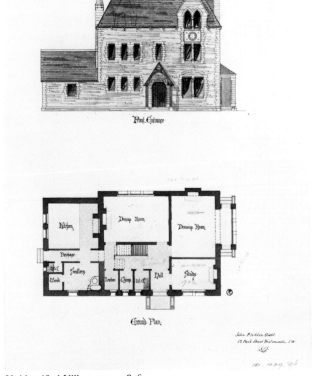

Unidentified Villa D.1039–1896

Garden front. Side elevation. Side elevation. Section BB. Scale ⅛*th*
18¾ × 12½ (47.5 × 31.5) D.1038–1896

Ground floor plan and *chamber plan* of a detached house. Scale linear. Insc. with measurements and names of rooms
Pencil, pen and ink, and water-colour on tracing paper
10¾ × 13⅞ (27.4 × 35.3) D.1479–1896

Sketch plans (on 2 sheets) for a house. D.1480 insc. with measurements and names of rooms
Pencil on tracing paper
7 × 8⅞ (17.7 × 22.5) D.1481–1896
6 × 10⅞ (15.3 × 25) D.1480–1896

Basement plan. Ground plan. *Plan of first floor. Plan of attics* of detached house. *Plan. Elevation. End elevation. Section* of *Stables.* Insc. with measurements and names of rooms. s. *J. P. Seddon Arch.*
Pen and ink and water-colour on tracing paper
13⅞ × 21¾ (35.3 × 55.2) D.1119–1896

Public Buildings

Sketch plan for a large public building, possibly an exchange or town hall. Insc. with names of some rooms and notes
Pencil
19¾ × 35⅝ (50.3 × 90.5) D.1403–1896

Roofs

Sections of *roof over centre shed. Roof over barn. Roof over cow houses.* Insc. *J. P. Seddon Archt. 12 Park St. Westr* and with measurements
Pencil and water-colour
17⅞ × 24¼ (45.5 × 61.6) D.1528–1896

Section and detail of a timber roof. Insc. in ink with width of span 12′ 6″
Pencil and water-colour
14⅛ × 20 (35.8 × 50.8) D.1532–1896

Section of a roof. Wm. *1891*. On the back drawings of another roof. Insc. with notes and measurements
Pencil and water-colour
20 × 14⅞ (50.8 × 37.7) D.1535–1896

Part sections of two roofs. Insc. with measurements
Pen and ink, and water-colour on tracing paper. Torn
14½ × 10 (37 × 25.5) D.1536–1896

Schools

Sketch ground plan for a detached building, possibly a school
Pencil and wash
8¼ × 21¾ (20.9 × 55.3) D.1478–1896

Elevation of a school
Pencil, pen and ink
12 × 13⅝ (30.4 × 34.4) D.975–1896

Design for school to accommodate 60 children. Ground plan. Front elevation. End elevation. Cross section. Scale ⅛*th.* s. *John P. Seddon Architect, 12 Park Street, Westminster.* d. *July 1873.* Insc. with names of rooms and measurements
Pencil and water-colour on tracing paper
11½ × 13¾ (29 × 34.7) D.1354–1896

Miscellaneous

Tracings (on 7 sheets) of ceiling and walls with classical/Pompeian decorations including putti
Pencil and water-colour
Largest 17 × 11½ (43.2 × 29.3) D.1665–1667, 1679–1682–1896

Sketch designs for *studio ceiling* and *dining r. with south aspect.* Initialled *J.P.S.*
Pencil and water-colour
8¼ × 8⅜ (21 × 21.2) D.1670–1896

Plan and elevation of *drawing room fireplace. Half plan* and elevation of *bed-room fireplace.* Scale *1½ inches to 1 foot.* Insc. with notes
Pencil and water-colour
14 × 21⅝ (35.6 × 55) D.1618–1896

Plans, elevations, sections and details (on 11 sheets) of doors or parts of doors. D.1578 s. *John P. Seddon.* D.1602 insc. *J. P. Seddon 1 Queen Anne's Gate Westminster* and d. *October 9th 1880.* D.1577 pencil, pen and ink. D.1578, 1581, 1599, 1602 pencil and water-colour. D.1583, 1586, 1607 pencil. D.1600, 1608 pen and ink. D.1607–1609 on tracing paper.
Various sizes
D.1577, 1578, 1581, 1583, 1586, 1599, 1600, 1602, 1607–1609–1896

Plan of part of a floor showing tiling
Pencil, ink and water-colour
14⅝ × 9 (37.1 × 23) D.1765–1896

Sketches of naturalistic stone carved borders (8) and a bracket. s. in mauve pencil *J. P. Seddon*
Pencil
12⅞ × 18½ (32.7 × 47) D.1934–1896

Perspective sketch of room interior with a bookcase apparently designed by J.P.S.
Pencil and water-colour
10 × 14¼ (25.3 × 36.2) D.2153–1896

Lift. (Dumb waiter?) *Plan. Side* elevation. Part *front* and *back* elevations. Scale *2 inch*
Pen and ink, and water-colour
18 × 12 (45.6 × 30.6) D.2154–1896

Sketch of towers in a landscape. Imaginary?
Pen and ink
6 × 8½ (15.4 × 20.6) D.1434–1896

Front elevation of small bell cover. Section. Front elevation of cover of larger bell. Insc. *Prichard & Seddon* etc. d. *6 June 62*
Pencil
11¾ × 16½ (29.8 × 42) D.851–1896

Plans, elevations, sections and details of *Verandah on entrance front.* Scale *1″* and *full size*
Pencil and water-colour
28¾ × 20⅝ (73 × 52.6) D.1598–1896

Plan and elevation showing proposed alterations to two windows of an 18th century gothik villa. Scale ⅛″ *to a foot,* ½ *in* and ½ *full size.* Insc. *Prichard & Seddon* and with notes and measurements. Initialled *J.P.S.* d. *Apl. 1860*
Pencil, pen and ink, and water-colour
10¼ × 12¾ (26 × 32.5) D.883–1896

Sketch plan and elevation of a gate and pier
Pencil, pen and ink
7¾ × 9¼ (19.9 × 22.6) D.1574–1896

Part sketch plan and elevation of a chimney. On the back elevations of wooden fittings including a display case with sloping top
Pencil and wash
10¾ × 15¼ (27.5 × 39) D.1612–1896

Plan and elevation of entrance gates and steps. s. *J. P. Seddon.* Insc. with notes
Pencil and water-colour
18¾ × 13⅛ (47.5 × 33.3) D.1596–1896

Plan. Front elevation. Section. Details of a timber porch. Scale *inch* and *full size*
Pencil and water-colour
20¾ × 15¼ (52.8 × 38.6) D.1343–1896

Sketch for decorative panels including fleur-de-lys
Pencil and water-colour
20¾ × 28½ (50 × 72) D.1693–1896

Designs for Applied Arts

(See *Architectural Designs* for applied arts designs for specific places and clients)

Designs for three bases in Stoneware D.1937–1896

Ceramics

(see also *Tiles*)

Sketch of a column possibly intended to be made in majolica. s. *J.P.* (the rest has been cut off) and insc. with notes
Blue and red crayon on tracing paper
13¼ × 5½ (33.5 × 14) D.1629–1896

Designs for three *bases in stoneware* including part side and quarter views. Wm. *1874*. s. *John P. Seddon invt.*
Pencil, pen and ink, and water-colour
25⅜ × 19⅛ (64.4 × 48.6) D.1937–1896

Designs for jugs (D.2133, 2146, 2148), vases (D.2134–2136, 2138–2145, 2147, 2149, 2150) and a flower pot (D.2137) possibly intended to be ceramic. D.2138, 2144, 2145, 2149, 2150 initialled *J.P.S.*
D.2133, 2137 crayon. D.2134–2140, 2142–2150 pencil. D.2141 pencil, and pen and ink. D.2133–2134 on tracing paper
Largest 28½ × 20½ (72.3 × 52) D.2133–2150–1896

Sketches for a lectern, possibly to be made in majolica. Insc. with measurements and *Pembridge Sqre* (?) the next word is illegible. On the back are sketches of parts of majolica columns
Pencil and water-colour
7 × 5 (17.7 × 12.5) D.1621–1896

Furniture

Bedroom
(see also Wash Basin Stands and Wardrobes)

Designs for a bed, wash stand and table
Pencil on tracing paper, torn
10¾ × 18 (27.2 × 45.7) D.1770–1896

Designs for a bed, small cupboard, dressing table, dressing table mirror, and wash stand
Pencil on tracing paper
10⅞ × 18⅜ (27.2 × 46.6) D.1771–1896

Designs for a bed, cupboard and wardrobe in a room setting
9⅛ × 14¼ (23.1 × 36.2) D.1772–1896

Design for bedstead in a room setting
Pencil on tracing paper
11⅜ × 7¾ (28.9 × 19.6) D.1773–1896

Designs for a cupboard and a towel rail
10⅜ × 13¼ (26.5 × 33.6) D.2152–1896

Blinds

Design for outside blinds. Scale linear. Insc. *Seddon & Co. London*
Pencil and water-colour
16⅞ × 13⅜ (43 × 34) D.1893–1896

Bookcases

Elevations of two walls of a room showing designs for bookcases. Insc. *Seddon & Co. South Molton St. London* and with notes. s. with a monogram of the letters *J.P.S.* d. *1864*
Pencil, pen and ink, and water-colour
19½ × 13⅜ (49.7 × 34) D.1808–1896

Alternative design to above. Insc. *Plan. Plan. Elevation. Elevation. Section. Section*
Pencil and water-colour
19⅜ × 14¼ (49.4 × 36.3) D.1825–1896

Design for bookcase. Insc. *Seddon & Co. London.* s. with a monogram of the letters *J.P.S.*
Pencil and water-colour
13⅝ × 19⅛ (34.5 × 48.5) D.1809–1896

Design for a bookcase with sketch details. Scale linear
Pencil and water-colour
18⅞ × 13 (47.9 × 33) D.1810–1896

Design for bookcase. Elevation. Section. Scale *inch.* s. with a monogram of the letters *J.P.S.* Insc. *Seddon.* d. *Jany 4th/65*
Pencil and water-colour
12⅞ × 18½ (32.6 × 47.2) D.1811–1896

Design for bookcase. Front. Side. ½ plan looking up. ½ plan looking down. Scale ⅛ *full size.* Insc. *Seddon*
12⅞ × 18⅝ (32.6 × 47.3) D.1790–1896

Bookstand

Design for a bookstand. Scale *2 inch.* s. *J. P. Seddon*
Pen and ink, and water-colour
12⅝ × 9½ (32 × 24.1) D.1775–1896

Cabinets
(see also Sideboards D.1792–1896)

Design for two cabinets with large mirrors above. Insc. *Seddon & Co South Molton St. London.* d. *1864*
13¼ × 19⅝ (33.6 × 49.7) D.1863–1896

Sketch front elevation of a small cabinet (?)
Pencil
12¼ × 10¼ (31.1 × 26) D.1872–1896

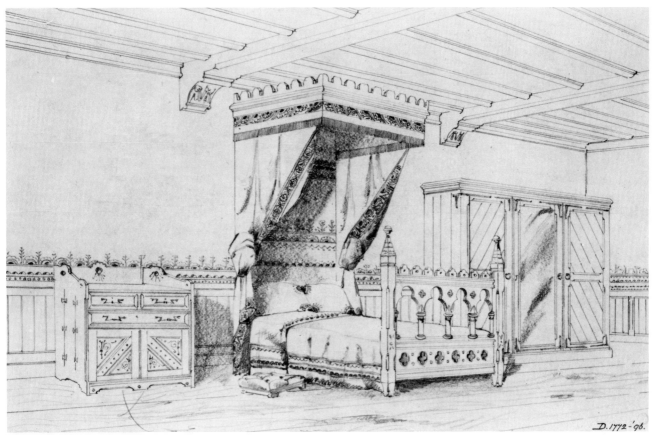

Designs for bed. cupboard and wardrobe D.1772–1896

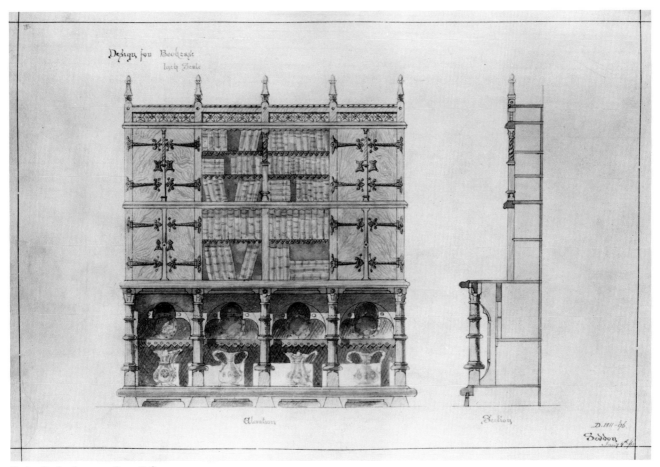

Design for bookcase D.1811–1896

Two designs for free-standing octagonal display cabinets. Insc. *design for centre cabinet, Seddon & Co. London* and with notes about the *top*
Pencil and water-colour
$12\frac{1}{2} \times 18\frac{1}{2}$ (31.7 × 46.9) D.1794–1896

As above but circular. Insc. *design for centre cabinets, Seddon & Co. London* and *this base not this* and *this octagonal*
Pencil and water-colour
$12\frac{1}{2} \times 18$ (31.7 × 45.7) D.1795–1896

Two designs for cabinets. Insc. *design for cabinet*. s. with a monogram of the letters *J.P.S.*
Pencil and water-colour
$18 \times 12\frac{1}{2}$ (45.7 × 31.7) D.1796–1896

Design for a cabinet. Front. Side. Scale *inch.* s. *J. P. Seddon 12 Park St. Westminster*
Pencil, pen and water-colour
$12\frac{7}{8} \times 18\frac{7}{8}$ (32.8 × 48) D.1805–1896

Designs [4] *for cabinets.* Insc. *Seddon & Co.* and s. with a monogram of the letters *J.P.S.*
Pencil and water-colour
$13\frac{1}{2} \times 19\frac{1}{8}$ (34.3 × 48.7) D.1807–1896

Design for cabinet. Design for cabinet. Both designs depict elaborate clocks. Insc. *Seddon & Co. London* and s. with a monogram of the letters *J.P.S.*
Pencil and water-colour
$19 \times 13\frac{1}{8}$ (48.2 × 33.5) D.1812–1896

Design for a cabinet with a circular glass panel in the front. Scale *inch*
Pencil and water-colour
$7\frac{3}{4} \times 9\frac{3}{8}$ (19.8 × 23.7) D.1774–1896

Front and side elevations of a display cabinet
Pencil
$11\frac{1}{4} \times 15\frac{1}{2}$ (28.7 × 39.4) D.1780–1896

Design for a cabinet with a sloping top
Pencil and water-colour
$9 \times 13\frac{1}{2}$ (23.7 × 34.3) D.1777–1896

As above
$10\frac{1}{4} \times 13\frac{1}{2}$ (26 × 34.3) D.1778–1896

Cupboards
(see also *Bedrooms*)

Elevation of a fireplace wall with two designs for cupboards
Water-colour
$8\frac{3}{4} \times 5\frac{1}{4}$ (22.3 × 13.4) D.2153–1896

Curtain Rails and Pelmets
Six designs for curtain rails and pelmets
Pencil
$19\frac{1}{4} \times 13\frac{1}{4}$ (49 × 33.7) D.1894–1896

Davenport
(see Sideboards D.1783–1896)

Desks
Desk. *Plan at AB. Plan at CD.* Elevations and details
Pencil
$20\frac{1}{2} \times 29\frac{7}{8}$ (52 × 76) D.1619–1896

Design for a pedestal desk
Pencil and water-colour
$10\frac{7}{8} \times 14\frac{1}{8}$ (27.7 × 35.9) D.1779–1896

Four designs for litany desks and four designs for pulpits. Insc. *Seddon & Co. South Molton St. London*
Pen and ink, and water-colour
$13\frac{1}{4} \times 19\frac{1}{2}$ (33.7 × 49.7) D.1625–1896

Dressing Chest
Design for dressing chests (2). Insc. *Seddon & Co.*
Pencil
$14\frac{5}{8} \times 9\frac{1}{2}$ (37.1 × 24.1) D.1782–1896

Hallstand
(see also Tables)

Design for a hall stand (?) with open shelves beneath and a row of hooks above. Insc. *Seddon & Co. 70 Grosvenor St.* and s. with a monogram of the letters *J.P.S.*
$13\frac{1}{2} \times 19\frac{1}{2}$ (34.4 × 49.5) D.1804–1896

Mirrors
Design for a mirror between two curtained windows. Insc. *Seddon & Co.*
Pencil and water-colour
$16\frac{1}{2} \times 12\frac{1}{8}$ (42.2 × 30.8) D.1892–1896

Design for bracket and glass. Scale $\frac{1}{8}$th real size. Insc. *J. P. Seddon 6 Whitehall*
Pencil and water-colour
$18\frac{5}{8} \times 13$ (47.3 × 33) D.1853–1896

Tracing of above coloured in a different way
Pen and ink, pencil and water-colour on tracing paper
19×10 (48.2 × 25.6) D.1854–1896

Elevation of one wall of a room showing a design for a mantlepiece mirror and two designs for mirrors and brackets. Scale $\frac{3}{4}$. Insc. *Seddon & Co. South Molton St. London.* and with a monogram of the letters *J.P.S.* d. *1864*
Pen and ink, and water-colour
$12\frac{7}{8} \times 19\frac{5}{8}$ (32.8 × 49.8) D.1855–1896

Front and side elevations of a tripartite mirror and bracket
Pencil and water-colour
$18\frac{1}{8} \times 13\frac{1}{4}$ (46.2 × 33.7) D.1857–1896

Design for a mirror
Pencil
$12\frac{7}{8} \times 10\frac{3}{4}$ (32.6 × 27.1) D.1776–1896

Portfolio Stand
Design for a [folding] *portfolio stand.* Elevations and sections open and closed. Scale $\frac{1}{8}$ *real size*
Pen and ink, and water-colour
$11\frac{5}{8} \times 18\frac{1}{4}$ (29.5 × 46.5) D.2156–1896

Screens
Design for screen. Front and side elevations. Scale $\frac{1}{8}$th full size. s. *J. P. Seddon.* d. *June 3rd 63*
Pencil and water-colour
$11\frac{7}{8} \times 16$ (30.1 × 40.7) D.1860–1896

Design for folding screen. The screen is shown placed in front of an open door. Insc. *Seddon & Co. London*
Pencil and water-colour
$13\frac{1}{2} \times 18\frac{1}{2}$ (34.2 × 47) D.1861–1896

Design for a fire screen. Plan. Elevation. Side elevation. Side view. Scale $\frac{1}{8}$ *real size.* s. *John P. Seddon.* d. *June/63*
$12\frac{1}{2} \times 18\frac{3}{4}$ (32.4 × 47.6) D.1862–1896

Seats
Design for an upholstered folding seat
Pencil, pen and ink, and water-colour
$12\frac{1}{4} \times 13\frac{3}{8}$ (31.3 × 34) D.1835–1896

Sketch of chair Holmes Patent. Front and side elevations. Scale $1\frac{1}{2}$ *inches to a foot.* s. in pencil *J. P. Seddon*
Pen and ink, and water-colour
9×14 (23 × 35.4) D.1842–1896

Sketch of church bench Holmes Patent. Scale $1\frac{1}{2}$ *inches to a foot.* s. *J. P. Seddon* in pencil
Pencil, pen and ink, and water-colour
$9\frac{1}{4} \times 16\frac{5}{8}$ (23.2 × 42.2) D.1843–1896

Sketch of patent church seat to fold up. Front. Side. Scale $\frac{1}{8}$th full size. s. *John P. Seddon*
Same design as D.1843
Pen and ink, and water-colour on tracing paper
$7\frac{7}{8} \times 11\frac{1}{8}$ (20.1 × 28.1) D.1834–1896

Design for a folding bench including front and side elevations and side elevation when folded up. Insc. *C. Seddon South Molton St. London*
Pencil and water-colour
11¾ × 19¾ (30 × 50.2) D.1844–1896

Holmes's patent church bench. Side view. Front view. Side when shut up. Scale *inch and a half*
Pencil and water-colour. Inscriptions in ink
13 × 18¾ (33 × 47.5) D.1627–1896

Holmes Patent church bench and chair. Front. Side. An upholstered chair. *Front. Side. Side (shut up).* Insc. *design for folding church benches on Holmes patent principle designed by J. P. Seddon. Manufacturer C. Seddon & Co. 58 South Molton St. London. These benches are as solid as ordinary church benches & will fold flat against walls so as to be stored with ease when not required. Sketch for church chair on same principle. Lounging chair on same principle.* Initialled *R.C.J.* Insc. *I. P. Seddon.* d. *1863.* Scale *⅛th full size*
Pencil, pen and ink, and water-colour
19⅛ × 13 (48.7 × 33.1) D.1628–1896

Holmes's patent church benches, so called because they were first patented by Richard Rivington Homes (later Sir Richard), are illustrated and described in the *Church Builder*, 1864, pp.29–30 in a note by Seddon. He ends by mentioning that C. Seddon and Co. were the sole agents for their manufacture 'appointed by the patentee'. None of these designs correspond exactly with those illustrated in this article although D.1627 illustrates similar incised decoration. No examples of this folding furniture are known.

Design for harmonium chair. Scale *2 inch.* Insc. *Seddon*
Pencil and water-colour
9⅝ × 12½ (24.6 × 31.9) D.1830–1896

Design for a chair. Side. Front. Scale *⅛th full size.* Insc. *Prichard & Seddon* etc.
Pencil, pen and ink, and water-colour
9⅛ × 13¼ (23.2 × 33.6) D.1831–1896

This chair was exhibited at the International Exhibition of 1862 and appears in the corner of a photograph of part of the Mediaeval Court pasted onto a sheet of furniture designs by William Burges in the Department of Prints and Drawings (8829.1). The chair and another like it, but without painted panels are discussed at length in the *Illustrated London News*, 18 October 1862, p.424. One like it has been acquired recently by the Department of Furniture and Woodwork.

Design for a chaise longe
Pencil
7¾ × 14¾ (19.7 × 37.3) D.1832–1896

Designs for four *hall seats*
Pencil and water-colour
9¾ × 13⅞ (25 × 35.1) D.1833–1896

Designs for *hall seat* and *dinner wagon*. Insc. *Seddon & Co.*
Pencil
14½ × 10½ (37 × 26.7) D.1836–1896

Design for dining room chair, including front and side elevations. Scale *2 inches to one foot.* Insc. *Seddon* and with a note in pencil
Pencil, pen and ink, and water-colour
11½ × 8⅞ (29.1 × 22.7) D.1828–1896

Tracing of above. s. *John P. Seddon*
Pen and ink and water-colour on tracing paper
11¼ × 8¾ (28.6 × 22.2) D.1847–1896

Sketch of part of a sofa
Pen and ink, and ink wash on tracing paper
7¼ × 8⅜ (18.2 × 21.2) D.1829–1896

Front and side elevations of a chair. On the back is a sketch of the back and seat of a chair. Insc. with notes
Pencil and water-colour
10⅝ × 14½ (27.1 × 36.7) D.1838–1896

Sketch of a sofa and chair. Scale linear
Pencil
11⅛ × 14¼ (27.4 × 36.5) D.1839–1896

Front and side elevations of an arm chair. Scale linear
Pencil
10¾ × 14⅜ (27.4 × 36.5) D.1840–1896

Design for an upholstered sofa. Insc. *C. Seddon South Molton St.*
Pen and ink, and water-colour
11⅛ × 14¾ (28.3 × 37.5) D.1841–1896

Design for dining room chair (on 3 sheets). Front and side elevations and two thumbnail sketches of alternative designs. Scale *2 inches to a foot.* D.1845 insc. in ink *I. P. Seddon.* d. *1863* D.1837 pencil. D.1845 pencil and water-colour. D.1848 pen and ink on tracing paper
Largest 12½ × 18⅝ (31.6 × 47.5) D.1837, 1845, 1848–1896

Front and side views of a chair. Insc. *Seddon.* Scale linear
Pencil, pen and ink, and water-colour on tracing paper
8¼ × 11¾ (21.1 × 30) D.1846–1896

Half front and side views of three designs for chairs, one with arms
Pencil on tracing paper
10⅛ × 12⅜ (25.7 × 31.5) D.1849–1896

Front and *end elevation* of an *Ottoman. Section* and front elevation of a *double bench with moveable back.* Scale linear. Insc. *Seddon.* d. *Decr. 15th/64*
Pencil and water-colour
18⅝ × 13 (47.3 × 33) D.1850–1896

As above but with two additional designs for *kitchen side table* and a *table* or *desk.* Scale linear
Pencil and water-colour
18¾ × 14½ (47.5 × 36.7) D.1851–1896

Back and side elevations of a chair. Front and side elevations of a desk or portfolio stand. View of a cupboard
Pencil and water-colour
15⅞ × 13¾ (40.3 × 34.9) D.1623–1896

Design for Archbishop's throne. Front elevation. Side elevation. Section. Details. Scale *inch & half to a foot* and *full size.* Insc. *John P. Seddon Archt.* and with measurements. d. *January 30 75*
Pencil, pen and ink, and water-colour
12¾ × 18½ (32.4 × 47) D.1626–1896

Sideboards

Front elevation of a buffet. Insc. *Seddon & Co. South Molton St. London* and with measurements. d. *1864*
Pencil and wash
18⅞ × 12¾ (48 × 32.5) D.1876–1896

Design for a sideboard (on 2 sheets). *Elevation. Side. Section.* Scale *inch.* D.1815 insc. *for Messrs C. Seddon & Co. 58 South Molton St.* D.1797. s. *Seddon* and d. */63.* D.1815.s. *John P. Seddon* and with a monogram of the letters *JPS*
D.1797 Pencil and water-colour. D.1815 Pencil, pen and water-colour
12⅛ × 18⅛ (30.9 × 46) D.1797–1896
12⅜ × 18 (31.3 × 45.6) D.1815–1896
This is similar to the illustration in the *Building News*, 2 June 1865

Design for a sideboard. Elevation. Side. Scale *inch*
Pencil and water-colour
13 × 18¾ (33 × 47.7) D.1798–1896

Design for a sideboard. *Half plan at A. Half plan at B. Section CD. Ende* [sic] *elevation.* Scale *inch* and linear. Insc. *J. P. Seddon Archt. 1 Queen Anne's Gate, SW*
Pencil
12¾ × 18⅝ (32.5 × 47.4) D.1799–1896

Design for a sideboard D.1821–1896

Designs for two sideboards, one with a hinged overlay with an alternative design for the top. Insc. *Seddon & Co Grosvenor St.* The overlay insc. on the back *35 Park St.*
Pencil and water-colour
$19\frac{5}{8} \times 13\frac{5}{8}$ (50 × 34.6) D.1802 and A–1896

Design for a sideboard. Insc. *C. Seddon South Molton St. London*
Pen and ink and water-colour
$13 \times 19\frac{5}{8}$ (33 × 49.9) D.1803–1896

Designs for sideboards (2 on one sheet). *Side.* ½ *elevation.* ½ *elevation. Scale inch.* Insc. *Seddon*
Pen and ink, and water-colour
$12\frac{7}{8} \times 18\frac{5}{8}$ (32.7 × 47.4) D.1813–1896

Front and side elevations of a sideboard. Insc. *C. Seddon South Molton St. London.* d. *1864*
Pencil, pen and ink, and water-colour
$12\frac{7}{8} \times 19\frac{3}{8}$ (32.7 × 49.2) D.1814–1896

Design for a sideboard for C. Seddon & Co. 58 South Molton St. Front elevation. Side. Scale inch. s. *J. P. Seddon, 12 Park Street Westminster* and with a monogram of the letters *J.P.S.*
Pencil and water-colour
$13\frac{1}{4} \times 19\frac{1}{8}$ (33.6 × 48.6) D.1818–1896

Elevation of one wall of a room showing design for a sideboard. Insc. *Seddon & Co. South Molton St. London* and s. with a monogram of the letters *J.P.S.*
Pen and ink, and water-colour
$13\frac{3}{4} \times 19\frac{5}{8}$ (35.1 × 49.8) D.1821–1896

Alternative design for the above. Insc. as above and *£54 with shelf abt. £4 more*
Pencil, pen and ink, and water-colour
$13\frac{1}{2} \times 19$ (34.2 × 48.2) D.1822–1896

Design for sideboard. Front view. Side view. Scale inch. s. with a monogram of the letters *J.P.S.*
Pencil, pen and ink, and water-colour
$11\frac{1}{4} \times 17$ (28.5 × 43.2) D.1781–1896

Design for a sideboard and mirror. On the back a sketch of a Davenport. Wm. *1863.* Insc. on the back *R.S.W. Franklyn, 55, Onslow Square Monday* and initialled *J.P.S.*
Pencil and water-colour
$10\frac{1}{8} \times 14\frac{1}{2}$ (25.7 × 36.8) D.1783–1896

Design for a sideboard. *Plan. Front. Side. Section. Scale* ½ *inch.* s. *John P. Seddon.* d. *1882*
Pencil
$8\frac{5}{8} \times 13\frac{1}{4}$ (22 × 33.7) D.1784–1896

Tracing of above. Scale linear
$8\frac{3}{4} \times 13\frac{1}{8}$ (22 × 33.2) D.1791–1896

Design for a sideboard bearing the inscription *Sit down feed and welcome to our table.* Part plan. Front elevation. Part side elevation. Insc. *Omit canopy*
$12\frac{1}{8} \times 16\frac{1}{8}$ (30.8 × 41) D.1786–1896

Front and side elevations of a sideboard. *Scale inch.* s. *J. P. Seddon delt.* d. *Sept. 61*
Pencil
$11\frac{5}{8} \times 16$ (29.6 × 40.7) D.1789–1896

Front and side elevations of a sideboard. Front elevation and *plan of cabinet.* Design for an arm chair. Numbered *14*
Pencil and water-colour
$19\frac{3}{4} \times 12\frac{7}{8}$ (50 × 32.7) D.1792–1896

Tables

Designs for tables. Dining table. Plan. Occasional table. Insc. *Hunt £8* and *Thomas Seddon, P&S.* d. *Oct 60*
Pencil and wash
$12\frac{1}{8} \times 9\frac{3}{4}$ (31 × 24.8) D.1868–1896

Design for hall table. Front. Side. Scale 1″ and *Pt. detail. Scale ⅛th full size.* Insc. *Hunt £10. Thomas Seddon. P&S.* d. *Oct 60*
$9\frac{3}{8} \times 12\frac{1}{2}$ (23.8 × 31.9) D.1869–1896

Design for a table. Front. Side. Section AA. Design for whatnot. Front. Plan. Section AB. Scale *1 inch to a foot.* Insc. *Seddon* and with a monogram of the letters *J.P.S.*
Pencil, pen and ink, and water-colour
18¾ × 12¾ (47.6 × 32.3) D.1889–1896

Designs for a *ladies work table,* a *work table with centre stand* and a *library lectern or book stand* in *pine*
Pencil and water-colour
18¾ × 13 (47.5 × 32.8) D.1890–1896

Design for a bracket table including elevations and top plan. Insc. with an illegible word and *P. &S.*
10 × 13⅛ (25.5 × 33.2) D.2151–1896

Designs for hall tables with metal hat racks. Insc. *Seddon & Co. South Molton St. London* and with a monogram of the letters *J.P.S.*
13¾ × 19¾ (34.8 × 50.2) D.2155–1896

Elevation of a circular table. Scale linear
Pen and ink on tracing paper
4½ × 7½ (11.3 × 19) D.1867–1896

Perspective of a table with legs in the shape of an 'X'
Pencil and wash
8¼ × 12⅜ (21 × 31.5) D.1866–1896

Top, front and side views of a table. Insc. *£10*
Pencil and wash
11 × 15 (27.9 × 38) D.1874–1896

Two *designs for occasional table* including *front, side, ½ plan of top* and *½ plan thro AA* of each. Scale *inch & half to 1 foot.* Insc. *Seddon* and with a monogram of the letters *J.P.S.*
Pencil and water-colour
18¾ × 13 (47.5 × 32.9) D.1878–1896

Small library table. End elevation of library table. Longitudinal elevation and *plan* of a desk. Scale *to elevations* linear, and *½ scale of elevation.* Insc. *Seddon* and with a monogram of the letters *J.P.S.*
Pencil and water-colour
18¾ × 12⅞ (47.5 × 32.6) D.1879–1896

As above but with design for another *library table* with *plan of angle & legs*
Pencil and water-colour
19 × 14¾ (48.4 × 37.5) D.1826–1896

Designs for five tables. Scale *inch.* Insc. with a note about the *legs*
Pencil and wash
18¼ × 12⅜ (46.3 × 31.4) D.1881–1896

Design for dining room table. Top. Elevation. Scale *⅛th real size*
Pen and ink, and water-colour
18⅝ × 13 (47.4 × 33.1) D.1884–1896

Design for table. Design for circular loo table. Plans and elevations. Insc. *Seddon.* Scale *1½ inches to a foot*
Pencil, pen and ink, and water-colour
18⅞ × 13¼ (47.9 × 33.6) D.1885–1896

Designs for a *circular table,* a *billiard table,* an octagonal *dining room table, servant's hall table with leaves* and another table. Wm. *1863*
Pencil and water-colour
19¼ × 13⅜ (48.8 × 34) D.1888–1896

Designs for two *dining tables* and a *wardrobe.* Insc. *Seddon & Co* and with notes about cost, etc.
Pencil
18¾ × 13 (47.8 × 33) D.1806–1896

Towel Rail
(see Cupboard)

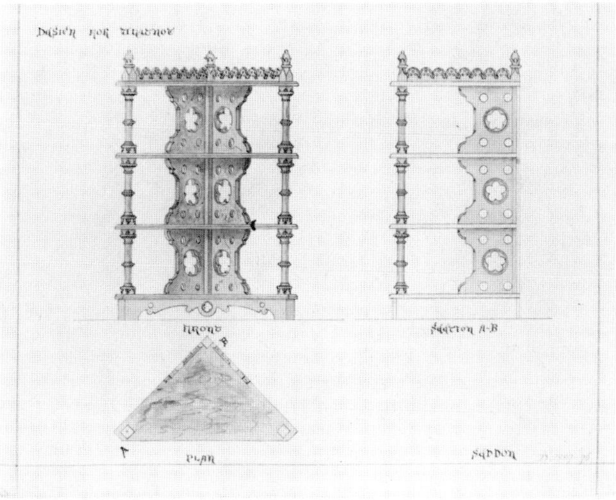

Design for a whatnot D.1889–1896

Wardrobes
See also Wash basin stand D.1827

Design for a wardrobe. Elevation partly without doors to shew internal arrangement. Side. Scale *inch & half.* Insc. *Seddon*
Pencil, pen and ink, and water-colour
12⅜ × 17¼ (31.4 × 43.8) D.1785–1896

Front and side elevations of a wardrobe. Insc. *C. Seddon. South Molton St. London*
Pen and ink and water-colour
13¼ × 14½ (33.7 × 36.7) D.1788–1896

Whatnot
(see Tables D.1889–1896)

Wash Basin Stands
(see also Bedroom D.1770, 1771–1896)

Design for basin stand (2).
One insc. *Birch abt. £6-15-0 Marble top.* The other *Birch abt. £8.* Lettered *Seddon & Co*
Pencil
12 × 9½ (30.5 × 24) D.1871–1896

Wash stand. Top, front and side elevations. Insc. with a monogram of the letters *J.P.S.*
Pencil and water-colour
9¾ × 14⅝ (24.8 × 37.3) D.1873–1896

Designs for *wash stand,* another wash stand and a *bedside pedestal.* Wm. *1862*
Pencil and water-colour
19⅛ × 13 (48.7 × 32.9) D.1877–1896

Design for basin stand with marble top. Top, front, and side elevations
Pencil on tracing paper
9½ × 14¾ (24.1 × 37.3) D.1886–1896

Design for bason [sic] *stand with tiles in back* (on 2 sheets). Front and side elevations and half plans
Pencil on tracing paper
9 × 14¼ (23 × 36.3) D.1820–1896

Design for bason [sic] *stand.* Front and side elevations. Design for *wardrobe.* Lettered in ink in a band *Seddon's Mediaeval Furniture*
Pencil
20 × 14½ (50.8 × 36.9) D.1827–1896

Metalwork

Door Furniture

Full size designs for two door hinges. Insc. *Hart and Son London* and with notes. d. *June 20 1868*
Pencil and wash
$19 \times 20\frac{5}{8}$ (48×52.3) D.1987–1896

Design for a door knocker. Scale *real size*. Insc. *Hart & Son. London*. d. *Oct 16th 1860*
Pencil and water-colour
$16\frac{3}{8} \times 12$ (41.5×30.7) D.1953–1896

Designs for four door knockers. Insc. *G. Smith & Sons, Deritend Bridge Works, Birmingham*. Numbered *5454, after 5656, 5653B, 5668*
Pencil and wash on tracing paper
$13\frac{3}{4} \times 9$ (35.1×22.8) D.1978–1896

Sketches of two handles and escutcheons
Pencil, pen and ink on tracing paper
7×12 (17.6×30.4) D.1968–1896

Sketches for a door handle, knocker and escutcheon
Pencil
$15 \times 9\frac{7}{8}$ (38×25) D.1951–1896

Full size design probably for door furniture
Pencil and wash
$25\frac{7}{8} \times 24\frac{7}{8}$ (65.7×63.3) D.1955–1896

Full size design for an ornamental hinge. Insc. with notes
Pencil
$13\frac{1}{4} \times 27\frac{1}{8}$ (33.5×68.7) D.1956–1896

Anchor bolt for door frame. Bolt with nut and washer. Side view of bolt. Plan nut and washer
Pencil and wash on tracing paper
$10\frac{1}{8} \times 8\frac{3}{8}$ (25.6×21.4) D.1604–1896

Fenders

Design for a fender
Pencil, pen and ink, and water-colour on tracing paper
$4\frac{5}{8} \times 8\frac{3}{4}$ (11.7×22.3) D.1944–1896

Design for a fender. Scale $1\frac{1}{2}$. *1'0"*. Insc. *Hart Son Peard & Co.* d. *March 5 1872*. Lettered *B*
Pencil and water-colour on tracing paper
$4\frac{7}{8} \times 11$ (12.4×28.1) D.1982–1896

Grate

Rough sketch for elevation of dog grate
Pencil on tracing paper
$35\frac{1}{2} \times 25\frac{1}{4}$ (90.2×64.2) D.1984–1896

Grating

Design for part of a cast iron grating (?). Insc. *Prichard & Seddon* and with notes. d. *Jany 61*
Pen and ink, and water-colour
$8 \times 8\frac{3}{4}$ (20.3×22.1) D.1969–1896

Lighting Fixtures

Design for a gas chandelier. Scale *one inch to a foot*. Insc. with notes and measurements
Pencil and pen and ink
$10\frac{1}{4} \times 8\frac{1}{4}$ (26×21) D.1947–1896

Design for a 29 jet lamp standard. *Plan of head of standard. Plan of base of standard*. Scale *1 inch to a foot*. d. *May 6 1878*
Pencil and water-colour
$15\frac{3}{8} \times 11\frac{1}{8}$ (39×28.2) D.1952–1896

Sketch for gas lamp bracket. Scale *3 inches to a foot*. Insc. *Hart and Son London*. Numbered *1*. d. *March 11 1864*
Pen and ink, and water-colour
$6 \times 8\frac{3}{4}$ (15.3×22.3) D.1945–1896

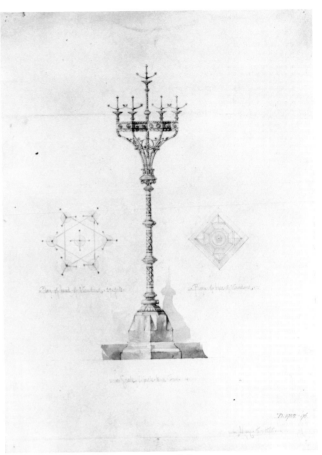

Design for gas standard lamp D.1952–1896

Design for gas lamp bracket. Scale *3 in to a foot*. Insc. *Hart & Son London*. Numbered *3*. d. *March 10th 1864*
Pen and ink, and water-colour
$6\frac{7}{8} \times 9\frac{3}{4}$ (17.5×24.9) D.1946–1896

Designs (on 4 sheets) for five suspended gas lamps. Scale $1\frac{1}{2}$ *inches to a foot*. Insc. *Hart Son Peard & Co London*. D.1957, 1976 d. *Jany 27th 1872* others d. *Jany 26th 1872*. Lettered *B* to *F*
Pen and ink, and water-colour on tracing paper
Largest $18\frac{3}{8} \times 9\frac{3}{8}$ (34×23.7) D.1957, 1958, 1973, 1976–1896

Designs (on 4 sheets) for suspended gas lights—two with counterweights. Scale $\frac{1}{4}$ *full size*. Insc. *Hart & Son. London*. D.1959 d. *April 19 1858*. D.1960 d. *April 7 1858*. D.1961, 1962 d. *October 8 1858*. Insc. with prices
Pen and ink, and water-colour on tracing paper
Largest $16 \times 10\frac{1}{2}$ (40.7×26.6) D.1959–1962–1896

Sketch for 4 light chandelier. Scale $\frac{1}{4}$ *full size*. Insc. *Hart and Son London*. d. *April 17 1862*
Pencil, pen and ink, and water-colour on tracing paper
$12\frac{1}{2} \times 10\frac{1}{2}$ (31.7×26.6) D.1963–1896

Designs for three standard lights. Scale $1\frac{1}{2}$ *inch*. Insc. *Hart & Son London*. d. *February 24 1860*. Numbered *1.2.3*.
Pencil, pen and ink, and water-colour on tracing paper
$14 \times 11\frac{1}{8}$ (35.3×28.4) D.1964–1896

Design for a single jet gas wall light. Scale $\frac{1}{4}$ *full size*. Insc. *Hart & Son London*. d. *Feby 25 1860*. Numbered *12*
Pen and ink, and water-colour on tracing paper
$4\frac{1}{8} \times 6\frac{1}{2}$ (10.4×16.6) D.1967–1896

As above but scale $1\frac{1}{2}$ *inch* and numbered *13*
$5\frac{3}{4} \times 5\frac{7}{8}$ (14.7×14.9) D.1971–1896

Designs (on 3 sheets) for three-light candelabra. Scale $1\frac{1}{2}'' = 1'0''$. Insc. *Hart Son Peard & Co.* d. *Feby 12 1872*. Lettered *A.B.C.*
Pen and ink and water-colour on tracing paper
Largest $10\frac{3}{8} \times 7\frac{1}{2}$ (26.3×19) D.1970, 1974, 1975–1896

Design for a lamp to be attached to a base. Scale $1\frac{1}{2}''$ to a foot.
Insc. *Hart Son Peard & Co. London*. d. *Jany 24th 1870*
Pen and ink, and water-colour on tracing paper
$11\frac{5}{8} \times 6\frac{1}{8}$ (29.6 × 15.6) D.1972–1896

Design for part of a gas chandelier with lustres. Insc. *Hart &
Son London*. d. *May 2nd 1862*
Pencil and water-colour on tracing paper
$24\frac{1}{4} \times 20\frac{1}{8}$ (61.3 × 51) D.1977–1896

Screen
Design for an ironwork screen. Insc. with notes about the
colour including *the foliage green with chocolate* [sic] *lines. The
vertical bars are all ultra marine blue. Horizontal* [*bars are all*]
chocolate [sic] and *Hart & Son, London*. d. *May 17th 1860*
Pencil, pen and ink, and water-colour on tracing paper
$15\frac{1}{2} \times 11$ (39.3 × 27.8) D.1980–1896

Tankard
Sketch of a tankard, possibly intended to be made in metal.
Insc. with notes about colours and *incised* and in *relief*
Pencil and blue crayon
$17\frac{1}{8} \times 11\frac{3}{4}$ (43.6 × 30) D.1624–1896
On the back of a drawing for pews at Llanddewi Felfre.

Stained Glass

Cartoon for a stained glass window depicting Christ blessing
Pencil and wash
$22 \times 16\frac{5}{8}$ (56 × 42.2) D.1762–1896

Sketch of three panels of stained glass filled with fruit and
leaves
Pencil, pen and ink, and water-colour
7×5 (18 × 12.8) D.1717–1896

Design for a window with ten coats of arms
Pen and ink, and water-colour on tracing paper
$12\frac{7}{8} \times 8\frac{3}{4}$ (32.8 × 22) D.1719–1896

Design for a window depicting two children kneeling with a
Roman (?) soldier's uniform. One is reading and the other
holding the helmet. Numbered *1*
Pen and ink, and water-colour
$8 \times 8\frac{7}{8}$ (20.3 × 22.6) D.1720–1896

Sketch of a window. Initialled *J.P.S.* and insc. *£40*
Pencil and water-colour on tracing paper
$10 \times 5\frac{3}{4}$ (25.3 × 14.5) D.1721–1896

Design for part of the top of an ogival headed window
depicting a bird in foliage and a border of grapes and vine
leaves. Insc. with notes and numbers
Pencil and water-colour on tracing paper
$19\frac{3}{4} \times 17\frac{1}{4}$ (50 × 43.8) D.1678–1896

Designs for four panels (on 2 sheets) possibly stained glass
D.1692. Insc. *S. Matthew* and *S. Mark* and D.1706 *S. Luke* and
S. John
Pencil and wash
$14\frac{1}{4} \times 21\frac{3}{8}$ (36.2 × 54.4) D.1692–1896
$12\frac{1}{2} \times 20\frac{1}{8}$ (31.6 × 51.2) D.1706–1896

Design for part of a six light window, the three lights in the
second tier insc. *Moses law giver. King David. Abimelech*. s. *John
P. Seddon*. d. *July 13 74*
Pencil, pen and ink, and water-colour
$17\frac{3}{8} \times 12$ (44 × 30.5) D.1698–1896

Sketch designs for parts of two tall narrow stained glass
windows
Pencil
$17\frac{5}{8} \times 9\frac{7}{8}$ (44.8 × 25) D.1699–1896

Sketch designs (on 1 sheet cut into two, and 2 further sheets)
depicting different designs for two lights of a three light
window. The design includes the words *Joy* and *Love*. D.1701
s. *John P. Seddon*
Pencil and water-colour
$12\frac{1}{4} \times 11\frac{1}{2}$ (31 × 29.1) D.1700 $13\frac{3}{4} \times 8\frac{1}{8}$ (35 × 20.7) D.1701
$21\frac{5}{8} \times 14\frac{7}{8}$ (54.9 × 37.8) D.1760 $21\frac{1}{2} \times 15$ (54.6 × 38) D.1761
D.1700, 1701, 1760, 1761–1896
On the back of D.1700, 1701 are plans of University College,
Aberystwyth and on the back of D.1760 a plan of part of a
church (?).

Sketch designs for parts of three lights of stained glass windows
for a church dedicated to *S. Mary on Hill*. Insc. *Windows in
Aisle*, and in ink *68 Bars 24½"*, and with other notes. Initialled
J.P.S.
Pencil and water-colour
$24\frac{1}{4} \times 17\frac{1}{8}$ (61.6 × 43.6) D.1702–1896

Sketch design for a stained glass window depicting a single
standing figure. Scale *2 inch* and $\frac{1}{6}th$ *full size*. Initialled *J.P.S.*
and insc. with notes
Pencil and water-colour
$18\frac{3}{8} \times 12\frac{5}{8}$ (46.8 × 32.1) D.1703–1896

Design for six stained glass windows with secular figurative
subjects
Pen and ink and water-colour
$10\frac{5}{8} \times 19\frac{5}{8}$ (27 × 49.8) D.1704–1896

Full size cartoon for a stained glass window depicting a
kneeling woman praying
Pencil, ink and water-colour
$19\frac{1}{4} \times 11$ (49 × 28) D.1705–1896

Design for a stained glass window bearing the insc. *Tabitha
Arise*
Pen and ink, and water-colour
$8 \times 3\frac{1}{2}$ (20.5 × 9) D.1710–1896

Design for a stained glass window depicting the Crucifixion
Water-colour
$4\frac{1}{4} \times 3\frac{1}{2}$ (10.7 × 8.9) D.1709–1896

Sketch design for a panel of stained glass with a geometric
pattern of circles and diamonds
Pen and ink, and water-colour on linen
$3\frac{3}{4} \times 5$ (9.4 × 12.8) D.1724–1896

Designs (on 3 sheets) for panels of stained glass depicting a
stylised tree. D.1729 s. *J. P. Seddon*
Pencil and water-colour on tracing paper
Largest $5\frac{1}{4} \times 5\frac{3}{8}$ (13.3 × 13.7) D.1727–1729–1896

Designs (on 2 sheets) for two small circular panels of stained
glass one depicting a pelican (?)
Water-colour on tracing paper
5×5 (12.5 × 12.5) D.1725, 1726–1896

Designs (on 4 sheets) for quarters of square windows with
circular centres. D.1754 insc. in pencil *These arrangements will
depend upon what colours Mr Rust can make for centres — say green &
purple the surrounding colours will be so as to throw those centres up*.
D.1753 s. *J. P. Seddon*. D.1752 insc. with notes
Pencil, ink and water-colour
Largest $15\frac{3}{8} \times 11\frac{3}{8}$ (39 × 29) D.1752–1755–1896
Jesse Rust was a well known stained glass maker at this time
for whom Seddon did a considerable amount of work
including the design of the front of his premises in London

Sketch designs for four stained glass windows depicting *Noah,
Abraham, Moses* and *David Rex*
Pencil
$13\frac{1}{8} \times 21$ (33.5 × 53) D.1757–1896

Sketch designs for six stained glass windows probably part of
the same set as above depicting SS Peter, Elizabeth, Mary,
Paul, Mark and an unidentified saint. Insc. *It would be better in
these windows to omit borders*
Pencil
$13\frac{3}{4} \times 21\frac{3}{8}$ (34.9 × 54) D.1758–1896

Window in chapel of 3 Kings [the next word is illegible] *from memory*. Initialled *J.P.S.*
Pencil and water-colour
7 × 5 (17.7 × 12.7) D.1708–1896

Textiles

Design for embroidery in the form of a cross. s. *J. P. Seddon Archt* and addressed *1 Queen Anne's Gate Westminster*. d. *10/7/76*
Pencil and water-colour on tracing paper
24⅜ × 23¼ (61.9 × 59.2) D.1898–1896

Design for an altar frontal, and thumbnail sketch of another design. Insc. with notes
Pencil, pen and ink, and water-colour
8⅛ × 12¾ (20.5 × 32.5) D.1906–1896

Design for a banner for the West Yorkshire Fire Brigade Friendly Society
Pencil
11⅝ × 7⅜ (29.5 × 18.7) D.1909–1896

Sketch designs (on 9 sheets) possibly for embroideries
D.1908, 1910–1912, 1914–1916 pencil. D.1913, 1917 pencil and water-colour.
Largest 30¾ × 26¼ (78.5 × 66.7) D.1908, 1910–1917–1896

Design for embroidered dossal. Scale *about ¼ full size*. s. *John P. Seddon*. d. *Apl 79*
Pencil on tracing paper
13⅜ × 9½ (34 × 24) D.1918–1896

As above different design. Insc. with notes
17½ × 11 (44.3 × 28) D.1919–1896

Tiles

For Godwin

Designs for two panels of tiles. Insc. in ink *reference as to fixing for Exhibition panels 1 & 2 let in 2 iron frames supported by the 2 pieces marked wood on each side of the drawing* and with measurements. Blind stamped *Hereford* the rest cut off
Pencil, pen and ink, and water-colour on tracing paper
5¾ × 9¼ (14.5 × 23.4) D.2102–1896

Designs for tiles. s. *John P. Seddon Archt*. and addressed *12 Park St. Westr*.
Pencil and water-colour on tracing paper
21¾ × 19 (55 × 48.3) D.2119–1896

Design for a panel of tiles. s. *John P. Seddon* and addressed *12 Park St. Westr*. Insc. with notes
Pencil and water-colour on tracing paper
28½ × 25¾ (72 × 65.2) D.2121–1896

Design for a panel of tiles. s. *J. P. Seddon*. d. *April 1870*
Pen and water-colour on tracing paper
21½ × 27 (54.6 × 69) D.2124–1896

Designs for tiles two insc. *W. Godwin* and a third *modified for W. Godwin*. Initialled *J.P.S.*
22⅝ × 22⅜ (57.5 × 56.8) D.2130–1896

Designs (on 3 sheets) for single tiles or groups of tiles
Pencil and water-colour. D.2111 on tracing paper
Largest 15¼ × 14½ (38.7 × 37) D.2063, 2082, 2111–1896

Design for a panel of tiles
Pencil and water-colour
18⅞ × 19½ (48 × 49.5) D.2132–1896

Design for an arrangement of tiles including the Sacred monogram. Blind stamped *Godwin Lugwardine. Hereford*
Pencil and cut out coloured lithographs pasted on
6¾ × 5¼ (17.3 × 13.4) D.2087–1896

Designs for three arrangements of tiles. Possibly for Godwin. Initialled *J.P.S.*
Pencil and water-colour
15 × 12⅞ (38.2 × 32.1) D.2049–1896
The top design appears to be a sketch for the design illustrated in the *Building News* 16 May 1874

Design for part of a tile border. Possibly for Godwin. s. *J. P. Seddon*. d. *Feb 1868*
Pencil and water-colour
26⅜ × 21⅝ (66.8 × 54.9) D.2072–1896
This design is very similar to D.2087 stamped *Godwin* etc.

For Maw

Designs (on 36 sheets) for single tiles or groups of tiles. D.2098, 2101, 2110, 2112, 2115 s. *J. P. Seddon*. D.2098 d. *Feb 64*. D.2101 d. *22 Feby 6* (the rest cut off). D.2110, 2115 d. *22 Feb 64*.
D.2112 insc. *Draw out all these designs complete & send a tracing to Messrs Maw*.
D.1661-63, 2002-9, 2011-26, 2034 pen and ink on linen. D.2076, 2112 pencil. D.2097, 2098, 2101, 2110 pencil and wash on tracing paper. D.2115 pencil and ink, and wash on tracing paper.
Various sizes
D.1661–1663, 2002–2026, 2034, 2076, 2097, 2098, 2101, 2110, 2112, 2115–1896
All these designs appear on the illustrative sheets listed below.

Three designs (on 4 sheets) for pages of illustrations of Maw's tiles. Insc. *Sketch showing arrangement of tiles for Messrs Maw* or similar. Numbered *1 to 3* and *6*.
D.2027 pencil. D.2052-54, 2056 pencil, pen and ink.
Average size 17⅞ × 12⅜ (45.3 × 31.4)
D.2027, 2052, 2053, 2056–1896
D.2052 reproduced *Building News*, 22 August 1873 and D.2053 *Building News* 14 November 1873.

Design for tiles for Maw and Company

For Minton Taylor

Designs (on 17 sheets) for single tiles or groups of tiles. D.2100 s. *John P. Seddon* and d. *Apl 7* (the rest cut off)
D.2118 pencil. D.1992–96, 1999–2001, 2035, 2036 pen and ink on linen. D.2044, 2070, 2073, 2100, 2104, 2122 pencil and water-colour. D.2100, 2104, 2118, 2122 on tracing paper.
Largest 39½ × 27½ (100.3 × 70)
D.1992–1996, 1999–2001, 2035, 2036, 2044, 2064, 2070, 2073, 2100, 2104, 2118–1896
All these designs appear on the illustrative sheets listed below

Designs (on 2 sheets) for pages of illustrations of Minton Taylor's tiles. Scale linear. Insc. *Design for encaustic tiles for R. Minton Taylor & Co. by J. P. Seddon Archt.*
17¾ × 11¾ (45 × 30) D.2054, 2055–1896
D.2054 reproduced in the *Building News* 25 December 1874 and D.2055 in the *Building News* 20 November 1874.

Design for an arrangement of tiles including examples made by R. Minton Taylor
Pencil, pen and ink, and water-colour
4⅜ × 4½ (11.3 × 11.4) D.2094–1896

Designs (on 45 sheets) for single tiles or groups of tiles. probably for Maw, Godwin or Minton Taylor. D.2043, 2061, 2062, 2081 appear to be designs for the arrangement of pages of a catalogue. D.2033 is a preliminary drawing for publication. D.2033, 2113, 2114, 2117, 2125 s. *John* or *J. P. Seddon*. D.2113, 2117. d. *Feb 70*. D.2033 d. *June 1873*.
D.1997, 1998, 2028–2032 pen and ink on linen. D.2033, 2047, 2103, 2106, 2113 pencil. D.2088, 2093 pen and ink and water-colour. D.2117, 2120, 2126 pencil and wash. D.2091, 2092, 2114, 2122 pencil, pen and ink, and water-colour. D.2105 water-colour. D.2090 on graph paper. D.2103, 2105, 2106, 2113, 2114, 2117, 2122, 2123, 2125, 2126 on tracing paper. D.2096 pen and ink, and water-colour with photographs pasted on. Rest pencil and water-colour.
Largest 36 × 27¾ (91.6 × 70.5)
D.1997, 1998, 2028–2033, 2040, 2042, 2043, 2046–2048, 2061, 2062, 2065, 2068, 2069, 2071, 2077, 2079, 2081, 2083, 2084, 2086, 2088–2093, 2096, 2103, 2105, 2106, 2113, 2114, 2117, 2120, 2122, 2123, 2125, 2126, 2131–1896.

Miscellaneous

Two designs possibly for tiles
Pencil and water-colour
8½ × 16⅛ (21.8 × 41) D.1653–1896

Design depicting three ears of corn possibly for a tile. Insc. in ink *8 to this. Please say if this is right & return Mary* (the rest has been cut off)
Pencil on tracing paper
9⅜ × 9½ (23.7 × 24) D.1668–1896

Design for a frieze of tiles (?). s. *J. P. Seddon* and addressed *12 Park Street Westminster*

Design for a panel depicting a six-winged griffin and bearing the insc. *Holy Holy Holy Lord God.* Possibly for a tile.
Pencil and water-colour on tracing paper. Torn
12¾ × 13 (32.5 × 33.1) D.1669–1896

Pen and water-colour on tracing paper, torn
9⅛ × 18¾ (23.1 × 47.6) D.1675–1896

Design for arrangement of plain tiles
Pencil and water-colour
27 × 24.2 (10⅝ × 9½) D.2039–1896

Design for arrangement of patterned floor tiles. Initialled *J.P.S.*
Pencil and water-colour
12 × 11¾ (30.3 × 27.2) D.2049–1896

Keys to arrangements of tiles around fireplaces (3) and to a tile panel. Each of the tiles or groups of tiles insc. with the title of its subject. The two fireplaces are further insc. *The tale of Beauty and the Beast. The History of Cinderella.* The tiles in the third fireplace are insc. *Head of S. Cecilia. Head of Chaucer. Head of Penelope.* The tiles in the wall panels insc. with the names of the months and *Town of Troy. Angel holding Moon. Ship in sail. Angel & sun. Town of Rome.* Insc. in pencil *Morris. Wm. 1862*
Pen and ink, and wash
13 × 13¾ (33 × 35.1) D.2050–1896

Design for an arrangement of tiles for publication. Initialled *J.P.S.* Insc. with notes including *Lithographers note all the photographs to be the same colors as this lamp.*
Pencil, pen and ink, and water-colour with lithographs and photographs pasted on.
5⅞ × 8⅜ (14.9 × 21.2) D.2080–1896

Sketch possibly for tile. Insc. *subjects*
Pencil and water-colour
3¾ × 5 (9.8 × 12.6) D.1673–1896

Drawings after other Artists

BURGES, William

(see also Topographical Drawings D.1000, 1001–1907)

Sections (2 on 2 sheets) of nave roof. Insc. *Brisbane Cathedral South Australia* and D.1498 *W. Burges Archt.* and D.1497 *Detail of Nave Roof ½ inch scale.*
D.1497 pen and ink and water-colour on tracing paper, torn.
D.1498 pencil, pen and ink and water-colour
15¼ × 10¾ (38.9 × 27.4) D.1497 27¾ × 30¾ (70.5 × 78.3) D.1498
D.1497, 1498–1896

LE DUC, Viollet

Copies (on 7 sheets) of wall and ceiling decorations from publications by Viollet le Duc. Insc. *Fontfroide, Carcassone, Commandery-* and *Castle at Concy*
Pencil and water-colour
Largest 16 × 26 (41 × 66) D.1647, 1648, 1654–1658–1896

PUGIN, Angustus Welby Northmore

Pattern upon dress of image in Choir of Cologne Cathdl. Scale *full size.* Insc. *From Pugins Glossary* [of Ecclesiastical Ornament]
Pen and ink, and water-colour
15⅞ × 13⅜ (40.3 × 34) D.1895–1896

STREET, George Edmund

Hanbury Church. Plan of *tile paving to chancel floor.* Scale ½″ *to a foot.* Insc. *from design by G. E. Street*
Pencil, pen and ink, and water-colour
21½ × 15⅛ (54.4 × 38.5) D.2128–1896

Oxford, St. Thomas's Church. Plan of tiling paffages. Scale ½ *inch.* Also a drawing of the *chancel floor Winscombe church.* Insc. *from a design by G. E. Street.* Scale ½ *inch*
Pencil, pen and ink, and water-colour
13 × 18¾ (33 × 47) D.1768–1896

New Church Stourbridge. Plan of *tile paving to chancel floor.* Scale *half inch.* Insc. *from design by George Edmund Street Archt.*
Pen and ink, and water-colour
18⅝ × 12⅞ (47.4 × 32.8) D.2059–1896

Upton Magna Church of St. Lucy *near Shrewsbury.* Plan of *tile paving of chancel floor.* Scale ½ *inch to a foot.* Insc. *from a design by George Edmund Street*
Pencil, pen and ink, and water-colour
18⅝ × 12½ (47.3 × 32.6) D.2058–1896

Plan of tile paving for chancel floor of an unidentified church. Insc. *from design by George E. Street*
Pen and ink, and water-colour
18⅛ × 12¾ (47.3 × 32.4) D.2057–1896

Plan of tile paving for chancel floor of an unidentified church. Insc. *from design by G. E. Street Archt.*
Pencil, pen and ink, and water-colour
18¾ × 12⅞ (47.5 × 32.8) D.2060–1896

Index of names and places

Abbeydore, Herefs. 20
Aberavon, Glam. 18
Aberdare, Glam. 26
Abergavenny, Lord 100
Abermad House 13, 22, 31, 44
Aberystwyth, Dyfed 11, 13, 20, 22, 23, 31–34
Addington, Surrey 23, 26, 34
Adforton, Herefs. 23
Arklow, Co. Wicklow 23
Arminghall, Norfolk 23, 35
Ayot St. Peter, Herts 23, 35

Baines, H. R. 17, 80–82
Barber, W. 88
Barfrestone, Kent 26
Bath, Somerset 24
Batson, Mr 74
Beckford Hall 35, 36
Belham, S. and Co. 61, 69
Berthwyd, Glam. 19
Betchworth, Surrey 24, 36
Birchington-on-Sea, Kent 14, 23, 36–39, 105
Birdhurst House 19, 20, 53, 54
Birkenhead, Lancs. 24
Birmingham, Warwicks 24
Bishopsbourne, Kent 22, 38
Blaina, Gwent 25
Bonvelstone 19, 20
Booker, Thomas 96
Borth, Dyfed 13, 20
Bradford 22
Brecon, Powys 20, 22, 26, 40, 41
Bridgend, Glam. 19, 42
Brisbane, Australia 118
Bristol, Avon 21, 26, 42–44
Briton Ferry, Glam. 25, 44
Broadstairs, Kent 21, 22, 44
Brock, Allan 21, 100
Broncroft Castle, Salop. 22, 45, 45
Brookfield 26, 46
Brown, Ford Madox 14
Brown, J. Norman 35
Burges, William 14, 29, 53, 75, 99
Burnley 24
Burrell, Sir Percy 23, 100
Burroughs, T. H. 22, 100
Butterfield, William 49, 86
Byass, R. B. 100

Caerleon, Gwent 19–21, 46, 47
Camrose, Dyfed 24, 47
Cardiff, Glam. 18–20, 24, 25, 47–50
Caröe, W. D. 47, 83
Carter, J. Coates 13, 24, 26, 46, 50, 86
Chalfont, Bucks. 24, 50
Chalgrave 26
Chance, Messers 84
Chance, R. L. 20, 100
Charlton 21, 50

Chepstow, Gwent 25, 50, 51
Chester 25, 51
Chigwell Row, Essex 13, 21, 51, 52
Clarke, Edward 52, 56, 70
Clayton and Bell 52, 75
Collman 44
Continent, The 29
Cork 20, 52
Cornish, J. G. 100
Crisp, H. 13
Croydon, Surrey 19, 20, 53, 54
Cwmafan, Glam. 17, 54
Cymmer, Glam. 18
Cynwyl Gaio, Dyfed 19, 23, 54

Day, Rev. A. B. 22, 57
Dering, George 61
Dillon, Lord 21
Dinas, Dyfed 26
Dingestow Court 19, 55
Dixton, Gwent 19, 55, 56
Donaldson, Thomas L. 11, 17
Donnington Priory 17, 56
Droitwich, Worces. 20, 56
Dytchley, Oxon. 21, 56

Eatington Park 12, 13, 18, 56
Epsom, Surrey 24, 57
Eythorne, Kent 25, 56

Fearon, Ann 53, 54
Ferguson, C. J. 32
Fisher, W. H. C. 13, 94
Fishponds, Avon 22, 57
Foll, Hattil 33, 36
Franklyn, R. S. W. 112
Freeman, E. A. 100

Gaye, H. 75
Gelligaer, Glam. 19, 57
Gilbert, Alfred 38
Glewstown, Herefs. 21
Godwin and Co. 35, 116, 117
Godwin, E. W. 13
Goodrich, Herefs. 24
Gough, H. Roumieu 13
Great Kimble, Bicks. 23, 57
Great Yarmouth 20–23, 58
Grosmont 12, 18, 20, 22, 23, 58
Guernsey 21, 58, 59
Gwerneshi, Gwent 17

Hales, John 12, 17
Hall, Sir Edward 25
Hammond 44
Hanbury 118
Hart Son, Peard and Co. 22, 114, 115
Harvey, L. 13
Haywood, C. Forster 14
Hemms, Harry 62
Henley-in-Arden, Warwicks 24
Hentland, Herefs. 17–19, 59–61

Hereford 25, 61
Herne, Kent 22, 61
Hoarwithy 21, 23, 61, 62
Holdgate, Salop. 20, 21, 62, 63
Holmer, Herefs. 20
Holmes, Richard R. 111
Hook, Surrey 26

Ingham, Norfolk 23, 64
Istanbul 18, 99

Jeffries, Gwyn 23, 97
Job, W. 101
Joldwynds House 19, 20, 63, 64

Kenmare, Co. Kerry 23
Kennardington 23, 64, 65
Kentchurch, Herefs. 18, 65
Keynsham, Somerset 18, 66
Kilpayson 18
Kilpeck, Herefs. 24, 66
Kingston Hill, Surrey 22, 66

Lacey Green, Bucks 22, 66
Lamb, E. Beckitt 13, 26, 79
Lavars and Barraud 56
Leaf, Charles 20, 101
Le Duc, Viollet 118
Lewis, Rev. 87
Lincoln 22
Little Dewchurch, Herefs. 20, 66, 67
Little Yeldham, Essex 25, 68
Llampeter Velfrey, Dyfed 19
Llanbadarn Fawr, Dyfed 22, 69
Llandaff, Glam. 11, 13, 17, 21, 24, 25, 69–71
Llanddewi Fach, Gwent 18
Llanddewi Felfre, Dyfed 19, 70
Llanddewi Rhydderch, Gwent 20
Llanddewi Ysgyryd, Gwent 23
Llandeilo, Dyfed 18, 71
Llandeilo Bertholau, Gwent 18, 71
Llandeilo Gresynni, Gwent 18
Llandenny, Gwent 19, 71
Llandogo, Gwent 19
Llandough, Glam. 19, 71, 72
Llandysoe, Gwent 18, 20, 72
Llanelen, Gwent 18, 72
Llanfabon, Glam. 20
Llanfaches, Gwent 20
Llanfair, Glam. 20
Llanfair Discoed, Gwent 17
Llanfihangel Torymynydd, Gwent 17
Llanfrechfa, Gwent 18, 72
Llangwm Isaf, Gwent 18, 74
Llangwm Uchaf, Gwent 18, 22, 23, 74
Llanharan 18
Llanisien, Gwent 17
Llanmartin, Gwent 18, 74
Llantrisant, Gwent 26, 74
Lloyd, Lewis 41
Lobb, Rev. S. B. 23, 65

London
  Aldersgate 24
  Architectural Museum 14, 25
  Buckingham Palace 11
  Ecclesiastical Art Exhibition 24
  Embankment 14, 24
  Fulham 21, 22
  Government Offices 10, 11, 18
  Hammersmith 24
  Kensington 26, 29, 74
  Kentish Town 17, 22, 26, 74
  Kingsbury 74, 75
  Lambeth Palace 23, 75
  Langham Hotel 20
  Law Courts 10, 11, 21
  Paddington 26
  Saint Paul's Cathedral 24
  People's Palace 24
  Tulse Hill 17, 18, 26, 75–77
  Wandsworth 76, 77
  Wells Street 23, 74, 75
  Westminster 14, 24, 26, 51, 78, 79
Long Melford, Suffolk 29

Margate, Kent 26
Marshfield, Glam. 19, 79
Martin, W. E. 38
Matthews, Rev. 23, 101
Maw and Co 21, 116, 117
Meeking, Charles 20, 101
Melbourne, Australia 24, 99
Melincryddan 25
Merthyr Dyfan 18
Mexborough, Yorks. 25, 79
Minton and Co 54, 117
Monmouth, Gwent 22, 80
Moore, W. F. N. 20, 101
Morel, Nicholas 11
Morris, J. Charles 71
Mottingham, Kent 17, 18, 80–82
Mountain Ash, Glam. 19, 82
Murray, H. G. 61
Murray, J. 13
Murray, Mr 26

Naftel, Paul J. 29, 58, 59
Nash, Gwent 20
Newchurch, Gwent 21, 83
Newport, Gwent 19, 21, 83
Newton 19
Newton, H. G. 24
Northampton 23, 84
Norwood, Surrey 19
Norwich 24, 25

Oldcastle, Gwent 21, 84
Orcop, Herefs. 17, 84
Overmonnow, Gwent 22, 80
Oxford 23, 118
Oxted, Surrey 19, 85, 86

Pace, G. G. 69, 70, 83
Paisley 24
Penarth, Glam. 21, 24, 25, 86

Penge, Kent 26, 86
Pentyrch, Glam. 12, 17
Peterstone, Glam. 18, 25, 26, 87
Pinner, Middlesex 18, 23, 87, 88
Ponsonby, Walter 95
Pontnewydd, Gwent 18, 88–90
Poole, Rev. 22, 59, 62, 101
Pope and Bindon 44
Powles, J. E. 56
Powys Keck, H. J. 23, 102
Price, I. 36
Prichard, John 11, 12, 14, passim
Pugh Pugh, Lewis 13, 31, 44
Pugin Augustus C. 12
Pugin, Augustus W. N. 118

Ransome 102
Ransome and Co 21, 104
Redbrook, Glos. 23
Redruth, Cornwall 24, 90
Rivers, Captn. 71, 76
Robinson, G. 24, 102
Robinson, J. G. 50
Rockfield, Gwent 23, 90
Rogiet, Gwent 25
Roos, Col. 49
Rossdohan House 23, 90
Rossetti, Dante G. 13, 38, 70
Rossetti, William M. 14
Rossiter, Mr 41
Rust, Jesse 24, 99, 115
Rylands, The 19

Saint Arvan's Gwent 24
Saint Lythans, Glam. 26, 91
Saint Mary Church, Glam. 20
Sandford, Rev. C. W. 22, 38
Savin, Thomas 13, 31
Seddon C. and Co. 21, 108–113
Seddon, George 11
Seddon, Major H. C. 36
Seddon, Thomas 11, 17, 112
Shields, Fredericj, J. 69
Shotley Hall 26, 91
Slough 22
Smith, G. and Sons 114
Smith, W. H. 25
Solomon, Simeon 38
Southerndown, Glam. 11, 17, 18, 25, 93, 94
Spiers, Richard Phené 13, 32
Sporun, Lewis 102
Stourbridge 118
Street, George E. 44, 49, 99, 118
Stroud, Glos. 25, 94, 95
Stutton, Suffolk 25, 95
Sunningwell, Berks. 23
Swansea, Glam. 24
Swindon, Wilts. 24, 95

Tait, Mrs 44
Taylor, John 38
Templeton, Dyfed 19, 96
Thornhill, Yorks. 21

Tintern, Gwent 19
Towyn, Dyfed 13
Tredegar, Glam. 25, 84
Trellech, Gwent 17
Truro, Cornwall 24, 96
Tynant, Glam. 17, 96

Ullenhall, Warwicks 23, 96, 97
Upavon, Wilts. 23, 97
Usk 70

Vaughan, David 87
Vaughan, E. Bruce 83
Verdon, Sir George 23, 102
Voysey, Charles F. A. 32
Vulliamy, Lewis 55

Walker, Thomas L. 12
Walton-le-Dale, Lancs. 25
Ware, Herts. 23, 97
Watson, Jonas 25
Weston-under-Penyard 19, 97, 98
Wetton, Champion 63, 64
Whitchurch, Herefs. 19, 99
White, G. 24, 57
Whitsun, Glam. 19
Wilde, S. C. 22
Wilkinson, Rev. 85, 86
Williams, David 31
Williams, Dean 25
Williams, Rev. J. D. 41
Williams, Thomas 44, 52, 56, 69
Wilson, Mr 38
Windsor Castle 11
Woolner, Thomas 13
Wyatt, James 58
Wyatt, Thomas H. 97
Wyesham, Gwent 23, 99

Ystradowen, Glam. 19